TRAPPED IN THE LOFT.

LIFE AND ADVENTURES

OF

LEWIS WETZEL,

THE RENOWNED

VIRGINIA RANGER AND SCOUT.

COMPRISING

A THRILLING HISTORY OF THIS CELEBRATED INDIAN FIGHTER, WITH HIS PERILOUS ADVENTURES AND HAIR-BREADTH ESCAPES, AND INCLUDING OTHER INTEREST-ING INCIDENTS OF BORDER-LIFE.

LARGELY COMPILED

FROM AUTHENTIC RECORDS HITHERTO UNPUBLISHED

BY

R. C. V. MEYERS, Esq.

WITH ILLUSTRATIONS.

PHILADELPHIA:
JOHN E. POTTER AND COMPANY,
617 SANSOM STREET.

COPYRIGHT
By JOHN E. POTTER & COMPANY
1883

PREFACE.

IN the preparation of this work, the author has had peculiar advantages. He has had access to a large collection of Miscellanies touching on early border times. He has had the opportunity of consulting rare authors on frontier life and warfare. He has derived considerable aid, in the disposition of his materials, from former writers on various subjects connected with the life and manners of our early Western settlers. He has also enjoyed a large acquaintance among those who are directly or remotely the descendants of the Wetzel family, and especially among the descendants of those who lived at the time when the hero of this work lived, or at the places he frequented. He has, therefore, been enabled, in many cases, to verify the truth of incidents which he found in books by these oral traditions, and in other instances he has carefully collated traditional reports with these written records.

But the author has had frequent occasion to congratulate himself on the possession of family documents in the form of diaries, or letters, written at the time. These private records give an idea of the times they were written in in that naive and simple style which pertains to all writings meant primarily but for the owner's eye, or those of his near friends. He has violated no confidence with these manuscripts; but, in several instances, he has been induced to quote, in the very language of the memoirs, certain portions specially bearing upon the subject in hand, and in many more he has given the substance.

From these various sources the author has collated the scenes and incidents and thrilling adventures of the celebrated scout. And with all due sense of his faults—and no one can feel these more than the author himself—he cherishes the hope, both that he has succeeded in forming such an idea of the times of Lewis Wetzel as is most consonant to the truth, and in representing these times in an intelligent and entertaining manner to the reader.

The author has not been able to regard Wetzel as a paragon of virtue, an erring devotee of a mistaken fanaticism, or so void of principle as to account the blood of his fellow-creatures cheap, provided it was flowing beneath a red skin. But he was a man of the times, one who proved a bulwark for the infant settlements, and a right arm for their defense—and in this sense, truly a hero.

And in his view of the Indian character, the author has also taken a middle course. He has been unable to see in the Indian all the simplicity which sentimental philanthropy affects to find there. But he has likewise failed to see all the fiendishness sometimes ascribed to that character by those who are interested in dispossessing the Indian from his soil. Much might be said in extenuation of the hostility of the savage. But there is also another side. And we fail as often when we lose sight of the character of the civilization of the pioneers as we do when we forget the law of human progress; for behind all we must bow with awe and reverence before that Divine Providence, who controls and bends the world to his will.

CONTENTS.

CHAPTER I.
From Old Things Unto New 9

CHAPTER II.
A Childhood 22

CHAPTER III.
The Bear 35

CHAPTER IV.
The Oath 49

CHAPTER V.
The Indian Scout 74

CHAPTER VI.
Martin Wetzel 104

CHAPTER VII.
A Massacre 125

CHAPTER VIII.
Crawford's Campaign 154

CHAPTER IX.
A Pursuit and an Escape 181

CHAPTER X.
An Indian Waylaid 199

CHAPTER XI.
Capture and Escape 229

CHAPTER XII.

Free 247

CHAPTER XIII.

The Hundred Dollars Reward 259

CHAPTER XIV.

The Turkey-Cry 276

CHAPTER XV.

A Chance for an Arrest 292

CHAPTER XVI.

The Indian Girl 300

CHAPTER XVII.

Trial and Acquittal 306

CHAPTER XVIII.

The Indian Camp 322

CHAPTER XIX.

The Hut in the Storm 331

CHAPTER XX.

The Story of the Lovers 343

CHAPTER XXI.

Wetzel's Brothers 359

CHAPTER XXII.

The New Orleans Episode 388

CHAPTER XXIII.

The Last Indian 401

CHAPTER XXIV.

Vale 407

LEWIS WETZEL:

THE VIRGINIA RANGER.

CHAPTER I.

FROM OLD THINGS UNTO NEW.

IN the early spring of 1764 a family of emigrants wended its way through the wilds of Pennsylvania out to the almost unbroken West. It was the family of a poor farmer, John Wetzel by name, from Lancaster, or its immediate vicinity,—an "up-country Dutchman," of more than average intelligence, bent on trying for a new home in the less claimed portions of his Majesty's colonies. There was the wife— a strong, helpful woman—and two children,—sons, —the older two years of age, the younger perhaps two months.

It is with this infant that this narrative has to do —when he had become a man moving through stirring scenes, a prominent figure, yet seeming alone and aloof from others. This day, however, he lay with his mother at the bottom of the wagon which contained all that belonged to his father, who drove the pair of hardy asses that plodded patiently along the heavy unkept roads, his two-year-old boy on the seat beside him.

They had started early in the morning of this bright spring day when all nature vied to keep and hold them back: the birds sang the songs they had known always; the dear old-fashioned flowers beckoned them only to stay; the dogs barked their remonstrances; the sad-eyed cows leaned over the rails, or raised their heads from the juicy young clover to low out a tender warning that though these travelers went farther they would see little that could claim their hearts so much as what they left behind.

There were also a few old men, with pipes in their mouths, moving across the gardens; and the sound of the heavy, rattling team brought pleasant-faced women to the doors, and all had a word for "the Wetzels" so fool-hardily turning their backs upon old associations to face vague and untried new.

But John Wetzel had ever been known as a stubborn, self-willed man, hard to turn, and ever since neighbors Eberly and Rosencranz had left for the proposed settlement in the western part of Virginia, he had chafed and looked with eyes averted on the smallness of his surroundings. He had neglected his tiny place with its two hogs and one cow and limited garden space, where only enough throve to keep the little household in food. He had neglected the tavern, where of evenings he used to make one of the many who planned and plotted better ways than were ever adopted to put down the Indians that were reported to treat the far-off settlers so shamefully, and whose depredations were not unknown here.

He went about the place moody and gloomy, paying no attention to anything, only fretfully chafing because of his environments.

"It's enough to kill his wife," asseverated neighbor Trull's wife, "and her in her condition too! Drat the man, he's a lune! He'd far better be a-doing something to put something in the mouths o' them that's depending on him, than namby-pambying around, as if he was rich as the Heisters. I've no patience with him, for my part."

Yes, and it was his wife's condition that made him so idle, that kept him from doing what he so longed to do, and what a letter from neighbors Rosencranz and Eberly had impressed so strongly on his mind that nothing could remove or efface it.

"I must wait! I must wait!" he said impatiently. "It's always the way with a man who sees his chance—he must wait. But in my case it can hardly be helped." And he sighed, and went for a long walk through places he had once loved, but which were now hateful and monotonous to a man who had imbibed suddenly a spirit of progress.

He waited weeks, he waited a whole month. Then the wail of a baby's voice was heard in the little house, and John Wetzel rejoiced. He waited two weeks more, and then one day while in the garden he looked up and saw his wife sitting by the window of their own little chamber, looking happy and bright, her face filled with mother-care.

He threw a little flower up to her.

"Come up," she said.

He entered the room where she was, and said kindly, but without preamble: "Wife, I have something to say to you which I have waited long weeks to say. And—but now, to-day, you are strong again, are you not?"

"Strong, John, with the grace of the Lord," she replied.

"And you are strong enough to move?"

"Move! and where to?—where can *we* move to?"

"There's land for the man who claims it—far away towards the setting sun."

"Not amongst the Indians?" she cried in terror,

placing her hand instinctively across the cradle where her baby slept the rosy sleep of childhood.

"Why not?" asked her husband in return. "The Indians are not God Almighty."

"John!" she gasped, "such profanity!"

"No profanity," he returned. "The profanity is in the fear we have for men who are only like myself; less than myself, because of their ignorance and perfidy and untruth. We place them on a plane with Deity in fearing them."

"Or demons."

"We should not fear the devil and his works."

"Oh, husband!" she cried, for in her eyes this was tempting the spirit of ill.

"This is neither here nor there," he went on, with a light in his eyes which the wives of strong men learn to know as a part of their husbands not to be tampered with; "the question is, will you go? You know how it is here—how poor we are, how restless I have ever been. Will you accept the profusion of the Lord, spread out for us for the accepting? Either we go, or others will—if not now, then at some future time."

"Nobody we know will ever go out to the wild Indian country," she insisted.

"We will, if you trust your husband," he rejoined, and turned to leave the room.

As he went out by the narrow door he felt a soft touch on his face. His wife had hurriedly snatched the baby from its cradle and placed its flushed cheek to its father's. He turned to her.

"This child will be poor as I am," he said bitterly, "or rich with plenty. It is for you to decide."

"No," she answered, "it is for you to say. I am only a weak woman, but I trust my husband with the strength of all women."

"And you will go?"

"'Whither thou goest, I will go; and where thou lodgest I will lodge,'" she said softly, and laid her baby closer yet to him.

So it came to be known in the place that the Wetzel family was absolutely proposing to emigrate just so soon as the baby was old enough to go on the long journey, which would be when two moons had rolled over its head. Every obstacle was paraded before the man who desired to better himself at the expense of personal comfort and the severance of familiar ties; sentiment was immediately called into play: and the bones of his ancestors, lying in the adjacent graveyards, were conjured up before him, how those bones might naturally be expected to "turn" in their kindred earth, did they know of this flagrant breach and go-ahead-ativeness on the part of a fool-hardy descendant not content to let well-enough alone!

A stern, stout, red-faced man came to the tavern and proclaimed: "I am a justice of the peace, friend John Wetzel, so listen to me. Ahem!"

"Yes, listen to the justice of the peace," cried all the idlers in the place, crowding around. The stout man hemmed.

"Your native place should suffice you," he said sententiously.

"It does; but I want more of it," responded John Wetzel.

"He wants more of it!" said the chorus of idlers, lost in astonishment; for they had never wanted more of it, and were content to live on half a head of cabbage when they could not get a whole, so that they only had a right to complain of the crops, and how it never rained when it should rain, or if it did rain it simply poured and ruined everything.

The stout man looked more a justice of the peace every second, and after the chorus had subsided into silence he brought a heavy look to bear on John Wetzel. Sentiment had failed; now cogent reasoning should be employed.

"I am a justice of the peace," he went on, "and I am supposed to represent wisdom—that is, I am a reasoner. Ahem!"

The chorus only looked at each other; this was going beyond them.

The justice of the peace now looked like a prime minister.

"Conceded I am wise, am I, then, fit to argify with you in this foolish determination of yours?"

The chorus was dumb.

John Wetzel was as dumb as the others.

With a look fit for a king, and a voice of thunder, the justice of the peace, throwing up his hand, said: "John Wetzel, I am wise. Are you? You go away from all you know, out to wild lands which—which—you do not know. You leave a house for—for—no house. For pleasant grunting hogs, fit for sausages and—and—other things, you will have buffaloes and—and—other things. For cows that yield streams of peaceful milk that oozes with richness, you will have buzzards and—and—things that yield no milk at all. Your wife—your *wife*, John" (here the justice of the peace got a quavering in his throat); "and your son Martin, John; and your baby Lewis, John—oh, upon what will they subsist? Can they make buzzard savory? Can they drink Indian? Nay, John, you will not, *cannot* go. I am wise; I cannot help being so. His Majesty may have heard of me. But are *you* wise?"

"Are *you* wise?" echoed the chorus.

"I never set up for a wiseacre," said John Wetzel, smiling, and moving towards the door.

"Yea, John," said the justice, "we cannot all be so. But it is conceded that I am wise, and——"

"The great Paul saith," went on John Wetzel, still moving towards the door, "the great Paul saith, 'If any man among you seemeth to be wise in this world, let him become a fool that he may be wise.'"

The justice of the peace, stared as who should ask if the world had come to an end, and looking very much like a justice of the peace after all, sank back into his chair at the head of the table, muttering feebly: "A fool! wise!" and closed his eyes.

"A fool! wise!" gasped the chorus, and began to think that Saint Paul as well as John Wetzel had much to answer for in saying such harrowing things of the justice of the peace.

"Where is he?" asked the justice, reviving.

"Saint Paul, your Honor?" returned one.

"Out upon you for a malefactor!" cried his Honor. "Where is the man John Wetzel, the reprobate?"

But no one could answer just then, for the door had swung open and shut again, and he was not there. Some one pulled aside the curtain, and they saw him striding on towards his home with the step of a boy.

But the justice of the peace was highly respected, and it seemed that Saint Paul had questioned his authority and dignity, and in so doing had been represented by John Wetzel. As the principal could not be touched, the representative was held answerable. So, very few people came to the Wetzels during their preparations for removal, and on the last day of their stay nobody but little Grizzie Heister came to say farewell. Grizzie was only fourteen or fifteen, a mere chit; but she cried a good deal. She had something in her pocket which bulged out. She kissed Mrs. Wetzel, and cried; she kissed little Martin, and cried. Over the baby she broke down completely.

"Oh, the Injuns will eat him," she wept; "the awful Injuns!"

"Or he'll eat the Injuns," grinned John Wetzel, now all animation and life.

"And his clothes 'll wear out, and he won't have anything but bear-skin to wear," said Grizzie.

"Bear-skin 's warm," grinned John Wetzel.

"He shan't wear bear-skin," shrieked Grizzie, "for I've brought this. It was in father's private room, and he gave it to me when I told him what it was for. Here! let me wrap it around little Lewis to keep him warm."

"This" was a small flag of Great Britain, and the baby looked gay in it.

"You've made an Indian of him already, Grizzie," said John Wetzel, "with all the bright red.

Yes, he can wear the flag of his country, though the flag never waved over much that he dared call his own." John Wetzel was one of those discontented colonists who did not feel glad at being oppressed.

So Grizzie went away, and the sun sank upon the last day of the Wetzels' stay here.

In the early morning they were on their way. When all the pleasant familiar scene burst upon the eyes of the adventurous man, who knows what his feelings were!

"Wife," he said once, holding in the team, "come sit here in front, for a last look."

She came out with her baby on her arm and sat beside her husband. She looked over the smiling landscape, over all she knew so well, all that she had ever known and loved. Then she looked into her husband's eyes.

"Must it be?" she asked tremulously. "Must it be?"

"The free land calls us," he answered, waving his hand westward. "Must it be, wife?"

"It must be!" she said, with compressed lips.

"Get up!" he cried to the team, and they were on their way again.

His wife still sat on the front seat of the wagon. She wiped her eyes once or twice, then she fairly broke down, hiding her face in her baby.

"That is no way to conquer rebellion," remonstrated her husband; "and we go out to conquer, not give in."

"It shall never be again," she said, and it never again occurred while he was alive. She was removing something from about her baby's shoulders. "My tears have wetted all the pretty flag," she continued. It was Grizzie Heister's gift, all sodden with the mother's tears.

"That flag has caused too many tears," said John Wetzel sententiously. "We will have it no longer, the ugly rag." And he tore it from the child and threw it into the dust at the feet of his team, with a look of contempt on his face that his wife could not understand.

There were few to prophesy of that more beautiful flag of thirteen alternate white and red stripes with "a union of thirteen stars, white on a blue ground, representing a new constellation," the first representative of which was to be made in the shop of Betsy Ross, in Philadelphia, when the little Lewis should be thirteen years of age.

But little knew John Wetzel of this as on his way to Wheeling Creek he conveyed his family that day from the old home they were never to know again.

Days and nights came down as the heavy wagon moved on slowly through the almost untrodden wilderness. The cry of wolves became of little account as farther and farther the patient asses took forward the little group. The strange herbage of the wilderness replaced the smiling fields and fragrant homely flower-gardens.

The peculiar freedom of everything around them insensibly crept over the husband and wife. The little boy in the wagon cried to get out for the pretty grasses, and walked along beside the wagon happy and free. The baby looked out on the sunny landscape and crowed. There were no poor men here, there were no rich men: all were alike. Every man was Adam; every woman, Eve. Abel lived in every little child, and Cain had not yet learned to be dissatisfied with the reception of his sacrifice.

CHAPTER II.

A CHILDHOOD.

JOHN WETZEL, going out with the determination to conquer difficulties, seemed to court those which were almost insuperable.

"Settle with us here, on Wheeling Creek," urged his old neighbor Eberly.

"No," he replied, "there are too many here already. I'm going farther up."

"But the danger——"

"Had I been afraid of danger I should never have come here. There seems to me more danger of staying with men than with nature."

"Then Indians will be your nature."

"I know very little about Indians. I know a good deal about white men."

"You are a strange man, Wetzel."

"I am as I am," he returned.

"And you do not see the wisdom of settling with us here?"

"I do not see the wisdom: it may be yours; it is not mine."

"Good-bye!" they shouted after his wagon.

"Good-bye!" he replied, and the asses moved on, and trod down the long grasses, and the few settlers after awhile lost sight of the wagon.

For miles the hardy man went on, and at last sighted a spot that pleased him. It was on Big Wheeling, fourteen miles from the river.

"You are not afraid?" asked he of his wife, as she stepped from the wagon and looked around her.

"What is there to be afraid of?" she asked in return, holding her baby closer to her.

"Nothing but want, such as we have left behind us," he answered.

She put her baby in the wagon with its little brother, and set about making a fire and preparing their meal.

They lived in the wagon for days, until a rude cabin had been erected by Wetzel, at which his wife was not behind-hand in assisting. In two weeks they were domiciled in a home.

"Thank God," said John Wetzel reverently, "we are free!"

If loneliness is synonymous with freedom, they were indeed free. The spot on which the cabin stood was the most exposed imaginable, on every side open to incursions from Indians, were they bent on hostility. The family was wholly beyond the reach of any prompt aid from the settlement and fort at Wheeling, should succor be needed.

But in a little while they made up their minds that they needed no aid. They had left the pent-in life of poverty behind them, and now they reveled in the wealth and prodigality of nature. Their lack of fear created a lack of caution. And in this cabin, so far removed from any signs of civilized life, they set about beginning life anew. It was a happy life for months, for years. They rarely saw any white man. An Indian now and then stopped at the door, accepted some tobacco, and moved off. Sometimes a stray squaw would come up with dried venison to trade for powder, and would ask to hold the papooses a little while. Then in fiercely cold weather even these failed. For months at a time no human being approached them. The husband and father at rare intervals went to Wheeling for necessary supplies: his wife never went, never had any desire to go. Her time was crowded with duties. Her little family gradually became a large one; five children were born here—Jacob, John, and George, and two daughters, Susan and Christina.

The father, too, had little time for visiting: his children were all too young to be of any assistance to him, and he was in a place where everything must come from personal exertion.

Towards the end of the fourth year the Indian visits were more frequent, and his herd was often stolen from him by night. Then, too, the braves were impudent, and their insults were often very gross.

He was also largely engaged in locating lands, and his frequent excursions into the wilds for this purpose constantly exposed him to attacks from hostile tribes, which, however, he seems to have escaped. He had experienced poverty, and to fight that off had been hard enough; now he was aiming at wealth and ease for his children, and for all he cared the exertion he had expended to thwart poverty might be increased a hundred-fold in the acquirement of plenty.

The Indian wars were in full rage after he had been here a few years, and nearer and nearer to him came the depredations of the savages.

"But I will *not* give in," he said. He gathered about him a numerous company of wild horses, reclaimed from savage state by arduous toil, and though these were often preyed upon by the Indians, he took it in good part.

"This was Indian land," he said, "and they let it go to waste. These horses they thought useless, but I reclaimed them. Now they claim but their own."

And the wife's labors! She cared for nothing else

but her family, and often left alone became reckless as her husband. She made deer-skin clothes for her husband and boys, and from the scanty supply of wool their few sheep yielded she spun and wove cloth for herself and her little girls.

The land produced little at first, because of their small means to procure the necessary implements to cultivate it, and often their few fowls were raided on, and there was but milk for food. Even that sometimes failed, or the cows got astray. In the latter case she would listen for the tinkling of the bells, and hearing them at a great distance in that immense solitude she would tie her babies in bed, her older children to the door-jamb, to keep them from being hurt or straying after her, and went herself in search of the cattle, and maybe hours would elapse before she brought them home, hoping that in the interval no hostile Indian had paid a visit to her cabin. The wolves, too, in hard winters, when they were famished and desperate, troubled her: often at night she used to bar the house, and sit beside the chimney feeding the fire with pine logs to keep the beasts at bay, her children sleeping on the floor around her, her husband she knew not where, nor whether alive or dead, the howls of the creatures outside, and their scratching at the ill-made door urging her on to make a fiercer, hotter fire, and not to sleep nor relax her vigilance a minute.

This was the home-rearing of Lewis Wetzel. It was breathing this atmosphere of daring that made him an object of terror to the bands of restless savages which roamed about the frontier homes,—a man without fear (as he was known to be),—a veritable tower of strength unto the infant settlements springing up around him.

For Lewis Wetzel came to be considered the right arm of defense by many of the settlers in the vicinity of Wheeling, and while he was never known to inflict any cruelty upon women or children, as has been charged to him, he was revengeful, with a deathless hatred, upon the Indians, because he had suffered an injury at their hands, the sense of which left him not a moment throughout his life, and which in time debarred him from the comforts and satisfaction of friends and lovers. He called himself an Indian hunter, as other men call themselves bear-hunters, snake-hunters, and the like; and while he would pass over a sleeping animal which it might have been death to him to pass by, and was in his power to procure immunity by killing, he never forgave a single Indian for the wrong he had sustained at the hands of a few. He put reason to shame, and called his wrong his reason.

He hated Logan, that noble man; he hated his

eloquence, and thought of him only as he thought of the veriest cut-throat in the Delaware or any other tribe with which he was daily brought in contact.

In his earliest youth he heard all the hopeful stories of Indian kindness,—how friendly tribes, meeting white settlers, took them to their camping-grounds, feasted them, treated them with all attention, asked no questions, as the code of Indians is, loaded them with presents, and let them go. He knew of the fortitude of the young Indian chiefs,—how much they were compelled to bear, how much torture they were to undergo before they were adjudged competent to call themselves leaders. A chief had once come to his father's cabin and called the Bible the *talking leaves*, and looked with awe at his mother as she read aloud the language of Christ speaking to her from the yellow and weather-beaten volume with all the tender love and care the disciples of old knew. He knew that prior to the intercourse of the Indians with the Europeans their weapons had been bows and arrows, clubs and tomahawks, and spears of wood, curiously ornamented with stones and shells; but that after they had begun traffic with the foreigners their rude weapons were laid aside for those of iron and other metals, and that before the commencement of the war with Philip, though the trade was strictly restrained by the government of the Provinces, the Indians had gotten many fire-arms, and learned how to use them, and not alone upon beasts of prey. He knew that many atrocities attributed to the wandering tribes were committed by renegade white men, who joined with the tribes for pilfer and carnage. He knew all this in his earliest boyhood, and had no hatred for the Indians, because his wrong had not yet come to dry up the fountain of kindly feeling for a mysterious race indigenous to the land they claimed for their own,—a race noble from very recklessness, claiming what they called theirs by right of precedence, and whose wild blood, like that of their bisons, refused to be tamed, or, tamed, was not to be trusted, because the wont of unchained freedom was liable to vent itself in fierce deviltry, when once the taming process had taught it cringing and deceit.

When his father's land-claims were becoming more and more extended, and he was oftener than ever brought into contact with the Indians who threatened to become hostile, little Lewis Wetzel looked on and listened, amused and entertained. When his father returned from any of his excursions, he would gather the children around him, and tell them the comic situations his prowess had led him into; and as Indians always largely figured in these narrations the most august chiefs were looked upon by the small folks of the family as court fools. And no hatred is ever bestowed upon that which gives us amusement; there might have been disdain, but surely not so great a passion as hate.

And when the father went on any of his quests, the children, standing in the little enclosure, would remind him not to come home without a fresh supply of "Injun tales," the fairy-stories of children of wild life.

It was always Lewis who called loudest, who ventured farther from the clearing with his father. For a great love had sprung up in the boy for the father who had waited until he was born, so that he could go away from old troubles and want and poverty's trials. It was Lewis who saw his father before the others did, watching for him at a little knoll a quarter of a mile from the house. It was Lewis who went to the Monongahela for fish for the expected father, who often came a month later than promised. The chair for father was always placed by Lewis; the hottest potatoes allotted to his share. The boy, hearing of the revolting colonies, had his father explain to him the right and wrong of it all.

"Oh, if I could go!" he said. "There are boys as young there?"

Yet when the father was eager to join the "rebels" it was Lewis who cried:

'No, no, no! Mother and the children need you—I need you."

When the father had once been to Wheeling, and came home with the startling news that the flag which had long been representative of his Majesty's dominion was now everywhere wildly torn down and dishonored, it was Lewis who heard it from the father first and retailed it to the brothers and sisters with the pleasing reflection that Grizzie Heister's gift long before had been dishonored.

And when once an Indian, claiming a hundred horses of his father, had been refused, and declared vengeance in consequence, it was Lewis who threw a stone for the indignity offered to his father by the great, magnificent man.

"My white brother had houses and lands and beasts; why should he take the red man's?" the Indian asked.

"My red brother is mistaken," answered John Wetzel; "for I have taken nothing belonging to him. These horses were wild and unclaimed by my red brother, till I took them and trained and tamed them and found a market for them. Surely, they are mine."

"My white brother shall have two hundred wild

horses for his hundred tame ones, if he will but give them to me."

"Why should my red brother give more of his property for what he claims as his. Surely, he is mistaken."

"My white brother has the talking hand. I cannot compete with his slyness. He has stolen our beasts, he has stolen our strength. The white man has come and turned us away from our own. The white man has stolen the red man's land; the red man will steal the landlord's," concluded the baffled Indian, striding away.

"Nothing has been stolen," cried John Wetzel after the retreating figure. "The red man threw away, and what he threw away the white man picked up."

The Indian gave him a significant look of scorn; how could he understand this logic?

What seemed to be a small affair was the beginning of almost ceaseless warfare. Egged on by a few Indians who had been aiding the British, and who had now deserted and come to their old forest fastnesses, the hitherto peaceable red men held John Wetzel and the other settlers in a constant state of siege. But it was only as play to the children. Martin and Lewis Wetzel had mimic fights between them, representing the Indian's and the white man's mode of warfare.

The two boys had educated themselves in all the slyness of the savages. Martin was now fifteen years of age, Lewis thirteen, Jacob eleven, John nine.

Yet the fun of the boys was the burlesque of tragedies. The Indians came nearer and nearer, were openly hostile, and fired on any of the little party that ventured beyond their own reserve.

In the midst of the now frequently-recurring attacks, Lewis was stricken down with small-pox, and his brothers and sisters contracted it from him. With this dreadful contagion, with a scarcity of provisions, and murderous Indians lying in wait, the sum of human misery might by some women be said to be complete. But John Wetzel's wife was not such a woman; she nursed her children, collected food somehow, and helped barricade the insecure cabin, for the cabin had never been thoroughly finished, as with these early settlers there were always so many more necessary and useful things to claim the attention of the husband and father. She had her cows brought nearer the house, her sheep tethered, and she watched. John Wetzel did not venture out so frequently now as formerly, but remained at home and protected his family. Almost daily, fierce, bright eyes could be seen lurking in the bushes, and the muzzle of a musket more than once was detected in the leaves of a tree. At nighttime the wolves howled as ever, but it was not certain that human voices did not utter some of the wolves' tones, or that the scraping at the door was not a wary Indian looking on the group within.

The tragedy was coming that turned Lewis Wetzel from peace and tenderness into an Indian scout; that earned for him the sobriquet of "Hunting Dog;" that embittered his life and left him little time for aught but revenge. Yet at this time he was a happy child, just recovering from a long illness, lying securely in his flock-bed at night, or gazing up the wide-mouthed chimney during the summer darkness, counting the twinkling stars and listening with awe to the sounds outside, and himself and his brothers and sisters telling stories of bad spirits of bad Indians, who, debarred the pleasures of the happy hunting-ground, remained upon the earth cruelly to keep little white children wide awake, and, shining like pretty, quivering lights, to lead them from their homes into deep bogs and quagmires.

CHAPTER III.

THE BEAR.

SURELY, at this time, John Wetzel, with all his bravery, must in his heart have regretted that he had always disdained the usual precaution of settlers,—that of placing his family in one of the stations or forts, instead of carrying them into the thick of dangers that threatened them on all sides when he was absent from them. During these absences, towards the last, he constantly found that he was fearing for their safety, yet the next minute trying to laugh away his fear and to persuade himself that they were safe, because of the very lack of precaution to protect them, knowing that the red foe sought their enemies, expecting to find them protected by the mass, and not in exposed, isolated cases; for the Indians had hitherto felt assured that those brave enough to be fearless were friends. Though at present he remained more than ever in his clearing, yet there were times when he must be away. In the fly season, his horses, maddened by the stings of the gauzy-winged creatures, broke from their fastenings and scampered through the high grasses and took to the Monongahela. The water offered no obstacle whatever to them; they swam away, threatened every minute with being scattered and the band broken and dismayed. He was often away for days on the mission of gathering the half-broken beasts together again. Then he had his sheep and cows to look after, and on account of the loose sheds he had erected for them, and which he now had no time to strengthen, there was always a likelihood of their straying away. Again, he burned for news as to the progress of the fight of the people against all England, and he would hurry to the settlements for tidings. The country in revolt, bands of desperadoes creating havoc all around him, his little clearing and hut had miraculously escaped visitation. Yet every day made him more apprehensive for its safety, and his fear led him into the recklessness of seeking in the far settlements for news, leaving his wife and children unprotected till his return.

"They are in God's hand," he would say, "whether I am near or far."

His wife might have pleaded now for removal, for the time being, to a settlement; but she knew little or nothing of what was going on so near home; and, strange as it may appear, so close to scenes of world-wide import, she was as far away from them in thought as though they had not been. She had her home to think of; that was enough for her. She had to try and instill her little knowledge into the minds of her children, to teach them to read from the old Bible, and to tell them that the wide-rolling country around them did not constitute all of the world. Her husband had always protected her, and now he told her little or nothing of what he heard at the forts or settlements. It boded only for her good. However, when he went away now, he would caution Martin to keep a wary eye on the place.

"Why should you caution him now more than formerly?" his wife would ask.

"Because Martin is fifteen years old now," replied her husband; "almost a man, and he should know some of a man's responsibilities. Suppose anything should happen to me, who would be left but Martin to look after things?"

"Oh, husband!" cried the wife, alarmed at such a possibility.

"But there is the possibility," he said. "And all the same, Martin must look after the affairs at home now when I am called away. When any danger arises——"

"What danger can there be?" she asked.

He dared not tell her. But when he was on his

way home he would look, his heart in his throat, for the first sign of life and peace. And that first sign would usually be Lewis on the knoll waiting for him. Thus until the close of the summer of 1777. The woods around were beginning to soften into mellow tints, the songs of birds were fewer, the rich, aromatic haze of dying summer was over all the landscape like a soft, iridescent veil. The corn stubble glistened with dew of early morning, and the crickets were bold and made music pleasant to the peaceful housewife, as she went about her multifarious duties.

It was the last part of August. One day John Wetzel made up his mind to go to Wheeling for news. He had not been away from home for a month, and he was anxious to know what was going on in the outer world away from his little cabin, and how the fight was going, if for the British or the colonists.

A herdsman after a stray flock had come to the cabin one night lately and told him that there were rumors that the fight promised to be a long one, and that eventually all the rebelling colonists would be shot down by his Majesty's troops, who were now in New York preparing for a general wiping-out of the whole system and the organization of a new.

The herdsman had also told how the report ran

that the Indians had been called in by the British in this work of extermination, first as guides in the wild parts of the country, then as partisans.

This last piece of startling news determined John Wetzel: he knew what the war would be if the hostile Indians took part in it; he must know more.

While the herdsman was talking, he looked over to his wife. No, she had not heard. She was busy with the children and the Bible. The little group was all about her knees learning the wondrous story of the wars of old, of King David, of wise Solomon, and the brave women of the times.

The soughing of the wind outside was very pleasant to listen to, and far to the north there was a faint crystalline line of light which proclaimed the advent of cooler weather,—the northern lights, the aurora borealis.

"Wife," he said suddenly, "I think I will take a run up to Wheeling the coming week."

"Very well," was all she answered, and went on with the old stories.

So she knew nothing of the herdsman's talk.

In the following week John Wetzel went away.

His eyes were about him looking inquisitively at every tree, every clump of bushes. But all was as usual.

He was away two days.

In those two days he had found ample corroboration of the herdsman's story, and his face was set and stern as he wended his way towards his cabin.

In that lonely ride home undoubtedly he made up his mind that now at last he must take his family somewhere for more protection than he could afford them. Filled with the tales of horror he had heard at Wheeling, he left the place, full of fear for his family. Yet as he plodded along on his horse and got farther into the country, and saw all nature at peace, not a sign of change, his fears insensibly grew weaker.

When he came to his clearing and saw afar off his little son on the green knoll, he laughed at his weak dread. His wife was at the door when he came up.

"Well," he said cheerfully, "back again. No news, I suppose?"

"Why, yes," she answered; "old Crumply overturned the milk-pail last evening, and the speckled hen was caught in the briars."

"Too bad," he rejoined.

"Yes," she went on, "and that old bear that came in last winter and went up to the fire and warmed himself, and you would not have him turned out—well, he's been here again this morning, and he was in the bushes outside the cow-shed, his old nose poked here and there."

"I don't think he looked like the old bear, but he was the same color," spoke up Lewis.

So the news was chronicled.

And all that came of it was that John Wetzel determined to kill the bear in order to keep him from becoming too familiar.

"Give me his skin," said Martin.

But Lewis was looking out towards the bushes and said nothing.

"Hang it!" exclaimed the father all at once, "what do you think I've forgotten to get at Wheeling?"

"Your head?" asked his wife.

"Something as important—powder. The first time I ever did such a thing. The news there clean upset me——"

"What news?"

"News! Oh, nothing much. I must start again to-morrow."

"Then, father, take the girls with you, and let them stay with Tom Madison's folks. There's Berta Rosencranz, a likely girl, would like to have them, I'm sure. You know you've always promised to take them."

"Can you have them ready in time?"

"Ready! Listen to him, now. Come, boys, help get this carpet-bag filled."

In the small cabin all was excitement to get the

little ones ready for the exhilarating trip. There was bread to bake, so that they might have some loaves, and long light spongy cakes to eat on the way, and a bottle of milk was to be tied around the neck of each.

Next morning the father and the little girls went away,—at the last minute little John crying so hard to go with them that he was packed off too.

It was lonely in the cabin without them, and Martin wandered off with his gun. But Lewis stayed.

"Why don't you go with your brother?" asked their mother of him.

"I don't want to go," he answered.

"The first time you ever felt that way. Are you sick?" she asked.

"No," he answered, and went and sat outside the door, his face towards the clump of bushes. Nearly all day he sat there. The next morning he took up his post there again.

"He's fretting for father," commented his mother, watching him.

Towards sundown John Wetzel, with his powder, came up to the door.

"I missed you from the knoll, Lewis, lad," he said. The mother made her explanation.

"I wasn't fretting about father," cried Lewis, "for

father's brave. I only fret about the weak ones,— the girls."

"Oh, ho! it was the girls, was it?"

And Lewis made no answer.

"And now how is the bear?" asked the father, laying down his powder.

"I watched for him," said Martin, "but I didn't get a chance at him."

"A chance!"

"Father, he dodged me when he saw me."

"That's a queer bear," said John Wetzel.

"I don't think it is a bear," said Lewis, speaking for the first time.

"What do you think it is, old man?" asked his father laughing. "A whale, maybe? Did you see his skin?"

"It's a bear-skin," replied the boy.

"A bear-skin carries a bear," said the father.

"I don't think it's a bear," reiterated Lewis.

"What do you think it is, then?"

"An Indian, with the bear's skin."

"Lewis!" cried his mother shrilly, "what do you mean by such nonsense? An Indian, indeed! If it's an Indian, why should he hide out there, you foolish boy?"

"He saw me watching him."

"You're dreaming," said his mother. But the father said nothing.

John Wetzel, when night settled down dimmer and darker, fastened the door securely, and for the first time in many months. His wife was astonished at his timidity, and laughed at him.

"And only a bear," she said.

She took up her station beside the fire, which felt very comfortable this chilly evening. Her husband sat on the opposite side of the fire, shading his face with his hand. The boys gathered about their mother, and soon the quaint old story of the wars of the Bible sounded through the place. All was peace and gentleness.

"Hark!" said the father once.

"What is it?" asked his wife pausing, with her finger on the word at which she had stopped.

"Go on," he said; "it was only a rustling outside."

"Why, John," she cried merrily, "you are as nervous as a cat. What is the matter with you? If this comes of going to the settlements, you'd better remain at home."

She took up her reading once more. For perhaps fifteen minutes she read aloud, the light of the fire shining on the page before her, and making huge shadows in the place, when an exclamation from Lewis attracted her. She looked up; her husband had gone from the fire-place, and was over against the door, his eye at a knot-hole there.

"Why, John," she began.

"Hush!" he whispered.

There was a rustling outside the door, and a pressure against it. She laughed.

"It's the old bear," she said, "and you ought to be ashamed of yourself to be thus easily scared."

"Come here," he said.

She went to him, and, guided by him, placed her eye to the knot-hole. Outside, one by one, tall shadows passed by the door. There must have been twenty-five shadows. Each shadow as it went along pressed softly up to the door, then joined the other shadows collected a little apart from the house in an ominous company.

"What is it?" she whispered, awe in her voice.

"Indians!" he whispered in reply.

"But why do they come thus?"

"Wait!"

They had not long to wait. The shadows again separated, and went to the back of the cabin. There came a wierd, soft tramp in the night, a soft tramp that carried a grim purpose with it. There came a burst at the door, and a plank gave way. Through the opening made thus John Wetzel fired his gun. There was a shriek outside.

"What have you done?" wailed his wife, wringing her hands.

"Murder!" he said, "and they will do more."

She ran back to her boys, and clasped them to her, wildly praying to the Supreme Power to guard them from all harm. She looked at her husband; he was white as death.

"You cannot hold out against them," she said.

"No," he answered.

"Then why not ask them what they want?"

"Look!"

There was a thin streak of yellow light shining in from the night outside, through the opening left by the shattered plank. Her look told her everything.

"Fire!" whispered John Wetzel.

"They are never going to burn us!" cried the agonized woman.

There was a rasping sound all around the cabin, as the silent fiends outside piled up the branches from the dry trees into a mountain over the little cabin. Then there came a tender crackling; then fifty thin threads of flame sprang up. Then for the first time there was a sound of voices outside: a shout of joy. Once again John Wetzel's bullet sped on its way. Even once more; and the place was as though filled with a great sun, so light the flames were. A great blazing log tumbled in on the floor; the roof was a mass of tinder. The place was scorching hot, and outside, joining with the shouts of the Indians, came the frightened bellowing of liberated cattle and the bleating of scurrying sheep; while the quick stamps on the ground told of loosened half-wild horses making for the river.

The mother had torn a blanket from the bed and thrown it over the boys to protect them from the flames. The smoke filling the place blinded her. She could no longer see her husband. A part of the roof fell in, and with it came a crowd of yelling savages.

"John! John!" she shrieked, and hurried towards the place where she thought he must be. She was jostled against by fighting Indians, who were now stamping on the fire to put it out. She caught a glimpse of her husband in the arms of three or four painted savages, hurried from the cabin struggling for his life. Shrieking, she was after him.

She had almost touched him, when a gleam of something bright blinded her,—a tomahawk in the hands of a fierce brute over her husband's head.

There was a quick movement of the Indian's hand, a whoop from his lips as the instrument descended with a dull thud and crashed through the skull of John Wetzel. Then she knew no more.

The early morning light brought its dew and songs of birds.

The wife and mother had fallen in the long rank grass and been completely hidden from her would-be murderers. She raised herself and looked around.

There was the mouldering cabin. That was all. She knew that her husband was killed, she had seen the deed done.

She thought her children were burned up with the cabin.

Groaning in her agony, she determined to make her way to Wheeling, where her other children were. Fierce and weak, clutching her arms, she fled on. On her way stray cattle came and looked at her; cows begging her only to stop and milk them. Wild-eyed horses gazed at her, their manes blowing in the morning breeze, and dumbly asking her where was the corn they had so long been used to of mornings. She knew these were a part of her home, now hers no longer. Stumbling on, looking straight before her, she made her way, a widow with three children less than she had had last night, into the fort at Wheeling, where she fell unconscious, moaning unintelligibly.

CHAPTER IV.

THE OATH.

BUT the boys had not been murdered, as their mother's despair had suggested to her. Martin, the eldest, in the earliest moment of the assault had dropped from a window and flown across the lurid meadow, the yells of the savages growing fainter and fainter as he sped along, his mother's cries the last sound that rang in his ears. In the morning he crept back to the scene of ruin and desolation, only to send his voice to heaven for his lost or slaughtered kindred.

But the two younger boys had been discovered by the Indians beneath the blanket in the burning hut, where Lewis had been struck in the breast by a bullet which tore away a piece of the bone.

The conquerers spared these boys because of their extreme youth, and drove them before the band across the country, captives.

On the way, by the light from his burning home, Lewis, looking down, saw in the crushed and trampled grass the mutilated body of his father.

The boy stopped abruptly, and seemed turned to stone.

He looked around, and in the red light as far as his eye could reach rolled the boundless prairie, with groups of beasts huddled close together, gazing with wild, affrighted eyes upon the strange light. Great birds swept by towards the burning building, wheeled about it afar off, the circles eddying nearer to the flame, nearer and nearer still, until, with shrill cries, they darted into the heart of the flame, and perished there. There was a soft crackling in the grass, and spots of fire leaped up here and there. The moon looked red and sullen through the smoke. That was what the boy saw. His brother at his side was bitterly weeping and cowering before their red enslavers. But Lewis Wetzel shed no tear, uttered no groan.

"Did you see father, there in the grass?" wept his brother.

There was no reply.

"Father is dead!" wept his brother.

Still there was no reply to his wailing. Yet in that instant of horrid sight there had come to the silent boy the bitter hatred that never left him thereafter,—something that had meant life and being to him went from him into the dead body of his father, as dead as that body. A hush came upon him that left its impression forever after in his face. The love he bore the murdered man lived with tenfold intensity, and deadened every other natural feeling. But that love, having nothing now on which to expend its wealth in fond endearments and happy hopes, turned immediately it knew the outrage done it into irrevocable hatred against the slayers and their whole kind,—a fiendish perfection of hatred that bordered closely upon madness, but which had not a grain of madness in it, any more than madness may be said to actuate any feeling of retaliation for wrongfully-inflicted suffering. In the simple and untutored communities, however, through which the scout afterwards moved, he was often said to be not quite sane.

"White boys hurry!" said the tormentors that night of the murder.

A brawny chief came up and caught Lewis by his hair and threw him forward. The boy was only convalescent from small-pox, and the wound in his breast bled profusely.

"White boy bleeds easy," said the chief; "his blood is thin," and gave the lad another thrust forward. Still there was no wincing, nor a sound of complaint. "Good!" cried the chief, with a sort of brute admiration. "White boy no coward. He will be chief yet. If he will not be chief, he will roast."

The Indians, though as a race peculiarly deficient in the comic element, and to a degree blind to the ludicrous, laughed at this sally of their chief, and further sought to provoke the boy in order to test his endurance. They received no notice for their manœuvres, although one of them caught up little Jacob and pretended to tomahawk him.

They then tied the arms of the boys with thongs drawn so tightly as to cause exquisite pain. The smaller boy wept in agony; his brother never winced. As a new variety of sport, the two boys were then bound about the knees, and, prodded from behind, were forced into a sort of jog-trot inexpressibly wearisome. To this latter torture the younger boy obeyed and trotted on as he saw the man aiming blows at him. But the elder did not accelerate his pace from the tired march they had been reduced to, and every effort to harass him was useless if intended to cause him to act as his brother did. He was switched, and stinging blows fell unheeded on his limbs: a knife was brandished before his eyes, and he did not wince; it is doubtful if he ever saw the knife meant to menace him.

It was not so much bravery in the lad that made him callous to all this: the shock of his father's death turned his nerves to iron. While the Indians admired his stoic bearing, the hatred for them almost burst his breast.

But the Indians grew tired of their sport, and made preparations for going forward.

"They're taking us from home," wailed little Jacob, clinging to his brother, and thus impeding their movements.

A blow from a brave separated the boys. Then, with hits and thrusts, they were driven on. Day came, grew to meridian, declined, and nothing was given the boys to stay the pangs of hunger. Night, and another day, and their mouths were parched, their limbs faint and trembling.

At night Lewis Wetzel crouched upon the hard, bare earth, for they were not allowed a blanket, and folded his brother in his arms and thus stifled the trembling, caused as much by weakness and even fear as by the cold dews dripping through the trees upon their defenseless heads. The younger boy slept at last, secure in the fold of his boy protector; but Lewis never closed his eyes, but crouched there watching the guard that every now and then threw a glance towards the two youthful captives who rested just beyond the fire, but too far removed from it to feel any of its warmth.

"Courage! courage!" Lewis Wetzel was heard to whisper; but whether the courage was invoked for himself or his brother that brother who heard did not know.

For two days after their capture the red-skins drove the boys along like stolen sheep, waving their murderous weapons over their heads, and yelling in their ears, delighted when they saw a sign of blanching and wavering. They compelled the children to sit close to them while they eat and drank, and offered nothing to the captives. Then from feasting they would arise and drive the boys on, prodding them with sticks if they showed signs of weariness. And so on till they were no longer in sight of the familiar homely clearing, and were sadly exhausted, footsore, tired, and hungry. They received kicks and cuffs for any approach to tardiness, up to the very last, and at every moment they expected death. But such was not to be the case: death was not for them in that guise. The second night after the murder of John Wetzel the Indians sighted the Big Lick, about twenty miles from the river, in what is now Ohio, and upon McMahon's Creek. Here they encamped, the youthfulness of the boys and their utterly spent condition causing them to relax their usual vigilance concerning prisoners.

"White boys hungry?" they asked, holding tempting morsels of deer's flesh before the famished children's eyes. "White boys' father lost his hair, eh?"

Jacob was crying from hunger and fright; but

Lewis paid no attention to physical want, as he never did thereafter, but stood there white and nerveless.

The Indians made their fire bright after they had eaten their fill, and sat down and smoked and talked far into the night. Then they wrapped themselves in their blankets, and stretched themselves on the ground. The sentinels paced up and down for a little while, scarcely vouchsafing a glance towards the two pale, faint boys clinging to each other outside the ashes of the fire, and hemmed in by the blanketed sleeping warriors, now snoring. Then these watchers would pause once in a while, and glance over towards their somnolent brethren by the warm ashes that dissipated the chilly dews falling through the woods.

Wetzel, to his last day, always remembered how he felt watching the sleeping Indians, many of whom had removed their moccasins and thrust their feet into the ashes, lying there in sensuous ease, while two forlorn children crouched together on the ground far away from the fire's generous heat, and exhausted, bewildered, wounded. The watchers, from looking at the evidences of the ease they coveted, paced irregularly their rounds. Then they sat upon the ground for a little while. Then two got together and spoke a word now and then.

The fire grew less, and sunk away into smouldering ashes; the sounds in the midnight wood were conducive to easy slumber.

One of the guards lazily watching the boys saw the bright light in Lewis Wetzel's eyes, and came over to him frowning.

"White boy sleep?" he asked.

He received no reply.

"White boy better go sleep," he said further. Then still seeing the eyes open, he struck the boy in the face as a reminder.

"Now sleep," he said; "a Indian brave cut out the white boy's eyes and make him sleep."

This remedy for insomnia seemed to be understood by the boy, for he *did* close his eyes, he *did* to all appearances sleep as his brother was sleeping beside him.

At last the watchers, from sitting on the ground, rolled heavily over, one by one, and slept with the others.

When they had lain there a few minutes, with no signs of awaking, Lewis Wetzel whispered into the ear of his brother:

"Get up; we will go home."

"There is no home," whimpered the little brother.

"Get up; we will find home," fiercely said Lewis, in so strange a tone that his brother obeyed him unquestioningly.

Captivity and Escape of Lewis and Jacob Wetzel.

They threaded their way between the sleeping Indians, guided by the glow of the hot ashes. Leaves crumpled under their feet, and they paused. No, no one was aroused. A bulky brave lay directly in their path.

This brave at first was a stumbling-block to the two boys. He was broad, his arms were stretched out beside him; the slightest touch might wake him. Even as they stood there, the boys saw this brave struck on the face by a falling leaf, and he stirred uneasily, without, however, opening his eyes. They would not go back, they dared not go forward. Minutes seemed to elapse, and still they stood there, that sleeping form before them, their minds strained to the last point, and almost beyond reasoning. At last, with a pulling of himself together, and a stern setting of his upper teeth in his lower lip:

"Over," whispered Lewis Wetzel, and he lifted his brother sheer across the body, stumbling after him. There was yet an outer circle of Indians to be crossed. This was done boldly, and the free land lay before them, and they had but to choose a way. They went a few hundred yards, when their wounded feet made them pause and sit upon a log. Their shoes were gone.

"We cannot go," said the younger brother, with age's desperation.

"Not barefooted," replied Lewis; "we must have moccasins."

"Where will we get them?"

"You stay here, and I will get them," said Lewis, in that same tone of voice that must be obeyed.

He went back to the camp-fire, crossing sleeping body after sleeping body. He found the moccasins set before the hot ashes to dry. He took two pairs, and came with them back to his brother.

"Here," he said, and knelt down in the darkness and fitted the moccasins upon the younger boy's feet.

They sat a little while longer on the log. Privation seemed to have dwarfed the energy even in so young children, and now that they saw a way out of captivity, the impulse to accept it seemed gone. At last the older boy aroused himself from the state of apathy they had fallen into.

"Now," he said, "don't move. Stay here till I come back."

"Where are you going?"

"We need protection, little Jacob."

"Where are you going?—why do you leave me here alone?"

"We must have a gun," he said, and disappeared in the darkness.

As in many other hearts brought to desolation,

the thought of a Supreme Being seems further removed than mortal revenge, and what mortal can do is of more moment than the power of Omnipotence; so was it with this boy when he left his brother, who depended upon him, alone in the darkness and the night. There flashed over him the stories he had heard his mother read from the Bible,—the stories of a just and all-powerful God. He thought of the prayer for protection he had early learned. Then:

"No!" he said bitterly; "I will not pray. Myself must do now."

The meaning of desolation, and the one power that delivers from it, was to come later in his life.

Again did he make his way back to the camp-fire. There was a musket lying beside one of the sleepers, and he stooped and picked it up, and prepared to move off. The sleeper stirred, and changed his position, so that his face turned up to the boy, gleaming like mahogany in the fire-glow.

All apathy was gone from the boy then. What had come to him when he looked upon his dead father awoke again. Grasping the musket in his firm, brown hands, he looked down at the face. Here was one of his father's murderers! Perhaps this very man had struck the blow; perhaps it was he who had first fired the cabin; perhaps it was he who had worn the bear-skin, and been watched for days by the boy who now looked upon him, holding him in his power. Might not the debt be paid now? Instinctively he raised the hammer of the musket. He lost sight of everything else around him but the man who lay in his power. That one face gleamed out at him, tempting him. A fierce longing came to him now—this moment—to place that gun-barrel close to that treacherous countenance, and send a soul out to the dread unknown in memory of his father. Fear was gone from the boy now, and he stood there as reckless of life as he was ever after. The helpless Indian face tormented him; more and more he burned to wreak vengeance. He looked about him, and saw the many recumbent forms. Oh, to kill all! At least, he might die in the attempt.

Then he thought of his relying brother, waiting for him on the log in the black, dense wood.

"I have no time now," he said, slinging his weapon over his shoulder, and leaping savage after savage with a step as light as the air, and, buoyed up, he came back to his brother. They set out immediately. Young as they were, they were sufficiently expert in tracking paths in the woods to find their way out. There was nothing but a charred ruin remaining of their home, but they were to make their way to their mother and sisters and brothers.

Again the leaves crisped under their tread; farther and farther from the light of the fire they went.

"Remember," said Lewis Wetzel once, "there must be no more whimpering. If you whimper, I'll leave you here."

"Are you afraid of them?" asked his little brother tremulously.

"It is because I want them to fear me that I mean to escape," was the reply.

So they went on, casting many a glance back through the ebon darkness, where the now dim light of the camp-fire was but as the glow of a candle they had often seen set in the window at home to guide them on their way from the hunting of a stray sheep or cow.

They had not been gone long when the Indian whose gun had been purloined awoke and discovered his loss. The fact of the escape was made known at once, and a pursuit instituted. The boys, going along, heard the Indians hard on their heels. Once they were almost overtaken, the Indians brushing closely past them.

"Down!" whispered Lewis, and he and his brother precipitated themselves into the sea of tall grass all around them, and which their pursuers beat with clubs without discovering the objects of their search. Long the boys laid there. Then the pursuing party passed on. "Up!" said Lewis Wetzel, and he and his brother fell into the rear of the searchers, and took up their travels again towards liberty.

Then they heard the Indians returning, cursing the guard and everybody concerned, for the loss of two captives who had not so much as left their scalps behind, but had stolen a gun and two pairs of moccasins—and only boys at that!

When the boys heard the angry voices returning, they precipitated themselves into the grass again, and a second time escaped detection. Then, when the party had passed by, they went feebly on again. They were then followed by two Indians on horseback, whom they eluded in the same manner. But these Indians drove their horses over the grass in a hap-hazard manner, and more than once the boys narrowly escaped death. But they did escape, and a day more found them beyond the reach of the braves.

They subsisted for days on roots, for though they had a gun they had no amunition but the one load in it, and that Lewis refused to use on mere game, expecting more deadly use for it were they pursued a second time (which was not to be), and, after slow marches and strong endeavors to counteract the weakness stealing over them, they reached the river. In their sorry condition, and knowing that that river *must* be crossed before they could be near friends, the two boys made a raft, the implement for making which was a jack-knife, and their clothing torn in strips to tie the planks together when the withes from the trees failed them. In this raft they crossed the river, two boys made men by sorrow and wrong. When they reached the other side, Lewis was nearly exhausted from the bleeding of the wound in his breast.

"We must reach Wheeling," he said to his brother, and despite pain and weakness they again pushed onward, and slowly, but surely, they sighted Wheeling and friends.

From afar off they saw the place, and could discern the people moving about.

"But it is so far," pleaded the younger boy.

"You will go, as I tell you to," said the other.

Nearer and nearer they went to the place. Once out of the tall grass, they could be seen, and a man saw them. They could see this man, his hand before his eyes, looking in their direction, and apparently hallooing to those about him; then the boys encountered grass again. When they emerged, they were within hailing distance; in a few minutes more they were in Wheeling.

There they were met by their mother and her friends. Freeing himself from the hysteric woman's embraces, Lewis Wetzel stood apart from them all.

"He is hurt in the breast," said a little girl—Berta Rosencranz.

"Never mind my hurt," he said to those anxious to attend to him. "I am thinking—of my father."

"He is crazed," said old Eberly, their one-time neighbor.

"He is *not!*" cried the little girl, stamping her foot, her eyes blazing.

For several minutes the boy stood thus apart, his mother bitterly weeping, her little family huddled up beside her, and the child Berta alone gazing on Lewis with understanding of the feeling swaying him. Suddenly throwing the Indian's musket from him, and raising his clenched hand, he cried:

"I swear to kill every Indian that crosses my path, so long as God lets me live!"

For a moment there was a stunned silence; the vehemence, the energy, and, moreover, a certain quality they had not expected from the lad, startled the rude sympathizers into a calm of wonder and awe. Then his mother broke out in wails, wringing her hands and declaring that her child was mad, and asking despairingly, "What shall I do? What shall I do?"

She grasped her other child, so recently recovered, and held convulsively to him.

"Lewis! Lewis!" she cried, "what does it all

mean? What can it all mean? First your father, then you. I am wild! I am wild! I am afraid for the first time in my life, and I don't know what makes me afraid."

His little brother, whom he had brought into Wheeling, broke from his mother, and stood beside him.

"Your oath is mine!" he said stoutly.

The girl Berta had thrown herself upon the ground weeping. The mother rent the air with her cries. How that oath was more than mere boyish bravado their after-life attested. The energy of youth kept alive their hatred, until it had become a characteristic defying age or calmer judgment to effect alteration or mitigation. Hurled at one fell swoop from childish inconsequence and carelessness, their childish natures forsook them; they were hardened men, with more than a man's ordinary responsibility. Young boys were men when they could do a man's work among the settlers; and what the endurance and trials of a bringing-up such as theirs had been inculcated in them made them like the savages whose childish rearing was not a whit wilder than that of these white boys'.

A descendant of old neighbor Eberly told the present writer, not long since, that an old paper, found among some family books, and written by Eberly's hand, has this note:

"Lowis Wetzell a prime young ladd made oath to-day that hee wold kill every Injun as come on his path. A bad beginning for so young a ladd. I spoke to him about it, and he ansered nothing. Hee seemed like to a grown man all to once. Hee had such an air about him that I could say nothing to dissuade him after a bitt. Hee has suffered much: hee never smiled all day, as childern will when surrounded by other childern and soon forgit their losses. And the strange part of it is that nobody thinks the oath out of the way nor odd for a ladd to make. It sounds odd, and it looks odd on paper. But looking at the ladd and seeing his harde face and harde eyes, it seemeth not so odd nor out of the way. The Lord be with us all, and rid us of our many troubles now clustering about these colonies that are no longer England's out-posts, praise the Lord!"

Yet De Haas, in his memoir of Lewis Wetzel, gives an account of the death of John Wetzel, the father, which carries the date of the massacre forward about ten years or so, thus making Lewis Wetzel far more mature when the famous oath was taken than the notes the writer has collected. It is even asserted that the family came to Wheeling from Washington, Pennsylvania; some, again, contradicting these, and giving the Pennsylvania side of Virginia as their home before going farther West. The writer has had it asseverated to him that Lancaster sent the family of Wetzels forth. Said an old woman in the old market at Lancaster:

"Wetzels? Yah! I know Wetzels. My mudder she lofe Jahn Wetzel's boy Lewis. My mudder she was gal, and used to watch for Jahn Wetzel's boy Lewis up Wheeling. He was big man wid long hair, and he mended my mudder's dolly-baby's legs. He mended every tings what want mending, and the wiming used for to say: 'It's time Lewis Wetzel he come now already, and we will get all our tings mended when he come once.' Vashingtown was Lewis Wetzel's home? Nein! nein! Lancaster was his home. You tink I lies? I got big blue pitcher, what Heister's gal she found in Jahn Wetzel's house when he goned away, and my mudder's mudder she kept it."

And she pulled her black hood further over her face and attended to a more paying customer, who wanted some of her beautiful eggs and golden lumps of butter.

Be it as it may, there is so much that is necessarily left to conjecture, and facts standing the chance of being doubted as much as hearsay, that only the most often vouched-for legends, with long strings of scarcely contestible proofs, can be taken as in any way authentic, even such facts standing the chance of having detractors arise, claiming more proofs than those which have almost established the authenticity of the accepted version. Yet the Lancaster authorities still say Lancaster, with show of reason. As to the death of John Wetzel, De Haas's statement is: "He was killed near Captina, in 1787, on his return from Middle Island Creek, under the following circumstances. Himself and companion were in a canoe, paddling slowly near the shore, when they were hailed by a party of Indians, and ordered to land. This they, of course, refused to do, when immediately they were fired upon, and Wetzel was shot through the body. Feeling himself mortally wounded, he directed his companion to lie down in the canoe, while he (Wetzel), so long as strength remained, would paddle the frail vessel beyond reach of the savages.

"In this way he saved the life of his friend, while his own was ebbing fast. He died soon after reaching the shore, at Baker's Station."

This is materially different from the other version, and depends mainly, as much as that, upon the gossip of the settlers, which has come down to to-day in legends. In the then state of the country it is just possible that a settler murdered was only a settler murdered, and that the mode of John Wetzel's death was little inquired into until after his son had come prominently before the country as his avowed and fatal avenger,—the care-taker of the weaker parts of the frontier, whose services might always be called upon, and relied upon, wherever there were signs of Indian depredation, or where widowed women and orphaned children had no one left to defend them. And he came without a word, their friend, and the ready executioner of their red enemies.

But all statements, from whatever source, and with whatever degree of proof, coincide with the main events here narrated; and agree that the murder of the father was the chief moving power of the whole after-life of the scout. And the taking prisoners of the boys is substantially the same in all accounts as is given in the present instance, the wound in the breast and the loss of a part of the breast-bone being spoken of in every version.

Yet it seems more than probable that the two boys were of a very tender age when captured, younger by far than De Haas in his narrative makes them, as their savage captors had dealt only too often with white *men*, and very rarely took them alive when they were defending their own property and lives. Nor is it scarcely as probable that the sly and ever-watchful red men would have been so lacking in their austere treatment of grown men as to allow an escape of two for want of adequate guardianship and bonds. The Indian guarders of white men were staunch as those of old Rome, who were accused by the Jews of sleeping around the tomb of the crucified Christ, which accounted for its vacancy. A Roman soldier to sleep!

Consequently, their youth is pretty well established by the fact of the escape of the two boys, the mode of it, and the long time of waiting on the part of Lewis Wetzel before he carried his oath into execution.

However, the incident of their capture and escape is in all the chronicles and tales, and in all, also, is the vouched-for truth that the times were such that small mercy would have been shown to even willing captives by the Indians, if those captives were men. But boy prisoners were often treated with unexpected leniency, after trial of their endurance, as in the case of these two, in the hope of their affiliation with Indian tribes and subsequent adoption of their habits, thus becoming warriors fiercer, more malign, than the natives themselves, as apostasy invariably carries with it a fervor unknown to original beliefs and modes.

It is said that Lewis Wetzel sedulously declined any treatment for his wound. Little Berta Rosencranz gave him lint, and cried when he dropped it on the ground. Old Eberly said that the wound had caused fever, which hurt his brain. And this fact he records also:

"The ladd his heade burnt like fire, and his eyes they burnt too. Settler Truman's wife she gif him some tea made off the tanzy plante and olde man; but he wold not drinke off it, which I done my own selfe for the rheumatiz."

This old annotator appears to have thought more of the family than the other did, and keeps them steadily in view. His notes being in private-family form necessarily contain much that should not be made public, and which would be uninteresting, save for the quaintness in them. The writer uses them solely because they throw a more human light on the times and people they speak of.

Three weeks after the arrival of the two boys at Wheeling, and when they had been seen but little in the community, old Eberly, going into the woods to trap a squirrel or two, stumbled across the dead body of an Indian. A few yards from the body Lewis Wetzel and his young brother were silently regarding the old man.

"I sed to them," he writes, "you raskels, why fore did you put to death innocent man?"

The answer is not recorded, nor is the denial of

the death at the hands of the boys. But at the girdle of the dead Indian was found a scalp of golden hair, that glittered and fell in pretty streams before the brave, and tied to the bright hair *the left hand of a young white girl*, the fingers crushed and broken, as though the owner of the small hand had been cruelly tortured before death, if the hand had not belonged to a girl still living.

"Oh, such times!" writes old Eberly, after shuddering over the little white hand. "And the oath of that ladd was not only mere child's-talk. What will come of that oath? And O, these troublous times!"

There had come into Wheeling, a few days after the restoration to liberty of the two boys, a white man, from whose mouth had been torn the tongue, and whose wrists were gory stumps, from which no hands extended. He could neither tell nor write the story of his wrongs. Yet no voice nor writing was necessary to tell that Indian cruelty had done the deed. When this man died, eyes blurred with passion, not with tears, looked on his corpse. At about the same time twenty horses belonging to a settler were found one morning hamstrung, so that the suffering brutes had to be killed immediately.

A field of grain was trodden down in one night by human feet, and no one had heard a sound in the night but the soughing of the wind and the peculiar hush of the darkness. A party of white soldiers in red coats, led by Indians, had come to a settler's house and taken the bread from the hungry children and marched the father off a prisoner and left the woman in the hands of the savage guides. Innumerable are the stories that have come down to us, and which are horrible to us at this remote time, when even to read of them makes us hasten to turn the page. What must it have been when that old man, in the midst of it, took his quill and poke-berry-juice, and wrote upon his coarse paper his trembling concern for " these troublous times"? And what were these times?

CHAPTER V.

THE INDIAN SCOUT.

THE times were such as admitted very rarely of any intermediate course of action whatsoever. It was either for or against. It was a time of peculiar unquiet and turbulence. The Revolution was at its height; it seemed doubtful which way the war must eventually turn, and desperation became synonymous with bravery in the urging of their rights by the colonists. The troubles in the interior called for all the aid the colonies could grant, leaving the frontier almost completely exposed and defenseless.

The British called in and stimulated the already reckless and embittered Indians to make inroads upon cultivated lands and tethered stock. These inroads left everything changed, and barrenness and waste were on every hand. Scenes of murder were of frequent occurrence, and death was not always the worst penalty inflicted upon the captive settlers. These were only too often mere women and children, the men having marched inland hastily, leaving their families in the hands of Divinity, while they were enrolled as rebels against his Majesty of England. There were renegades, too, among the early settlers, who, being offended by slights, real or imaginary, inflicted by their brother emigrants, were the most energetic of the advisers of the Indians in their barbarous mode of warfare, and were benefited by the lion's share of the spoils. Simon Girty is one of these men. Because of some offered slight, the nature of which is mostly conjectural after this long period of time, and few authentic proofs being at hand, if any in existence, he deserted and joined the Indians, and became a horror to his former white associates. His exquisite cruelty was something original in the simple annals of the first settlers. His fury against the whites resembled more the paroxysms of a maniac than the deliberate cruelty of even a naturally ferocious temperament. No inquisitioner of old could have enjoyed more unmoved the throes of agony wrung from the tortured white man than did Simon Girty, as, mounted on his horse, he would look on at the barbarous scenes enacted by the raging Indian braves. With all their wiliness and suspicion of the whites, the red-skins seem to have reposed confidence in this man, strange as it may appear. His fiendishness may have awed them, and made them look to him as the incarnation of their own worst traits, which worst traits are oftener obeyed than better ones. At any rate, they held to him, and were willing to be guided by him in depredations they would never have thought of but for him.

He appears to have lost all moral sensibility, to have been deaf to the voice of friendship, save on one occasion. And that occasion is, that Kenton, who, as Girty's fellow-spy, went by the name of Butler, was at last taken prisoner by the Indians in a raid he had instituted against them, and, after being mercilessly tortured, was condemned to the stake, and besought Girty's intervention. Girty really did work hard to save his friend, and brought the influence of the noble and simple chief Logan to bear in his case.

"Young man," said Logan to the captive, "my people seem very angry with you. What cause have they?"

"They are angry,—I don't know why," said Kenton respectfully, and looking over to Girty.

"Tell me the truth," said Logan.

"I only know I have fought with your people, then became their enemy and fought against them," returned Kenton boldly.

"Be of good cheer," said the chief; "a man is not base for fighting against his enemies. My people speak of burning you at Sandusky, but I will send runners before, and they will speak you fair at Sandusky."

By dint of wily and yet brave manœuvering and risk, Kenton escaped, and Girty was his savior.

But Girty was not the only man who acted so insanely against his brethren. With such men in their midst, often unknown to be anything but their warmest champions, what had the settlers not to fear?

The money of the British doubtless played a leading part with many of these spies. Old Eberly writes:

"To-day I buried my britania tea-pot, for I mortally fear to bee called on to deliver it up, it being of a tempting richness, to the British spies that seem to bee here, there, and everywhere, without us knowing who they bee."

There was no use in making any complaint, for there was no one in authority with whom to lodge complaint. If a spy were discovered, the only righteous mode of dealing with him was to kill him as a dangerous reptile, without waiting for any intervention of so-called law. For there was little or no law now within reach of the frontiermen, and each was compelled to be soldier, prosecutor, and judge in his own defense, and to use his strong arm in the interests of his hard-earned property and his helpless family. As the Indian code was one of total extermination, the white settler was compelled to adopt the red man's tenets, and no mercy nor parley was granted.

From this only further cruelty, barbarity, and hatred could arise. And there sprang up among the settlers, after a night of horror and devastation, the Indian scout,—a man sworn to hunt down the Indian, to destroy him upon his own ground, to have no mercy, to be an avenging fate to wrong-doers. The services of these scouts were wholly voluntary, and their supplies were furnished by themselves at their own cost.

There was a settler who sold all his little belongings and came with the money procured therewith in his hand, and, handing it over to a man in authority, said:

"This is all I have. I give it to you if you will let me be a scout. If I die, the money can be divided between you. Should I live, then I can work for myself and gain more."

It was known that a woman who had suffered intense wrong at the hands of the Indians had vowed a fierce revenge. A scout was encountered in the Indian trails who spoke to no man; stern, sad of face, heavy-browed, he went on his way, ferreting out stray Indians and killing them without mercy and in silence. He associated with no man, he spoke not of his prowess; he never made a display of the scalps of his victims, if he ever took any; he was scarcely seen to eat, and when he slept no one conjectured. Stern, ruthless, he killed and spared not men, women, and even little children—all fell before the rifle that never left his hand. It was said that a score of Indians bit the dust in his track within a month, and still he went silently on.

Once, a cold, stormy night, another scout came across him going through the blinding snow towards an Indian camp, a heavy bag thrown across his shoulders, his gun no longer by his side, his right hand grasping the bag and holding it in place, his left hand hidden in the breast of his coat. His fellow-scout spoke to him, and he turned jaded eyes upon him and smiled,—the first smile that any one had seen on his face since he had mysteriously come into contact with the other scouts. He was asked where he was going. He pulled his left hand from his coat, and pointed towards the Indian camp—his hand had been shattered by the premature explosion of his gun, and was powerless henceforth. What, then, could he be going for in the direction of the Indian camp? He passed by his fellow-scout and went through the snow. The other man turned and sought shelter, and, wrapping himself in a blanket, slept.

He knew not how long he slept, but all at once he was awakened by an earthquake: he thought that heaven and earth had come together. But everything was still when he opened his eyes. For all that, his heart was beating wildly, and he could not think he had been dreaming. But no repetition of the sound occurred, and still the soft white snow fell gently and softly outside. He argued with himself that he had been dreaming, and that the start he had experienced when the other scout had shown his shattered hand had produced the dream—he had imagined the exploding gun.

But when it was light, he went towards the Indian camp discovered the night before. The snow had wiped out the track of the silent traveler encountered last night; the snow had wiped out most of the marks of devastation that wounded, silent traveler had caused. For the scout came across the form of the man, dead in his path, covered with snow, and with limbs and members of five or six Indians near by.

The bag on the silent scout's back had been filled with gunpowder, which, knowing that his useless hand would forever debar him from the use of the rifle, he had collected in some manner, and, as a last revenge, had gone to the camp-fire and thrown it in, taking death thus, himself perishing with the last fruits of his undying hatred. This the man who found the body readily understood, and gazed with awe upon the wild work of the strange being who rested under the snow before him. He leaned down before that form and scraped the snow away from the face. He opened the coat, then started back in horror: for the silent scout, the deadly destroyer of all Indians, man, woman, and child, was the woman who had been most foully wronged by Indian braves.

This story was brought into Wheeling along with the body of the woman. Her death made more scouts than her life could have made. A thirst for Indian blood arose; men coaxed for the privilege of being recognized as avengers of white men's blood. Even children were told their duty was to kill. All this argued that it was animal against animal. But such is not the case: it was awakening intelligence against rudely-awakened intelligence.

There are people, even at this late day, who hold that the Indian is a wronged man and a brother, and that the most uncivilized mode has ever been adopted to civilize him. He was naturally a brave and reckless man, protecting his rights and allowing no encroachment upon what he claimed as his own. He did not hate the whites, the "long knives," till he thought they usurped his privileges. Day by day his lodge was moved farther and farther towards the setting sun, his ranks thinned of his young warriors and maidens by the promises, honest and specious, of the whites. He could not accept civilization because, like the bison, civilization meant a bridle to his personality. "War was the favorite pursuit of this martial people, and military glory their ruling passion. Agriculture and the laborious drudgery of domestic life were left to the women. The education of the savage was solely directed to hunting and war. From his early infancy he was taught to bend the bow, to point the arrow, to hurl the tomahawk, and to wield the club." He was also taught to track his enemy's footstep through the almost impregnable forest; to mark the faintest indications of danger; to find his way by the appearance of the trees and by the stars. He must endure fatigue, cold, famine, every privation.

The Indians had an exalted spirit of liberty, which revolted against all control. They considered themselves sovereigns, accountable to no one but Manitou, the Great Spirit,—God! The dusky brave despised death, and during his life regarded it with the indifference of the Moslem. He seldom committed suicide, because patience and endurance are the first duties of a warrior, leading to high rewards, and none but cowards yield to pain and misfortune. He was taught from early infancy that the Great Spirit would be offended by any change in the red man's mode of life handed down by ancient tradition. He believed all the wild and debasing superstitions his wise men taught him. He left tobacco on rocks as a sacrifice to invisible spirits. His every act must conciliate some spiritual influence. He was willing in the beginning to act as guide to the chance white man, and looked upon the interloper, at first, almost as a superior being.

Roger Williams says: "I have been guided by them twenty, thirty, and forty miles, through woods, on a straight course, out of any path. When the English first came to this country, it was admirable to see what paths their naked feet had made in the wilderness, in the most stony and rocky places. On the whole, we may speak of them as a brave, reckless, generous, and unfortunate people."

Imagine such a people suffering under an imaginary wrong, thinking their simple lives set aside and circumvented by cunning and fraud. What they claimed by the law of primogeniture was taken from them, and they were forced to make treaties with the stranger, who had no right to anything, in order to insure possession of what had always been theirs.

Ignorant, as we reckon ignorance, filled with their own importance, what could they not become when desperate? A simple, holy nature perverted becomes more vile than the veriest reveler in all villainies. The whites who came to them with offered services when they were fighting off the settlers that daily encroached a little upon their reserves were of the most depraved nature, and sided with them only to wreak some petty vengeance upon their brothers, or to gain by foul means what they dared not claim by fair.

The Indian, a lover of bravery, must have seen in all the whites but prototypes of those who claimed their aid in their own quarrels. They became the fiends we know them during the Indian wars. All the unbridled passions of man, often more fierce than those of beasts, were given full license in their determination to wipe out the encroacher. They knew no reason, they saw no rights but their own. They were frequently imposed upon, in the childishness of their trust, and they became suspicious of all. But in their cowardly slyness, as we now call their stratagems, some of the old attributes must have survived, for the very reason that the brave of to-day has in some things a likeness to the warrior of a century ago. He endures: that is the likeness to his progenitor which survives and renders him above scorn for treachery and utter profligacy.

The writer has in his hands a little pamphlet, written by an adjutant in a Western military reserve, and circulated by his superior officer, describing a peculiar dance which he witnessed in the Unquepapa country, where he was stationed in 1871. Some of the features of this ghastly saturnalia are gleaned from it here as a sample of human endurance.

The sunflower dance is one of the most important dances or ceremonies among the American Indians, and at this dance new braves are admitted to an equality with those already proved as braves, who are called soldiers or principal warriors, and have an extra lodge—a large wigwam—in every big tribe, where no women are admitted, and where they hold their councils. It is called the "sunflower dance" on account of the season in which it occurs, that is, in the month of June or July, when the river edges are decked with a species of sunflower which the Indian maidens use for decorating themselves on this occasion.

The ground chosen for the dance is a level stretch of land without tree or shrub, except one young ash of about thirty feet high, and devoid of limbs and branches for twenty feet from the ground.

A short distance from this ground the narrator referred to saw several Indian grave-mounds, raised on high sticks above the ground, and each covered with red and white blankets. Skeletons of horses were lying at the foot of some of the graves, indicating that some one held specially dear, as mother, father, great warrior, or pretty woman, is buried there.

It is the custom among these Indians to kill a fine horse or a good mule on the graves of their best friends, and give in this manner the coyote and buzzard a feast, to keep them for awhile from attacking the bodies of the beloved ones. In communities of brave, simple people, however, even from Homer's time, animals belonging to the dead have been slaughtered, and with a noble and more poetic meaning than the one quoted above, which may be only as the practical white American understood it.

About 11 A.M. the Indians began to assemble from all parts of the country, almost all on horses or ponies, the men and women riding alike, astride.

The spectators posted themselves on the nearest hills, from which they could best see the proceedings. Those more immediately concerned in the dance dispersed themselves, parading over the festival grounds, all gayly dressed, and exhibiting on poles their enemies' scalps. After gravely taking whiffs from a pipe, which was passed from hand to hand,

and blowing the smoke in two streams from the nostrils, and raising their heads to the sun, by which they meant to offer a sacrifice of incense to the Great Spirit above, a drum was placed in the centre of the braves, and each warrior produced a thin ash branch, one end decorated with red ribbon. The women sat on the ground, forming an outer circle around the warriors, and began to sing, the men beating the drum.

A chief, named Kill Eagle, now rose from the ground, and stood looking around him for some time in mute dignity, until a silence as of death prevailed. He stands still, scanning the multitude for perhaps ten minutes; he does not speak, yet the people evince no impatience—they are as still as the hills around them.

At length the chief begins to speak in low but impressive tones, which become louder as he proceeds, and furious and menacing as his subject affects him. The substance of his discourse, which lasted more than an hour, being the past glories of the Sioux nation, the triumphs of their fathers in war and in the chase; the courage displayed by his people, and their honorable deaths in battles against their foes; or in their lodges in their old age, surrounded by their children and the scalps of their enemies.

He did not want his young men to think that he alluded to his white brethren, with whom he desired his people to be at peace, as it is the wish of the Great Father that they should live as brothers. But he meant those thieving, robbing Indians of other tribes, whom it would please the Great Spirit that they should punish for past crimes, such as stealing their horses, carrying off their young women to other tribes, and killing, when they could, any hunter of his people whom they might find alone on the prairie.

To punish those bad men they should have brave men; and as the number of his braves was getting small, through the death of those lost in battle and from old age, he wanted young blood in their braves, to uphold the honor of his nation. They did not want women to do their fighting, nor men with women's hearts in their bosoms, but men of tried courage and bravery.

He said that any of his young men that wished to prove themselves as braves might prove it as their fathers before them had done; that any of them that did not feel his heart big should stay among the women, and those who did come for trial should remember that the eyes of their fathers, mothers, sisters, sweethearts, and friends would be upon them.

He said they should prove themselves as men able to endure, as brave men would do; that the Great Spirit despises cowards, and forever banishes them from the happy hunting-grounds.

The time has sped on, and it is half-past twelve now, and further crowds by this time have streamed in.

The medicine-man now stands up and calls the young men who are anxious for the trial.

About sixty stalwart young Indians from different parts of the crowd now enter the ring and throw off their blankets. These are the candidates. Drums beat, squaws sing; each youth has a wreath of green leaves placed upon his head; the pipe is passed around; four warriors step into the ring, two carrying lassoes; the first two approach the line of young men leading forth the first to the stake, and the medicine-man throws the youth on his back on the ground.

The medicine-man bending over the prostrate man cuts two slits in his right breast, about an inch apart and three inches long, and the blood flows freely and trickles to the ground. Then he cuts two more slits in the left breast like those in the right, running the knife up and down under the skin to raise it from the flesh. Next the end of a lariat is passed under the skin, drawn across the breast and passed under the skin of the other cut, and drawn so far through, as is sufficient to knot it to the other part of the lariat in front of the breast.

He is then fastened by the lariat to the bare ash-tree and is expected to free himself by breaking the holds on his breast, for he cannot break the lariat. He pulls and pulls, yells and jumps, but the skin is tough. The crowds scream with delight. He tries again, and breaks one hold.

The loss of blood and the pain weakens him and he seems doomed. But two stout warriors seize him by the shoulders and fling him from them with ponderous force until they break the other hold.

He rises from the ground, picks up his blanket coolly, and retires.

The next young man steps forward. He has cuts made in the calves of his legs to which are fastened the skulls of buffalo-heads, and he is left to dance and jump about till he breaks loose from the skulls.

One young Unquepapa Sioux was so eager to distinguish himself, that when he came to the trial he walked in between four posts, having two in front and two in the rear, and had four holes cut in his breast, and four in his two shoulders; through each of these holes a lariat is drawn and fastened to the posts, having about three feet of the lariat slack to allow him to move back and forth. He began to jump and leap, sometimes straining on the lariat in front, and then on the ones fastened to his back; at other times jumping high, bringing the strain equally on all the fastenings. So he continued to jump and leap thus, like some wild animal trying to leap out of a trap, for perhaps a half-hour, but could not get one of the fastenings loose, and at last he fainted from pain and loss of blood.

A crowd of warriors gathered around him and soon restored him to consciousness by pouring cold water over him.

The lariats are still fastened to him, none daring to loosen them, unless he desires it himself, or until he dies. He is very weak now and is not able to make any more efforts to free himself.

He calls for his horse, a stout snow-white Indian pony, which is now brought into the ring, and two of the lariats are unfastened from two of the posts in his rear, and fastened to the pommel on the saddle on the horse's back. The horse is turned from him and gets a cut with a whip from one of the warriors, and makes a leap forward.

These two lariats tear out from the young brave's back, and he is lifted up from the ground where he has tumbled, and the other lariats fastened to the saddle.

Then the horse is cut again with the whip, and runs and plunges, and the young brave is free.

He is picked up by some warriors and carried from the ring, to all appearances dead, amid grunts of approval.

This is the dance, as it is called, which causes the mothers and fathers of the competing braves to feel for many days prior to the trial uneasy for fear of their sons failing to come off creditably to their manhood.

And these mothers, wishing to show that they share their sons' sufferings, often have half a dozen cuts made across their arms and breasts at the time their offspring are under the torture.

But the young man who presents himself for such trial and has not the courage to carry it through is cut loose from his fastening with the knife; he must give up all his horses, that greatest pride of the Indian; and should he be a chief's son his hereditary title is taken from him. He cannot join any war or hunting party, nor can he wear those ornaments that distinguish a brave, such as eagle feathers or council dresses, and he is no more considered in the tribe than a woman, until such an occasion as the present is offered again, when he has another chance to redeem himself as a man and a warrior.

And this after all the intermixture with civilization and its modes and chances to make life easy and to shirk traditional duties and consequences!

A hundred years ago, and at the period with which this part of this narrative deals, the endurance was there; but the perverted nature was fresher from the source of perversion, more deadly because of the newness of the perversion, than it is now when savage life is only so by the protection of laws of civilization. The state of the country and the unprotected condition of the people were to a great degree the impetus to get back possessions which the red man claimed as his own still, and to get them back the vaunted civilizing reason must not be called into play, for reason had done little but defraud them of what they now determined to have again. So they resolved to deal with the whites as they would with beasts of prey, and the whites learned to look upon the Indian as a reptile, possibly as a lion regards a viper.

"You cannot reason with an Indian," says a writer of the times; "he will listen to you with due attention, whittling a stick as he does it, nods his head, and grunts approval. The stick he is whittling is an arrow with which to pierce your heart when you have done speaking."

A missionary speaking with a young brave about the wrong of his present line of action was rejoiced to see the red man hold down his head and come before him submissively.

"You are sorry for what you have done?" asked the missionary.

The Indian gave a grunt of affirmation.

"You wish to change your mode of life?"

The same grunt of affirmation.

"You wish me to extend the right hand of fellowship and acknowledge you a member of the family of God's children?"

A third time the Indian gave his grunt of approval, and came closer yet.

"Then," said the missionary, "let my red brother approach me, feeling sure that his sins, though they be as scarlet, shall be made white as the driven snow. Let my red brother give to me the tomahawk in his hand."

"My white brother can have it," said the savage, raising his head for the first time—raising his hand at the same time to bury the tomahawk in the brain of the missionary.

To be as deceptive and treacherous as an Indian, in the eyes of the white settlers, was eminently necessary for self-protection.

The Indians sent forth spies in every direction,

and the wary white man never passed a day without feeling assured that his most secret acts were that night chronicled and commented on around wigwam fires amid the dusky shadows of the woods.

This organized system of Indian spies placed the settlers in the hands of the savages, and a reaction was necessary, an offset to counteract the baneful effect.

That counteraction came suddenly, and effectually, in the person of the Indian scout.

He was not a scout, a murderer from choice, because he wished a change from the monotony of life; the times allowed of little monotony. More often than otherwise he was the victim of some base outrage at the hands of the red man, entailing the loss of wife, child, parent, or all together; and instead of the love for those now dead implacable hatred found a place in the breast.

There is the story of a man who, out hunting one day, came home at night and entering his cabin found no light there, and called aloud to his wife and children, but received no response. He knew that he must wait until morning to know what had become of them; so all night long he paced up and down within the narrow confines of the one room. In the early light of dawn he saw upon the wall of the room he had walked for hours in the darkness the hanging and mutilated bodies of his family, suspended by spikes through their hands. That man became a scout.

Another man saw his youngest child dashed to pieces from a rock where an Indian ran with it, pursued by the father. That man also became a scout.

A short time after the murder of John Wetzel and capture and escape of the boys a conclave of settlers was called in Wheeling one morning. They met with closed doors.

In the midst of a harangue urging the necessity of more protection against the hordes of wandering Indians the door noiselessly opened and some one entered.

The little place was crowded, and so intent were the men, that they hardly knew of the entrance of any one, till, working his way through them, a young man, a mere boy, stood before the officers of the meeting.

He was a dark faced lad, his eyes gleaming, his hair matted with neglect and forest dews and even then remarkably long and black.

"I wish to proclaim myself an Indian scout," he said to the astonished men.

One of them took him by the shoulder. "How did you dare to come here?" he asked.

The lad shook off the hand.

"Will you recognize me as a scout?" he asked.

"Boy, do you know what you say?" returned one of the elders.

"I wish to become a scout!"

"Go away!" commanded the elder; "you are a boy with a foolish man's tongue. You are dazed by the talk of those around you. The life you would lead is not all of romance. Go home!"

"Home!" echoed the lad bitterly. "Do you know where my home is—that I have a home?"

"Go to your father then, and bid him keep a stricter watch over you."

"Go to my father? I wish I could!" said the boy in louder tones and resisting those who would have silenced him. "I tell you I have no father; he is dead; I wish to hunt down his murderers—and I will do this whether you recognize me as a scout or not. Only I felt that a man as old as my father was should sanction what I do."

The men were quieter now around him and did not offer to turn him away.

The president of the meeting said, not unkindly:

"I am sorry for you, my lad. But if you loved your father properly you would know that murder and blood would scarcely purify your memory of him. Doubtless your love has crazed you."

"I am sane."

"Wait then, my lad, until a time when you are calm."

"Calm!" he cried. "I shall never be that until I avenge my father."

"'Vengeance is mine,' saith the Lord."

But the lad did not heed him, but stood panting before them all, clutching his musket up to his breast, his nerves alert, his head thrown back.

"My mother used to read that when I had a home," he said. "You speak of the love I may have had for my father. You do not know how I loved him; nor do I. I only know that the loss of him has killed whatever made me love him. It is also thus with my brothers. We were a strong, loving family. We were happy, careless boys; my father's death has made us reckless men.

"My father came from his birth-place, where everything was well known and where he had toiled and troubled for years; he came out to these wilds to encounter willingly far greater toils and troubles to secure to us children ease and comfort. Our father died in attempting this for us.

"Our mother was a brave woman who cared for no possible trouble; she never quailed in difficulty and distress, which was often all around her. She loved my father: that made her brave. My father's death has made her a weak, trembling, frightened woman. She saw him die. She is broken, and her bravery died with what gave it to her—our father. We wish to avenge a brave mother. Does not the Bible say 'an eye for an eye, a tooth for a tooth?' Did not the Bible men avenge their fathers and mothers and ruined homes? Is not Christianity avenging by civilization the murder of Christ? You have no right to deny me that which the Lord tells me is my right, not merely my privilege."

The men looked at him in astonishment. Never before had a boy spoken thus before men,—a boy reared in these wilds at that,—a boy who had been educated only from the Bible. They could not treat him as a boy. That speech earned for him the respect due to a man. It seemed almost as though he pleaded for his father's life, as though the privilege to hunt down the Indians were a prescription that would restore his dead father to life.

There was a kindling in the eyes of those about him. But the boy minded not that—only his desire for respect, for his preferred calling was uppermost in his mind, and all things else meant nothing.

"Sit down!" said the president, pushing a chair towards him. The lad seemed not to hear him, and continued standing. What answer ought they to give a boy with noble instincts but perverted reasoning?

"Who was your father?" at last asked the president.

"He was John Wetzel; he helped to found this place," said the lad.

There was a murmur. Half the men there had known John Wetzel personally, at one time or another.

The president of the assembly himself was not a stranger to the reckless man who had withstood the advice of his friends and chose to settle beyond their reach and protection. He looked down at the lad, standing before him, and could not but feel that John Wetzel's death had been not altogether as other men's—he had seemed to purchase it by his very hardihood. But what of the lad?

Whatever the president might have said was unavailing, for he looked into the eyes of those around him and saw but one answer to the prayer of the boy who stood there: the boy was not to be treated as a child. There was the respect due to a man which he claimed and meant to obtain.

There were cries of "Treat the boy square! Don't go agin the lad."

"Go!" said the president to him. "You may do what you think best."

"Do you give me the privilege of a scout?" persisted the boy.

"You are too young——" began the president, when his voice was drowned by cries of "Give it to him! Give it to him!"

"Very well, Lewis Wetzel," said the president, "we recognize you as an Indian scout, and here's my hand on it."

He held his hand out, but the lad seemed not to see it.

Shouldering his old musket, he walked through the lane made by the men, without a word, unlatched the door, and walked away. Straight on he walked, and the men gazing after him were silent as he.

He went determinedly to his mother and told her what he meant to do, and left her trembling and weeping.

"He did not even kiss me," she mourned; "and he was always the most affectionate of the children. And he was always the leader. If he goes, his brothers will not long remain here with me. I shall be a widow and childless; my brave boys will not close my eyes in death, and I have tried to be a good mother to them. It is bitter, bitter! All my energy, all my life, is gone from me. Oh for the old time of my early married life! Oh for the time when that boy rested a babe in his cradle in the poor little home far away! Oh for the time when his father asked me would I come here, or stay in the home that had known us both so long! Better had we died among friends, though poor, than to die here! For are we richer here? Is there as much mine now as there was when I had my one cow and two pigs?"

"But he's gone because he's brave," said a little maiden weeping with her and her little girls. It was little Berta Rosencranz.

But no grief could bring him back again, no prayers avail to turn from his purpose the boy whose mind was so steadily set towards revenge. His little sisters had gathered about the disconsolate woman, and were holding to her in perturbation, not yet accustomed to the change in her, but doubtless wondering where was the active, tearless mother of old.

Berta had run to the window, though, and was straining her neck far out to catch a glimpse of the boy now far off.

"I see him!" she cried; "he's going through the grass towards the river." Then he disappeared from her eyes.

He took the trail that led to his old ruined home, and went and sat there and looked on the charred embers that alone remained to tell the story of onetime shelter and love. He sat there until night, drinking in all the sense of desolation, no longer a boy, but a man, with a wronged man's deadly sense of one never-dying purpose.

And at that same time, with his lonely mother, the bright-eyed maiden sat and soothed, with pretty words, the older woman's sorrow.

"I should be proud of him," said the girl.

"Not if you were a mother," sobbed the woman.

"If I were ten times a mother," said the girl, "I should be glad to know that all my sons avenged their father's death. What are women for if they cry because a man steps up and defends them? If I were a man, I'd do—I'd do——"

"What would you do?" complained the mother. "Would you break your mother's heart? That is what children do most of all."

"Then mothers ought to get tougher hearts, if they know what they've got to expect. If I was a mother ten times over, I'd be tougher every time a child would rise up to protect me. And if I was a man I'd do as Lewis Wetzel has done—I'd be where Lewis Wetzel is at this moment."

"And where is he?" asked the mother. Thereat the girl threw herself into the woman's arms, weeping her pretty eyes dull with a passion of fruitless tears.

But no sound of all this reached the man who caused it, as, sitting before the ruins of his one-time home, he let the desolation of the scene enter into his soul like the iron into his of sacred story.

CHAPTER VI.

MARTIN WETZEL.

YET of Lewis Wetzel no specially remarkable action is recorded from the time of his escape from Indian captivity till the year 1782, when he was eighteen years old. It would seem that he disappeared from the eyes of those who knew him, until he could command a man's attention. His boyish strength may not have been sufficient for his would-be enterprise. And doubtless he recognized the fact, and daily increasing his bodily endurance patiently waited for the coming of manly vigor which should gain him the vengeance he desired. He said in after-years that this waiting time was the discipline of his life.

There were raids on the red-skins all around him when he again appeared, and he took a general part in them, and never save in company with others; but nothing was done to distinguish him from the other half-wild boys of the settlers, who fought, like him, for the honor and safety of those most dear to them,—these boys who so often did the work of men in tilling the soil and tracking the game necessary for the daily food of the families.

Logan was the second son of Shikellimus, and this is the same person whom Heckewelder describes as "a respectable chief of the Six Nations, who resided in Shamokin, Pennsylvania, as an agent to transact business between them and the government of the State."

In 1747, at a time when the Moravian missionaries were the object of much groundless hatred and accusation, Shikellimus invited some of them to settle at Shamokin, and they did so. When Count Zinzendorff and Conrad Weiser visited the place, several years before, they were very hospitably entertained by the chief, who came out to meet them (says Loskiel) with a large, fine melon, for which the count politely gave him his fur cap in exchange; and thus commenced an intimate acquaintance.

Logan was a shrewd and sober man, not addicted to drinking, like most of his countrymen, because he never wished to become a fool. Indeed, he built his house on pillars, for security against the drunken Indians, and used to ensconce himself within it on all occasions of riot and outrage.

Logan inherited the talents of his father, but not his prosperity. Nor was this altogether his own fault. He took no part, except that of peacemaker, in the French and English war of 1760, and was ever, before and afterwards, looked upon as emphatically the friend of the white man. But never was kindness rewarded like this.

The countless stories that have come down to us relative to this chief are doubtless not unknown to many who read this narrative. For scarcely a book that refers to Indian life is complete without a story or anecdote of Logan. Yet one that has received little attention, if any, came to the present writer from the lips of an old trapper, whose father had told it to him one day when they entered their claim for a tract of land upon which had once stood the cabin of the chief, no traces of which were now to be seen amid the rank vegetation that covered the place.

Logan had built his house and had moved his family into it, trying to live like the civilized white men. He had made three chambers in the house, one for himself and his wife, a second for that of his children, while a third was reserved for any chance stranger, Indian or white man, who might crave shelter at his hands.

The trial must have been severe; four close walls were suffocating to a man who had doubtless rarely slept under a roof before, and in whose veins ran the blood of an ancestry that had known nothing of houses. But he was determined to act like a civilized man, and to represent the progressive element of the times. For nights he never slept, and he could hear his wife complaining at his side; while in the adjoining chamber the rest of the family were moving about discontentedly. After a repetition of such a night on five successive occasions, Logan arose at last one night, after tossing about for hours, and, hearing no sound from his wife, who had laid herself upon the floor to try and snatch a little sleep, which the newness of a bed had destroyed, he concluded that she was happily resting.

"Lucky woman," he said. He moved carefully about. He was determined to sleep, too, but he could not sleep under a roof. Cautiously going to the hole that served for a window, he threw himself out upon the ground, dragging his blanket after him, and, reaching a little hollow in the ground formed by the trunks of some massive trees, he laid himself down for a nap.

But he made up his mind not to sleep long, for the wife and family must not know of this proceeding, as he had determined when he built the house that civilization must be followed, and that no infringement upon it dare be allowed. He would rest for an hour or so, and then he would regain the house and nobody be the wiser.

It was comfortable here on the hard ground,

beneath the twinkling stars, the free, fresh breezes fanning his face and entering his nostrils. How he enjoyed that sleep! He slept, at least, as he thought he had never slept before; certainly as he had not slept since his house had been built. How long he slept he did not know. He woke with a start. The day was breaking, and in the east a faint pink glow was spreading like the blush of a baby over the clear sky. He gathered his blanket around him, and ran precipitately toward the house. Suppose he had been missed! If any of those inside knew of this escapade, there would be no discipline of civilization thereafter.

But none of those inside were to know. For, on nearing the place, in the faint, early light, he saw a shadow upon the wall. He looked up, and there was his wife's blanket hanging over the eaves, while one foot peeped down at him: she had got up in the night and sought the roof for a bed. He was startled; but he was startled the more when, on hearing a suppressed yawn near at hand, he looked about him and saw suspended from the window of the second chamber two blanketed forms,—the other members of the family.

The story does not go on to say how insomnia under a roof was cured after this. But it is known that this same house was presented by Logan to the missionaries, and was held by them while the family of the chief went farther up the country and built another house there.

This second house claiming the admiration of the missionaries, it was likewise presented to them. The houses had been built with great exertion, and months had been taken up in their construction. But so reverently did the chief regard the men who had come to instruct the savage tribes and teach them the truth of a God who kept not perpetual hunting-grounds as a reward for the brave men he called children, but who held in reserve peace and rest for oppression, and long-suffering for those who did their best towards establishing peace and rest upon the earth, that he regarded his own worldly possessions as nothing if they could contribute to the comfort of these teachers of the universal religion.

Logan and his family worked for the white teachers, gave them of their substance, and protected them from the incursions of warriors who did not understand the teachings other than as further modes of cheating and getting the upper-hand. Logan stood the friend of these savages, too, however, and tried to make them comprehend, and pitied them when they could not, as in very many instances was the case. The settlers knew of all this, and regarded Logan kindly.

This was the man Lewis Wetzel had heard of all his life, and had been taught to believe in implicitly. But now he doubted him and classed him with the other red men, his sworn enemies, whom he meant to kill. And others, too, now saw as he did. For events had been represented to the simple settlers in such a perverted form that rage burned in the bosoms where affiliation had long endeavored and desired to assert itself.

In the spring of 1774 a robbery and murder occurred in some of the white settlements on the Ohio which were charged to the Indians, though, perhaps, not justly, for it is well known that a large number of civilized adventurers were traversing the frontiers at this time, who sometimes disguised themselves as Indians, and who thought little more of killing one of that people than of shooting a buffalo. A party of these men, land-jobbers and others, undertook to punish the outrage in this case, according to custom (as Jefferson says in his Notes), in a summary way.

Colonel Cresap, a man infamous for the many murders he had committed on that much-injured people, collected a party of white men and went in quest of vengeance. A canoe of women and children was seen coming down the Kanawha, and there was laughing and happiness, the little floating party not at all suspecting an attack from the whites. Cresap and his party concealed themselves on the bank of the river, and the moment the canoe reached the shore, singled out their objects, and at one fire killed every person in it.

This happened to be the family of Logan, innocent and friendly inclined. Shortly after this, another massacre took place, not far from Wheeling; a considerable party of the Indians being decoyed by the whites, and all, with the exception of a little girl, murdered. Among these, too, were both a brother of Logan and a sister, the delicate condition of the latter increasing a thousand-fold both the barbarity of the crime and the rage of the survivors of the family.

Logan, therefore, came sternly from his cabin, where he had meant peace, and distinguished him-himself by his daring and bloody exploits in the war which now ensued between the Virginians on the one side and a combination of Shawnees, Mingoes, and Delawares on the other. The civilized party prevailed, as usual, and wiped out a considerable number of Indians. But "many of their dead they scalped, rather than we should have them," says the white historian; and naively goes on to narrate: "but our troops scalped upwards of twenty of those who were first killed."

Thus did the superior whites imitate what they looked upon with abhorrence at the hands of the base savage. It was at the treaty after this battle that Logan, the much-injured man, made this noble speech:

"I appeal to any white man to say if he ever entered Logan's cabin hungry, and he gave him not meat; if he ever came cold and naked, and he clothed him not. During the course of the last long and bloody war, Logan remained idle in his cabin, an advocate for peace. Such was my love for the whites, that my countrymen pointed as they passed, and said: 'Logan is the friend of white men.' I had even thought to have lived with you, but for the injuries of one man. Colonel Cresap, the last spring, in cold blood and unprovoked, murdered all the relations of Logan, not sparing even my women and children. There runs not a drop of my blood in the veins of any living creature! This called on me for vengeance. I have sought it; I have killed many; I have fully glutted my vengeance. For my country I rejoice at the beams of peace. But do not harbor a thought that mine is the joy of fear. Logan never felt fear. He will not turn on his heel to save his life. Who is there to mourn for Logan?—Not one!"

The eloquence in this speech is incomparable.

No wonder the man was called a prophet! He was a man in advance of his times, and the times were sufficiently startling for the settlers, and they had not the leisure nor inclination to study out the excellences of one character when they had all they could do to subvert the evil intentions of characters less prone to good. He stood alone, aloof from friends and foes, unknowing friends, with foes on every side. It is probable that his own blood hated him more than the strangers did; he represented the progressive element, and such an element must ever appear more aggressive to friends who do not partake of it than to foes who are in a like state of ostracism from its influence. If the man understood his own inclinations, it is as much as—indeed, more than—could have been expected of him in the minds of calm, rational reasoners.

In the most peaceful and settled age, when art and science both contend to make thought the common property, a new element appearing creates in the minds of the mass a wonder not unmixed with ridicule. Any subversion of established usage excites, first, opposition, which means oppression; then ridicule, which is the loosening of the oppression, and the establishing of the principle upon the plane of equality; then adoption of the principle, which is its elevation to superiority over its surroundings.

Logan thus represented principle, but it is doubtful if he ever got beyond the first grade, that of oppression, with his fellows. He had every right to look to civilization to uphold him, but the acts of his own people had caused civilization to pause; and a pause in any attempted improvement is a retrogression. He appealed to the white settlers; he said that he wanted to be as they were; he wanted their sympathies and their most thoughtful encouragement. He claimed a standing with them because he knew the workings of his own mind, and what he most deserved at the hands of the whites.

But what could such noble words mean to the uncultivated settlers? They had received too much wrong, vengeance intended for aggressors, not themselves, to see any nobility in any red man. Logan represented merely one of his abhorred race. They knew far more of the wrongs they themselves had suffered than of the deceits practiced upon the Indians, for with the honest settler there was too much to do about his own little preserve for him to bother himself even with deceit to the savages. And so Logan might speak of the loss of his family, but had they not lost families too? How could Logan's empty wigwam appeal to the boy Lewis Wetzel? There were not even the blackened walls of his own happy home remaining, and heavy, tall grass obliterated the very landmarks his father had set up by dint of months and years of toil. And what of Logan's murdered family? Where was the father who had been watched for day after day, month after month, year after year, by the boy on the little green knoll?

The line of argument most popular at this time was:

"Can we trust Logan?"

"Can Indians be trusted?"

"They cannot."

"Therefore we cannot trust an Indian."

"Must we pity Logan?"

"Do Indians pity us?"

"They do not."

"Therefore we cannot pity an Indian."

"But should not Logan, at least, be tolerated?"

"What is toleration? It is trust and pity. To tolerate Logan is to trust and pity an Indian."

The boy Wetzel heard all such arguments around him, and was too young to understand anything but the rights of the settlers which had been infringed upon and violated by Indians. He hated a word in favor of the red man; he is known to have engaged in bitter quarrels with people who advocated a peaceable adjustment of difficulties. For peace meant a giving-in, an acknowledgment that the Indian had not been treated fairly; when, in fact, the Indian had been treated so fairly that he was allowed to live, and every white man's hand by rights ought to be raised against a red man.

"It must not be!" he said; "it shall not be! When my time comes it will not be. There is no peace for an Indian but what a bullet gives him."

So Lewis Wetzel bided his time and waited for a man's strength.

And it was even as the mother had said. Martin, too, was bent on revenge. An expedition was set on foot in 1780 to proceed against and destroy the Indian towns situated on the Coshocton, a small branch of the Muskingum River. The main place of rendezvous was Wheeling. Colonel Brodhead, a soldier of more than local distinction, assumed the command. Martin Wetzel was a volunteer in the campaign. The officers of those wild frontier armies were too often only such in name; for every soldier under them acted as seemed right in his own judgment and particular case.

Cheered out of Wheeling, this little army of four hundred men immediately took up the line of march and went forward rapidly in order to fall upon the Indian towns by surprise, and before any of the red spies, ever on the alert, should apprize the aggressed of the approach of foes.

Colonel Brodhead, taking his men secretly along, soon surrounded one of the Indian towns before those inside were at all aware of the proximity of any danger.

"Every man, woman, and child were made prisoners, without the firing of a gun." (Pritt's Border Life.)

We read further on: "Among the prisoners were sixteen warriors. A little after dark a council of war was held to determine on the fate of the warriors in custody. They were doomed to death, and by the order of the commander were bound, taken a little distance below the town, and dispatched with tomahawks and spears, and then scalped."

The first tomahawk raised was in the hand of Martin Wetzel.

In the grim work of death, with a kind of fiendish pleasure, he sunk into the heads of the unresisting Indians a weapon which in hands like theirs had caused the death of his father.

For the tomahawk was as much used by the whites as by the red men, and with an equal dexterity.

"Early the next morning an Indian presented himself on the opposite bank of the river and asked for the 'Big Captain.' Colonel Brodhead presented himself, and asked what the Indian wanted. To which he replied: 'I want peace.'

"'Send over some of your chiefs,' said Brodhead.

"'Maybe you kill,' said the Indian.

"He was answered: 'They shall not be killed.

"One of the chiefs, a good-looking man, came over the river, and entered into conversation with the commander in the street; but, while engaged in conversation, Martin Wetzel came up behind him with a tomahawk concealed in the bosom of his hunting-shirt, and struck him on the back of the head.

"The poor Indian fell, and immediately expired.

"This act of perfidy and reckless revenge the commander had no power, if he had had the disposition, to punish, as probably two-thirds of the army approved the treacherous deed."

The next day the army commenced its retreat from Coshocton.

Colonel Brodhead committed the prisoners to the militia.

They were about twenty in number.

After they had marched about half a mile, the men commenced killing them.

Again was the deadly weapon of Martin Wetzel crimsoned with the blood of his life-long foes.

And, like his younger brother, such was his indomitable spirit of revenge that no place nor circumstance was sacred enough to preserve the life of an Indian when once within his grasp, and the word "treachery" was never employed by the settlers in any act that decoyed an Indian into their power.

In a short time they were all dispatched except a few women and children, who were spared and taken to Fort Pitt, and after some time exchanged for an equal number of their prisoners.

Some years after this horrible bloodthirsty action, but which in the eyes of the settlers the circumstances of the time seemed to render unavoidable, Martin Wetzel, hunting in the forest, was surprised and taken prisoner by a party of predatory Indians.

He remained with them a considerable length of time, and by his great cheerfulness and apparent satisfaction disarmed their suspicion, acquired much of their confidence, and was adopted into one of their families, as was sometimes the case when the mode of savage life seemed congenial to a captive.

But all this seeming gratification was the veriest dissimulation; although Martin Wetzel showed a cheerful countenance, in his heart was the brooding spirit of revenge, and plans for his escape engaged every minute of his captivity.

He desired, too, to make that escape memorable by some tragic action of revenge.

How much he overreached, by his acting, the credulity of his entertainers, the sequel will show.

He was to all intents and purposes free; he hunted with them, he danced and frolicked, and appeared thoroughly satisfied with the course affairs had taken, never showing distaste, although the Indians knew who he was and what had been the fate of his father.

In the fall of the year his dread chance came.

He and three young chiefs set out to make a fall hunt to supply the winter stores of flesh.

They pitched their camp near the head of the Sandusky River.

During the hunting he was careful to return to the camp in the evening, prepare the wood for the night-fire, and do all the other duties of camp necessity; for he knew that, although he was trusted, his companions were ever on the alert, and that maybe he had been taken on this hunt merely to test the truthfulness of his protestations, and should any slip occur he would suffer for it.

By the line of conduct which he adopted he lulled any suspicion they might have entertained of him, and little by little he saw the half-averted glance of discretion give way to open looks of full confidence.

One evening, while hunting and belated, he came across one of his Indian camp-mates.

The Indian was full of their mutual exploits, and praised the white man's wondrous aim.

MARTIN WETZEL'S TERRIBLE REVENGE.

"My father taught me," said Martin sententiously.

The Indian looked at him, for he knew the tale of John Wetzel's fate.

But Martin's face was calm and unperturbed, and the chief went on with his talk.

The white man watched for a favorable opportunity, and, the Indian's attention being called in an opposite direction, he shot him down, scalped him, and threw his body into a hole made by the tearing up of a tree by the wind, and covered the motionless form with logs and brush.

He then hurried to the camp, and prepared the wood for the night-fire as usual.

When night came down, and the missing one not returning, Martin expressed great concern at the absence of their companion.

"Does my white brother worry about a warrior?" laughed one of the Indians.

For they did not appear in the least out of countenance or disconcerted on account of the non-arrival of the other, and dismissed the subject entirely from their minds as too trivial to entertain, ate their supper, and lay down to sleep.

Martin had gone too far now to retreat. He lay down with the others, but sleep was never further from his brain. The two Indians were soon unconscious. Being now determined at all hazards to escape, the question for Martin Wetzel to decide in his mind was whether he should attack both Indians while they slept, or watch for an opportunity of dispatching them one at a time.

The latter plan seemed likelier to thwart failure. Early the next morning he prepared to execute his desperate plan. He was still apparently anxious about the continued absence of the chief, who had failed to come last night.

"It makes my white brother whiter, this fear," again laughed one of the remaining Indians, looking on the pallid and set face of the determined man.

Wetzel made no reply, merely turning away. Then the two red men set out on their hunt alone, while death pursued them in the shape of Martin Wetzel, creeping like Fate through the brush after them. All day he followed stealthily, keeping them in view. Towards night he came boldly up to them, and began speaking and asking about their day's sport. One of the Indians sauntered off, and Martin detained the other over some imaginary game until his fellow was far away. Then, with one fell sweep of the tomahawk, he laid the red-skin lifeless on the ground.

"This for my father!" he said, and scalped the savage and threw the body into a sink-hole, and made his way through brake and briar to the camp to meet the remaining Indian.

He had not come when Martin arrived there, and, throwing branches on the fire, he sat down and waited, and soon saw the brave, by the light of the fire, now fiercely flaming, coming slowly on with a burden of game thrown across his shoulders. With a strange, half-stifled cry of joy, the white man hurried forward, under the pretense of aiding in disencumbering the hunter of his load.

"Stoop!" he said; "stoop!"

When the Indian stooped down to have the game detached from his back, the tomahawk, already so imbrued with the blood of his kin, sunk into his brain, and Wetzel stood alone in the blackness of the night, guiltless in his own eyes. There was no danger of pursuit, so he proceeded very leisurely, and packed up whatever of the camping implements he deemed he most needed and could most conveniently carry, and made his way to the white settlements with the three Indian scalps dangling from his belt of wampum, after an absence of a year. Those who saw him coming over the hills, and recognized him, despite his Indian trappings, cheered and greeted him as a hero. For the men who rid the country of a pest and protected otherwise defenseless women and children were the right arm of the law, the strength of an exposed people. What they did, by whatever means they succeeded, could not be thought other than brave, the risks of success alone being considered, let alone their willingness to endure for the sake of those they resolved should endure no suffering.

Thus Martin Wetzel's acts of comparative perfidy, as it seems to us afar off, could meet with nothing but the approval of his countrymen upon this and similar occasions, and the greater his ingenuity and cunning to meet a like ingenuity and cunning, the greater the meed of praise and approval.

CHAPTER VII.

A MASSACRE.

AT last, at the age of eighteen, and when his oath, if it were yet remembered in the community, was thought of as the mere explosive impulse of a boy, and his seeking for the title of scout but a like impulse, Lewis Wetzel comes upon the stage, a man, hardened by enforced exposure, strong of sinew, stern of mind,—a warrior.

He was moulded of the stuff that makes men gods in the eyes of their contemporaries, and the question naturally arises, whether, had the cause of his provocation been directed at another time and season, and against a more civilized people, he would not have lived in the annals of history a figure for the admiration of future ages, instead of gaining the mere local fame of a harassed and nervous community.

His bravery was never questioned, his endurance was marvelous, his intensity and perseverance unsurpassed, his cool-headedness and calmness in refusing to wreak his vengeance upon those in his power, unless they were of his sworn enemies and men, proved the attributes of a successful general and an idol of a thinking people. But the people who most relied upon him were more active than thoughtful, more grim than sentimental; and while he defended them they considered that he was revenging his own wrongs; and while they admired him they resolved that had they felt as he did their acts would have been as his. They did not deprecate him; they appreciated him to the full. But he was only one of themselves. They had known him from his earliest childhood. His bravery was often said to be mere recklessness of consequences, and to idolize the man would have been to fall down and worship qualities which every man, as wrought upon as he, possessed in common with him.

Those who saw him come into Wheeling in the spring, when he had turned his eighteenth year, described him as being a harsh-featured man, taciturn, and not given to indiscriminate conviviality. He joined in none of the few enjoyments which mankind, no matter how oppressed and overridden, will institute; he rarely held converse with those about him. But children and dogs loved him, and women pitied him, as women so often will find a subject for pity in what men call uncongenial and above or beneath them.

Again must old Eberly come to the fore: "Lewis Wetzel," he writes on the leaves of coarse paper which are now crumbling and difficult to transcribe, "is not so bad as hee is represented. Hee is often where there is sickness, and a man that had small-pox·had no other nurse, and no one knew it until the man hee was well once more."

He appears to have loitered about the settlements for awhile, and then he saw his chance. He enlisted as a soldier in that disastrous campaign of Colonel Crawford in 1782. His mother, hearing of this enlistment, paid little attention to it.

"He never minded me," she said, "and he don't care if I am murdered, so that he can go do murder himself. It is his place to stay here and protect me and his sisters, and provide a home for us, instead of doing as he does. Are there no other men to do the work? We have suffered enough, I should hope. I have no patience with him."

This change from her old life of bravery was only another impulse to lead her son away from her to revenge the brave woman she had once been, and who had now sunk into the utterer of chronic complaints, never weary of lauding her dead husband's virtues and comparing them to the lack of them in her sons. She was never to gauge the feelings of a mind like that of her son—how many of those around him did? He was one of many—that was all they saw.

It is said of him that he had placed a pile of stones on the spot where his father's body had lain in the grass after the murder, and this shrine he appeared to regard with something of the superstition of the Indians themselves. He did not offer propitiatory sacrifice upon it, it is true, but when he was tired out and breathless from any exertion he had taken in order to test his strength he would wend his way to this pile of stones almost as though he went to conciliate his father's troubled spirit that might not rest until it was avenged.

Under this pile of stones, too, it is also asserted, he had contrived a receptacle for his powder and bullets, and he made his bullet-moulds here and heated the lead upon the pile. Often at night there would be seen the little thread of flame leaping from the pyramidal heap as he poured his metal and shaped the leaden messengers of death.

The Indians saw that flame, we may be sure, and investigated it. Whether they understood it or not is not for us to say; but it is also said in tradition that the savages rarely came into the immediate vicinity of that stone heap, and that more than one brave has been seen speeding away in the darkness when he had come to ascertain the meaning of the

THE TRAGEDY AT WETZEL'S HOME.

weird light and found a haggard boy silently standing before the flame, his face stern as Fate and as relentless. He had thousands of bullets stored away in this place, and when he left the neighborhood the settlers were at liberty to help themselves to what remained.

This was when he was as yet young and the time was heavy on his hands; when he had grown older, he had more to do than spend his days in idle pouring of lead; he then deemed that the mound was sentimental, and so he tore it apart and scattered the stones. At the time of Crawford's expedition he had obliterated this mark of his memory of his father.

He had now gained a man's strength, a man's steadiness of nerve and purpose, if he had lacked these last two essentials before.

As a short preliminary to Crawford's failure, it may be well to speak briefly of the events which led to this campaign, in which the Moravian Indians were so terribly avenged.

Somewhere about the year 1772 some devout Moravian brethren succeeded, after untold hardships, in establishing a little Indian community which embraced the faith and collected in three villages on the Muskingum.

The villages were known as Schoenbrunn, Salem,

and Gnadenhuetten. Here they lived amicably with all men, the precepts of the Mingo chief, Logan, entreating them to give up war and cultivate the soil.

Their number, increased by new accessions, in a short time was not less than four hundred souls.

They thus occupied a position midway between the advanced posts of the whites and the camping-grounds of some of the hostile Indians, and, practicing a quiet, peaceful demeanor, hateful alike to their white and red neighbors, they were accused alternately by each of privately favoring the other.

In the latter part of the year 1781 the bands of militia of the frontier came to the determination to break up these peaceful Moravian towns. They were called the "half-way house of the warriors," and the term was used in deadly derision by the fierce and lawless frontiermen, who despised the peaceable Indians for supposed treachery because they opened their doors alike to every comer.

A detachment of men, under the command of Colonel David Williamson, went out from the border with the avowed intention of inducing the Indians by calm reasoning to move farther off, with the further cool alternative that if they refused to accede to the militia they would all be brought prisoners to Fort Pitt.

When they arrived at the Moravian towns, but very few Indians were found, and these mostly infirm or old, the main body having removed to Sandusky.

These few remaining ones were taken to the fort and apparently well treated by the commandant, and afterwards they were allowed to return to their homes.

This manner of proceeding against the red man greatly incensed the country people who still adhered to the rule of total extinction as regarded Indians once reduced to captivity.

Colonel Williamson, who, prior to this episode, had been one of the most popular of men on account of his brave war record, now became the object of popular hatred and suspicion, and his leniency towards the Moravian Indians was held up as his reproach, and wholly obliterated his well-known bravery.

On the other hand, the peaceably inclined Indians fell under the dire suspicion of the Indian warriors who had been pressed into the service of the British against the colonies, or States, as they now began to be called, and also of the English commandant stationed at Detroit. To this commandant it was viciously reported that the pious teachers of these Moravian Indians were in close confederacy with the American Congress, for the purpose of preventing, not their own people alone, but likewise the Delawares and a few other nations of red warriors, from entering into war against the rebelling American colonists.

The many and frequent failures of the hostile Indians against the white settlements were attributed to the Moravians, who sent runners to Fort Pitt to give notice of their approach and thus prepare to receive them; and this charge was certainly true. In the spring of 1781 the war-chief of the Delawares apprised the missionaries and their proselytes of their danger, both from the angry whites and the hostile Indians, and advised them to remove to a place of security.

This advice was not acted upon, and what the chief prophesied was fulfilled to the letter; for in the fall of that same year (1781) the Moravian settlements were burned by upwards of three hundred Indian warriors, their peaceful villages laid waste, their smiling fields of grain desolated, their beasts taken from them, and the bewildered and unhappy converts to Christ turned into the trackless wilderness once more, murmuring against the power of the God of the white man for not protecting them in their time of need, and doubting the good missionaries for fools and madmen.

Winter came on, and they still trudged from place to place seeking staying-ground, and finding none. Many of them perished from cold and famine. But the tender teachings of Christianity could not become wholly erased from their minds, and while they felt degraded in the eyes of their hostile red brothers, they yet looked upwards for that aid and succor which the missionaries had told them would surely come, and consequently they would not disavow their belief and join their savage brethren.

But the missionaries were not with them now: they had been taken prisoners, robbed of nearly everything they possessed, and then sent to the commandant at Detroit, where, after being strictly examined by a council of British officers, they were permitted to go free.

This removal of the Indians from their peaceful Christian villages was instigated mainly by three white men,—Alexander McKee, Matthew Elliott, and the renegade Simon Girty.

The hostility of these three men to the Americans was unbounded, and they were continually (before their plans reached fruition) plotting the destruction of the Christian Indians as the means of inveigling the Delaware nation into a bloody war with the patriot colonists. A plot was laid at Sandusky to waylay and murder the missionary Zeisberger and bring in his scalp; and Simon Girty himself conducted the party to Sandusky for that purpose, the frustration of which chagrined him and added new fuel to his fiery spite.

In the latter part of February following, the famished condition of the Indians wandering over the bare plains of Sandusky compelled about a hundred and fifty to return to their ruined towns on the Muskingum to try and find among the desolated hearth-stones a few remnants of their once plentiful stores of food for their rapidly-starving families.

They came in the night, and, numb with the piercing cold, they gathered a little wasted corn. They were discovered in the morning, and, without any further provocation, and wholly without resistance, nearly a hundred of these unoffending, starving creatures were deliberately murdered—by white men.

There had been some murders committed by the red enemies of these peaceable Indians, near the Ohio, in the month of February, and the visit for food to their broken homes by the Moravians created a pretext of charging them with the crime.

Accordingly, between eighty and ninety men were hastily gathered together and placed under the command of Colonel Williamson, who was told that this was his chance to vindicate himself in the eyes of the people.

The company encamped the first night on the Mingo bottom, the west side of the Ohio, about sixty miles below Fort Pitt.

The second day's march took them to within a mile or so of the central Moravian town.

Early the following morning the men were divided in two equal parties, one of which was deputed to cross over the river about a mile above the town. The remaining party was cut up into three divisions, one of which was to make a circuit of the woods and reach the river a short distance below the town, on the eastern side; another division was to fall into the centre of the town; and the third and remaining division was to enter the devastated place at its upper end.

Thus the physically weakened Indians, who had embraced the faith professed by these militiamen, were hemmed in on all sides, and while they searched for food to keep off starvation, they were approached as though they had been tyrants on the defensive.

When sixteen of the party designed to make the attack had crossed the river, their two sentinels came across an Indian called Shabosh.

The man was eating raw maize. One of the sentinels broke his arm by a shot, but, heedless of the pain, he kept cramming the maize into his dry mouth with his sound hand, looking wildly about him.

The other sentinel then fired and killed him.

The two together then tomahawked and scalped him.

Fearing that the firing of the guns which had done this deed would warn the Indians in the town of their approach, they went hurriedly to the party who were to begin the attack and advised them to move on immediately, which was done.

In the meantime the little party which had crossed the river marched to the main town, on the west side. Here they found a company of the Indians gathering the rotting corn left in their fields when the British Indians the previous fall had driven them away.

The white party, coming up, professed delight at coming across the Christian Indians who had been so savagely treated and told them to have no fear.

"Peace be with you," said the leader of the white band; "we have come to lead you to a place where all is plenty, and where corn is wasted for want of use. We will take you to Fort Pitt, where friends are waiting for you."

"Has the peaceable Indian a friend?" asked an Indian emaciated and worn. "Are not his white and his red brethren equally his enemies?"

"Those enemies are not the professors of a faith like you," was the reply.

"And is our faith yours?" asked the red man eagerly.

"Do we not offer you shelter and food and protection?" responded the white man.

The Indian looked wistfully around at his own little party, so cold, so sick, so famished. Then he held his hand out to the white man, saying:

"The white man's God is true, after all. We had begun to doubt if all the missionaries told us could be true. In our desolation and wanderings, thrust one way, then another, we feared the tales of a guarding and forgiving God were but as a legend, and that He was as revengeful as the Indian's 'Manitou.'"

The white man was evidently disconcerted by the simple faith of the Indian, and he turned aside. But the stern faces of the men under him left him no choice.

"We have no legends," he said to the Indian; "we have no souls that go to birds and beasts at our death, as the tales of the Manitou have."

"The white man's God takes the souls of those who trust in Him to himself," said the Indian.

Again the white man turned away.

"Maybe my white brother never heard the story of the whip-poor-will?" said the Indian, smiling conciliatorily, a bird far off piping a melancholy note.

"What is it?" asked the white man; "the tale?"

"In a few words I will tell it. A white trader sold liquor and beads to Indians for their peltries, —the skins of the animals the Indians had captured. It said the white man always made the Indians drunk before he traded with them and thus gained advantage over them. The white man was called Wilhelm; he was a Dutch settler. When the Indians upbraided him because of his perfidy, he would say: 'You can whip poor Wilhelm if he is not honest.' So he went on and prospered thus, and he became very wealthy from the sale, at a high price, of the skins he gained fraudulently. For years his lodge was visited by the red men, and each time he made them drunk, and then swore that he had not cheated them, in the same words: 'You can whip poor Wilhelm if he is not honest.' At last, one day when the red men were become poorer and poorer and had no meal, no tobacco, and Wilhelm had money and glittering stones and lodges unnumbered, a red man came to him towards the close of an afternoon when the storm was shaking the tree-tops and birds were frightened and flew screaming through the air, their feathers all broken and ruined. It was dark and dismal around the trader's lodge, and a pool of water beside it was black and heaving with the wind that moaned and shrieked. The trader came to the door of his lodge when he saw the Indian approaching.

"'It is an awful storm,' he said.

"'Is not the white man afraid of the spirit-voices abroad?' asked the Indian. 'For perchance among them there is the voice of a spirit which the white man loved not, and which he treated unfairly when it inhabited the body of flesh. Is the white trader not afraid?'

"'I am afraid of neither man, God, nor devil! You may whip poor Wilhelm if he is,' said the trader, laughing, and shaking his fist up to the sky.

"The wind blew louder and louder; birds fell dead at their feet. One little bird was whirled through the air apparently dead, but it touched the Indian on the eyes as it was descending, and then it appeared to live, and immediately circled about his head and flew to a tree above the pool of black, agitated water.

"'The little bird lives, but its voice is dead,' said the Indian to the trader. 'The wrath of Manitou has ruined its voice.'

"'Ha, ha!' laughed the trader; 'the wrath of Manitou indeed! Come, chief, let me see the peltries. Hold on, though!'

"He went into the lodge and brought forth a bottle of fire-water.

"'I want none,' said the red man. 'I can make my bargain without that.'

"'But I always treat,' said the trader.

"The red man, however, refused to touch it, and began to untie the bundle which he had upon his back. He spread before the gloating eyes of the trader such a pile of skins, and of such magnificent quality, as human eyes never before beheld. The trader could not speak for a few minutes, so lost was he in admiration. And the storm seemed to increase in violence, the trees bent shrieking to the ground, the lodge shook on its firm foundations, the door opened and shut violently, the pool of black water tumbled and tossed, the little voiceless bird fluttered its wings and flew incessantly from its tree to the Indian as though it wanted something which he alone could give it.

"When the air was thick and black and the storm very great, the trader suddenly roused himself from his admiration of the skins.

"'Drink,' he said, with trembling voice, holding out the fire-water. 'I never bargain without drink. It is dark, too, and the drink will keep off fear.'

"'I bargain without drink,' said the red man.

"'It is not good skins you bring,' said the trader.

"'You lie!' said the red man, in a stern voice.

"The trader looked at him.

"'It may be because it is dark and I cannot see well,' he said. 'And oh, *do* drink a little rum!'

"'If it is too dark, behold the light,' said the red man, and struck upon a flint and lighted an overturned bush, which, strangely enough, burned brightly, though it was damp.

"The flames leaped up, only to show the storm to greater advantage. The little voiceless bird hovered about the flame. The flame shot its rays through the open door of the lodge and lighted on huge piles of gold which the trader had been counting when the Indian had come up, making the room glitter like a fallen sun. The trader now closed the door.

"The sight of his gold in the light from the flaming bush seemed to have made him bolder.

"'No,' he said; 'the skins are very bad—the worst I ever saw.'

"'You lie!' said the red man again.

"The trader leaned over the skins, exulting, and thinking he must be bold indeed to bargain with this chief.

"'I will give you a bottle of fire-water and a

quart of beads for these,' he said. 'They are not worth so much.'

"'You lie!' again said the red man.

"The trader looked up: the red man's form had expanded; it rose above him; it towered above the highest trees; it seemed to reach the very sky and take away the awful storm-clouds and break and crush them.

"Even in his fear the trader defended himself.

"'I do not lie,' he said.

"The red man's hand caught up the burning bush, and it glittered and turned into a tomahawk in his hand. The little voiceless bird hovered around the tomahawk, pecking at it.

"'I do not lie!' now shrieked the trader, his voice rising above the storm that had burst in all its fury, the rain pouring down, the clouds broken by the red man's head, the heavens seeming to war with the earth; the lodge rocked upon its foundations, the pool of black water hissed and hissed, blackness all around, with wild cries of animals, and the hiss of snakes that crawled in fear even into the lodge.

"'I do not lie!' shrieked the trader. 'You may whip poor Will——'

"He got no further, his voice crying plaintively the beginning of his common plea, for the tomahawk of the red man crashed through his skull, and he fell back dead within the door of his lodge, which rocked and shivered and snapped, and pitched headlong into the black pool with all its shining gold and precious stones, and the pool roared as though it laughed, and opened to receive it all, then closed over it and grew black and peaceful as the storm rolled away and the moon and the stars came in the sky, where the red man had ascended like a long gray trail of smoke.

"But all through the dripping wood, now here, now there, was the plaintive cry of 'whip-poor-will, whip-poor-will.'

"It was the voice of the little bird that had been voiceless; and the last words of the white trader who had so long cheated the Indians were thereafter always loud in the land at dark of night or early morning,—a warning to the world of a soul that in pain saw, when it was too late, the error of its way, but even at the last could think of no words but those of old falsehoods, and tried to cheat even the Manitou with words that had ever cheated his children. For the huge red man had been Manitou. That is all the story. There!—there is a whip-poor-will. Hear it!"

"We have lingered too long," said the white man, who, as the tale had proceeded, had gained composure; "and now come on."

The party then took up the line of march, the Indians hemmed in by the militia.

But there was no doubting on the part of the starving Indians as to the sincerity and good intentions of the band of militiamen who had promised them so much and listened patiently to a story of their tribe, and they walked patiently along, after delivering up to the whites their scanty arms and ammunition, and thanked them over and over again.

"Stop!" said the chief; "the white brethren are hungry."

So the command was given to halt, and the Indians began with all speed to prepare a savory mess for the friendly white men from the little store of corn they had collected, and packed some away for the cold journey through the biting blast.

A party of white men and a few Indians were immediately dispatched to Salem, a short distance from Gnadenhuetten, the central town, where the Indians had also come back to look for corn. These were easily persuaded to come to Gnadenhuetten, especially as the white men professed to be exceedingly religious, and Moravians, admiring their spacious and cleanly hut of worship as it once had been, and discussing fluently on the goodness of the missionaries, saying frequently:

"The good Indians are indeed good Christians, and well beloved at the fort, where our white brothers and sisters await them."

Some of them on leaving Salem set fire to the few yet standing houses and the portion of the church still remaining, which, on signs of disapproval from the Indians, they explained that no harm or sacrilege was intended, only that they must destroy any lurking-place liable to be made use of by the enemy of the good Indians.

On their arrival at the bank of the river opposite Gnadenhuetten they came across the body of Shabosh.

"What is this?" asked a stern-eyed Indian. "Do my white brothers murder in Christ's name?"

But it was too late: they had given up their arms, they were in the power of men who now began to be less religiously inclined, and, mentioning God less, proclaimed a knowledge of a lower power which proved a long familiarity with it.

The Indians were taken over to Gnadenhuetten, where the white men threw off all pretensions to friendliness.

The captive men were divided from the women and children, and shut up in two houses some distance apart. These houses the whites called slaughter-houses.

The prisoners being thus securely taken, a council of war was immediately called to decide on their fate.

The officers of the militia were unwilling to take on their own shoulders the whole responsibility of the decision, and agreed to refer the question to the men in a body.

The men were accordingly drawn up in line, and were full of merriment over the success of the escapade.

The commander of the party, Colonel Williamson, who was supposed to be anxious to retrieve his lost reputation, put in full parliamentary form the question:

"Shall the Moravian Indians be taken prisoners to Pittsburg, or be put to death here?"

There was a silence at first.

"All who are in favor of saving these lives will now step out of the line and form a second rank," commanded Colonel Williamson. On this, sixteen, some assert eighteen, stepped out of the rank and file.

"Down with them!" cried those in the rear, and these formed a line of majority beyond the eighteen—for death without mercy. The fate of the Moravians was thus decided, and they were told to prepare for death.

"We expected it," said they calmly.

For the prisoners, from the time they were placed in the guard-house, foresaw death, and began to sing some simple hymns they had learned, praying and exhorting each other to place a strong reliance in the saving mercy of the Christ they had been told of.

On being accused of having aided the hostile Indians they declared their innocence; they were then told that they had property of the whites in their possession.

They said they could render a satisfactory account of every single article they called their own— where, or from what trader they had purchased it.

But the number of horses, the Indian's sole delight, and other creatures which they had once possessed, were brought to bear against them by their accusers, who concluded that "when they killed the Indians the country would be theirs; and the sooner this was done the better."

Accordingly they told the poor half-starved creatures they must die.

Finding that all entreaties to save their lives were to no purpose whatever, and that some, more bloodthirsty than their companions, were anxious to begin the slaughter, they united in begging a short delay that they might prepare themselves for death, which request, at length, was granted. They asked pardon for whatever offense they had given or grief they had occasioned to each other; they knelt down, offering fervent prayers to God their Saviour, and, kissing one another, under a flood of tears, fully resigned to his will, they sang praises unto Him, in the joyful hope that they would soon be relieved from all pains and join their Redeemer in everlasting bliss.

They were not quick enough for their captors, who, impatient, during the time granted for the last devotions consulted as to the mode of death for the praying band of people. Some suggested the setting on fire of the two guard-houses they were at present confined in, thus burning them alive and saving the waste of time for burial.

But others said no, for they wanted to take home the many scalps as a proper confirmation of their triumph. Some, again, opposed both these plans, which had many adherents, and declared that they would never be guilty of murdering a people whose innocence was so satisfactorily proven, and proposed setting them at liberty, or, if that was not to be thought of, at least to hold them as prisoners, and deliver them up to the proper authorities.

But, as is usually the case with the most human of men in their treatment of those in their power, they who entertained the last proposition were declared weak by the majority, who advocated death in one form or other, and despised the idea of holding these Indians as they would other foes, rejecting any proposal which should suggest a line of treatment opposed to the alleged deserts of a hated people. Thereupon those who desired no personal violence called upon the God of the red and the white man alike to witness that they were innocent of the blood of these harmless Christian Indians, and withdrew to some distance from the scene of slaughter, like so many Pilates, who had the will to propose a humane action, but not the strength of will that dared put the action into execution in the face of popular protest.

The murderers, impatient to make a beginning, came again to them while they were singing and praying, and, inquiring if they were now ready to die, they answered in the affirmative, adding that they had commended their immortal souls to God, who had given them the assurance in their hearts that He would receive their souls.

One of the party, taking up a cooper's mallet, saying: "How exactly this will do for the business," began with Abraham, and continued knocking down one after another until he had counted fourteen that he had killed with his own hands.

He now handed the instrument to one of his

fellow-murderers, saying: "My arm fails me. Go on in the same way. I think I have done pretty well!"

In the other house, where mostly women and children were confined, Judith, a remarkably pious, aged widow, was the first victim. Christina, who had formerly lived with the sisters in Bethlehem, and spoke English and German well, fell on her knees and begged for life in vain.

But two of the Indians, both lads, escaped, each about fifteen years of age. One, hiding himself in the cellar of the house where the women and children were murdered, beheld the blood run in streams into the cellar, and, waiting until night, escaped through the window. The other, receiving but one blow, and not being scalped, recovered his senses; but, seeing the murderers return and kill a man named Abel (what fitting personal nomenclature!), who was endeavoring to raise himself up, he lay still until evening, when, the doors being open, he escaped into the woods.

The many particulars noted down with scrupulous fidelity are too horrible to reproduce at this late date, even when all the actors in the affair have been called to answer at a higher tribunal than man's opinion. Suffice it to say that in those two houses, where songs and prayers had sounded so earnestly in the praise of Christ, who died for all mankind and suffered for red man and white man alike, so that his people but take up the cross and follow Him in meekness and well-doing, all was silent when night came down, and the tired executioners slept from their labors or counted their scalps and made sure of the welcome that awaited them in the fort, while ninety-six dead bodies—forty-one men, twenty-one women, and thirty-four children—attested the weariness that seized their hands and arms.

"Thus, O Brainerd and Zeisberger, faithful missionaries, who devoted your whole lives to incessant toil and suffering in your endeavor to make the wilderness of paganism ' rejoice and blossom as the rose,' in faith and piety to God—thus perished your faithful followers, by the murderous hands of more than savage white men! Faithful pastors! Your spirits are again associated with those of your flock —' where the wicked cease from troubling, and the weary are at rest.' "

The Indians waiting in the upper town, Shoenbrunn, ten miles farther up the river, expecting the aid promised their brethren in the other two towns, were apprised of the danger, and escaped just in time to keep their scalps intact.

For a large division of the militiamen arrived at

Shoenbrunn on the very day the Indians had left, and were wild with rage at having been betrayed, as they termed it.

They collected together what plunder there was for them and with it returned to their companions.

After the work of wholesale slaughter was consummated, and no other Moravian Indians presenting themselves, the buildings in the town of Gnadenhuetten, including the two slaughter-houses, were fired, as those had been in Salem.

Thus the ninety-six dead bodies were consumed, and what the fire failed to reduce to ashes the wolves howling in the wilderness beyond promised to look after.

The party of whites then moved forward, and proceeded to Pittsburg, where, on the opposite banks of the Ohio, they attacked the peaceable Delaware chiefs and a number of friendly families, all under the protection of the government, killed a number, among them a promising young chief, and then went off.

Lewis Wetzel heard of this affair, and shuddered as he, too, tracked the Indians who had wronged him.

He declared that he would never have attacked innocent people, and he was known never to have been cruel to women and children; but possibly had he been detailed with the marauding party the sight of a red-skin would have blinded him and deafened him to the calls of mercy, and only his wrongs would have stood before him, calling out for him to avenge them, and he might have deemed the claim of religion on the part of the Indians but another trick to catch the principles of the white men, as he could remember how, long ago, a bear lurked about his old home, and how wolves' cries sounded about the door, when human beings imitated beasts to carry out the plots of their own nefarious treacheries.

He knew that in this party of men who brought into the vicinity of Fort Pitt nearly a hundred gory scalps there might be some bent on revenging a long line of affronts offered, like his own, by the Indians; but he also knew that men of the Simon Girty stamp were foremost in it, and that torture and bloodshed were the sole incentives, as they wantonly loved the contortions of a snake which was impaled to the ground and gradually died in agony.

He had little time to think of a matter which appealed to all thinking settlers at the time, but was quickly dismissed because of more personal troubles; for he was preparing for his own first campaign, which promised to inaugurate the infliction of his penalties on the makers of his broken home.

CHAPTER VIII.

CRAWFORD'S CAMPAIGN.

AFTER this excusable digression, we come to the period of Crawford's campaign, in which Lewis Wetzel and probably one or more of his brothers were engaged.

It was well known at the time that this stern campaign was intended to represent almost a second Moravian extermination, for a few false Indians claiming to belong to the Christian settlements had committed depredations which involved the whole party in the general accusation.

The settlers had stood too much and too often seen their rights set aside by both villainous whites and Indians to bear with aught more without most strenuous efforts to punish the malefactors.

Wetzel's peculiarly lonely condition, for he made few friends while among the peaceably inclined settlements, had attracted the attention of many around him. His isolation from the few simple gayeties, his keeping apart even from his relatives, singled him out as a peculiar character. The story of his father's death and the stern determination of the young man may have caused the gentle smiles which greeted him, as women ever pity loneliness and pain; which kindliness, however, seldom received a reward from him; for he noticed it not—he did not understand it.

Among the maidens at Wheeling was one black-eyed, little figure which came to be called "Wetzel's shadow." She was the daughter of the neighbor Rosencranz, who had been so well known in Pennsylvania before the Wetzels had come West. She had been born and reared here, and, her father and mother dying, the fact of the family of Lewis having known her parents in their days of greater domesticity may have attracted her to them. But she was not attracted to the other members of the family as she was to the young scout. It was she who mended the torn garments of the young boy, as she was so much with his mother; it was she who listened to the stories of his youthful prowess, and whose eyes gleamed when she heard the story of his oath.

When he went away through the forest on the scent, restless and ever provoked to activity, she it was upon whom his eyes first lighted on his return to Wheeling, she it was who offered to relieve him of his gun, and whose blushes made him often blush himself, not understanding nor liking her effusion.

She was always in his footsteps, shy but resolute. He often found her in the natural bowers of vines prone upon the ground crying her pretty eyes out, and wanting comfort; and yet he could not ask her what ailed her, nor disturb her at such moments.

He would creep away when he found her thus, going softly over the twigs and grass so as not to make a noise and let her know he was in her vicinity. He did not know why he avoided her, only he saw soft pity in her eyes for him, and he frowned at pity expressed on his behalf. When Crawford's campaign was broached and he signified his intention of joining it, the maiden Rosencranz was wild. She knew of the horrors of the late Williamson campaign, and to think that Lewis Wetzel would voluntarily murder innocent people was almost as bad as to think of him murdered himself. After days of conflict with herself, and when she could not go to the other women, who, older than herself, could only give her practical advice and tell her that Lewis Wetzel knew his own business best and that his affairs belonged to no woman, she resolved to go in person to him and remonstrate with him.

It may have been that his preparations for the

campaign had kept him busily employed with the other men, and he no longer frequented the haunts where the women oftenest went, and that she missed him sorely.

However that may be, she sought and found him.

At first she could not speak for crying, and only stood before him broken with her tears.

"What ails you, Berta Rosencranz?" he asked.

Then she found her tongue, and burst out with:

"Oh, this dreadful campaign — this dreadful colonel!"

"Colonel Crawford is a brave man," smiled Lewis. "He was born in the same year with General Washington, in the same Virginia too."

"That makes no difference," spitefully cried the little maiden; "and I wish he had been born in the same year with Adam, so I do."

"Why, he would'nt be here now," said foolish Lewis, lost in astonishment.

"I don't care," she said, growing angrier for some reason or other. "The idea of such a man going and killing! I wish I had him here—the traitor!"

"He is not a traitor, Berta Rosencranz, and his record is good. Did he not, in '58, go with Forbes's expedition, which captured Fort Duquesne? Did not General Washington often visit him in Fayette? Was he not a colonel of the Continentals? Whom do you call a traitor?"

"Well, I don't care, Lewis Wetzel; and you needn't stand up for everybody I don't like."

"Why don't you like everybody, then?"

"That's my own business. What right has he to take everybody away from everybody, and——"

"He does not. What do you mean?"

"Why does he lead people into temptation, then? I never was so angry as I am now, and it is all his fault. He ought to be ashamed of himself, so he ought."

"What makes you angry?"

"How should I know? I wouldn't ask silly questions if I was you, Lewis Wetzel. Don't the Bible tell us not to be silly? My goodness! The Bible! How can you bear to mention the Bible!"

"I did not."

"Well, you ought to have done so, then. A man who does not mention the Bible ought not to be trusted. I know I wouldn't trust such a man."

"I did not ask you to trust me, Berta Resencranz."

"Oh, Lewis Wetzel, how can you bear to hurt my feelings so?" cried the poor little thing, in tears again. "You know very well that I trust you, and you know I've always trusted you, and dear knows I haven't many people to trust."

"Why?"

"Because; that's why."

"Is it?"

"I'd never call myself an Indian scout if I couldn't tell that much. If I was an Indian scout, I'd know everything, and I'm sure I wouldn't be all the time giving every blessed friend I had the heart-ache?"

"Do I give every blessed friend I have the heart-ache?"

"Don't you?"

"Do I?"

"How should I know? I'm not every blessed friend a man has. You ought to feel ashamed to accuse me of anything of the sort—just as though I was an army."

Lewis was standing first on one foot, then on the other.

Berta was looking at him from the corner of her eye, while her face was buried in her apron.

He did not make an attempt to break the silence which had now fallen.

At last she said plaintively:

"Say, Lewis Wetzel, if anybody trusts us, we must do all we can to deserve that trust, mustn't we, eh?"

"I suppose so," he answered. Clearly he was tired of this nonsense.

"And if we don't deserve a trust we—we don't, eh?"

"I suppose so."

"Then if I trust you you will be very glad to do me a favor, eh? Upon your word of honor you will be glad to do me a favor?"

"Oh, yes."

"Then don't go with this campaign, Lewis. Just you stay here and be happy: you don't know how easy it is to be happy if you only try right hard. And who knows but there may be people around who would die to make you happy."

"It wouldn't make me happy for people to die—unless they are Injuns."

"Then you know, Lewis, I can make real nice molasses cakes—just as mother said they make them in Pennsylvania; and you know you liked them there."

"Did I? I must have forgotten."

"Of course; you were very young then, Lewis."

"Yes?"

"You know you were; you ought to be ashamed of yourself not to know that. So, as you will try to deserve the trust people repose in you, and you love the molasses cakes I know how to make, and just as you liked them in Pennsylvania when quite young, you will stay here and eat and be merry, and let old Crawford and his old campaign go without you. Oh, how nice of you, Lewis!"

He broke from her then, seeing a certain meaning in her fresh cheerfulness.

"I never said that I would stay," he said frowning. "I will not stay. You have no right to take up my words so. No; my duty calls me away, and I go. You, all the women, need the men for protection; and I go to keep your enemies from you. No, Berta Rosencranz, you cannot detain me any more than any other woman, any more than all the women in the world could detain me. Good-bye!"

And, turning on his heel, he left her sobbing, with her pretty head up against a tree.

He went immediately to Colonel Crawford and his men. He knew that the work he volunteered to do meant murder and plunder, and the destruction of the Wyandot towns on the Sandusky. But his vow had never been forgotten, and his chance was come.

It was the universal resolution of every man concerned in this expedition to spare the life of no Indian who might fall in his way, whether friend or foe, demoniacal as this may appear.

But it will be seen in the sequel that the result of the whole campaign was entirely different from that of the Moravian campaign in the preceding March. And while at this long distance from the troublous, exciting times of Lewis Wetzel's day we see only the horrible actions of the white men who acted the savage, yet the long continuance of the Indian war had debased the larger number of the white population to the almost savage state of nature. They had lost so many relatives by the Indians, they had been witnesses of such horrid murders and other depredations by the red foes, that they were in constant dread for their women and little ones; their flocks and crops were not assured to them, but were liable to be stolen and ruined in one night, and they insensibly became subject to that indiscriminate thirst for revenge which is such a prominent feature in the savage character.

The men were all mounted on the best horses they could get, the settlers furnishing steeds to those who owned none.

Lewis Wetzel had saved one colt of his father's, and this trained beast bore him.

On the 25th of May, 1782, not a cloud in the sky, the day tender and full of the scent of green-growing plants, and peace and plenty making a panoramic picture of wondrous beauty, four hundred and eighty men mustered in the old Mingo towns on the western side of the Ohio river.

They were all from the immediate neighborhood, with the exception of one company from Ten Mile, in Washington County, Pennsylvania.

Colonel Crawford had accepted the command with apparent reluctance; but, as an election had been held and votes cast for Colonel Williamson or himself to assume the office, and he being duly elected, he dared scarcely to deny the popular voice, and so he acceded to the will of the people.

The line of march was taken up, and the horses tramped along through "Williamson's Trail," as it was then called, until they arrived at the upper Moravian town, in the fields of which there was still corn on the stalks, upon which the host of horses was plentifully fed during the night of encampment there.

Shortly after the army had halted, three men, who had walked some distance from the camp, discovered a couple of Indians, and fired at one of them, without wounding him, however.

As soon as the news of the discovery of Indians reached the encampment, more than half of the men rushed out, without any command, and in the most tumultuous manner crashed through the stubble to see what the report meant.

From this open breach of discipline Colonel Crawford anticipated the defeat which followed. "They obey nothing but their own base instincts," he said, "and these instincts, like all impulses, do little for safety without a cool leader."

The whole fact in a nutshell is that the Indians were beforehand. They had seen the gathering on the Mingo bottom, and knew their number and destination. They saw from writing on the trees, that no quarter was to be given to any Indian, whether man, woman, or child.

Into June, however, the militia roved along, instead of meeting with Indians and plunder, coming across nothing but desolation. Where Indian villages had been, the place was covered with high grass, and there were only the ruins of a few huts. The Indians had tramped off to Scioto some time before.

At last the officers, gathered in council, determined to march one day longer in the direction of Upper Sandusky, and then, if nothing noteworthy presented itself, they would begin a retreat forthwith.

Through the plains of Sandusky they were to be seen early the next morning, going along out of humor, and expecting to come across nothing but the usual dull sameness. But about 2 o'clock in the afternoon the advance guard was fired upon by Indians, who, in large numbers, were concealed in the high grass, and driven back. The Indians, after this attack, made for a dense piece of woods almost entirely surrounded by plains, and here they would have had the vantage-ground. But the white men, by a rapid movement, headed them off.

Then the battle began by a heavy fire on both sides. A few Indians at the outset of the fight had gained a portion of the woods, but these were dislodged with slaughter. They then attempted to reach a small skirt of wood on the right flank of the army, but were prevented from doing so by Major Leet, who commanded the right wing of the army at that time.

The firing was incessant and heavy all day, and only when darkness fell was it discontinued.

Both the red and white armies slept on their arms that night, and waited impatiently for the morning. Large fires were kindled all along the line of battle by both parties, and chief among the workers and tenders of the fires of the whites was a dark, silent young fellow, who did his work quietly and effectually, only now and then pausing to shade his eyes with his hand and scan the opposite hills where the red man waited, and whose encampment was plainly visible in the glare of the fires.

"It is coming! It is coming!" he would mutter to himself, and then resume his work of piling on the logs.

Fiercer and hotter roared the fires all night, and the country was one big bonfire, by the flame of which the contending parties watched each other and prepared for the promised encounter of the following day.

There was a looking-after of muskets and a storing of powder and balls on the part of the white men. But not alone was these so-called civilized instruments of death attended to, as though any weapons designed to destroy life can be properly deemed civilized! But knives were sharpened, even tomahawks ground down, for hurling the tomahawk found many adepts in this little party, and when necessity compelled a cessation of powder-firing the Indians' own weapon of defense and attack was as efficacious in the hands of the foes of the Indians as in the hands of the dusky denizens of the forest themselves.

In the early morning the white party prepared for the defensive.

But the Indians made no attack until late in the evening, while all day long large parties of them were seen traversing the plains, like ants establishing a city, and some of them carrying away the dead and wounded of the day before. Their numbers now seemed uncountable and still increasing, and the officers of the white army anxiously called a council.

"We must retreat," said they with one voice.

"Why?" asked a calm voice.

"Who spoke?" demanded Colonel Crawford.

There was no response.

"We must retreat," again began an officer, and again came the interruption:

"Why?"

The men who had pressed in to the confines set apart for the council of war now drew back, all save one figure, a young dark-skinned man who had fed the fires the night before. He had been the speaker.

"How dared you interrupt?" was asked him, not that any court-martial was possible in such an army for breach of discipline.

"I meant no disrespect," was the reply; "only it hardly becomes men who go out to fight with an enemy to fall back because of a trifling superiority of numbers."

"A trifling superiority of numbers!" repeated the officer. "What do you say to that?"

He raised his hand, and all eyes were directed towards the point he designated. They could see from afar off the Indians pouring in from all directions until the opposite field of hills was one dense mass of humanity, which was gradually put into squares with considerable dexterity and military skill.

There was no response from the dissatisfied men,

and in silence they stood for some minutes regarding the manœuvres of the savages.

The council of officers was then convened again, the men excluded, and a guard stationed to prevent any intrusion from outsiders.

Colonel Williamson then proposed taking a hundred and fifty men and marching to the Upper Sandusky. The commander-in-chief interposed a refusal.

"I have very little doubt," he said, "but that you would reach the town, but you would find nothing there but empty wigwams, and, having taken off so many of our best men, you would leave the rest to be destroyed by the host of Indians with which we are now surrounded, and on your return you would meet the fate which had been ours during your absence. They care nothing for defending their towns, for the simple reason that the towns are worth nothing. Their squaws, children, and property have been removed long since. Our lives and baggage are what they want, and if they can get us divided they will soon have them. We must stay closely together, and do the best that existing circumstances will permit."

During the conflict of the day before the expeditionary force lost three men and had several wounded. Preparations for retreat were now made by burying the dead and burning fires over their graves to prevent discovery. Once, in the midst of one of these fires, a man was seen surrounded by flames, shaking his clenched fist towards the foe.

"Who is that man?" questioned Colonel Crawford.

"Can't say," returned the man addressed, "but from this distance it looks like a young fellow named Wetzel."

The retreat was to begin deep in the night. But the Indians seemed to scent the intention of the white men, and about sundown attacked the army with savage force and fury in every direction excepting that towards Sandusky. There was confusion, and momentarily consternation seized the troops, and as a result firing on their part was very desultory.

As hurriedly as the excitement incident to the assault would permit the line of march for the retreat was formed. When this was accomplished, the guides were instructed to take the course to Sandusky, the only opening between the masses of Indians. The army then took up the march for about a mile, wheeled about, and by a circuitous route gained the trail by which they had come.

They retreated the whole of the next day, pursued by the Indians, who kept up a steady fire into the rear-guard, which often had to be replaced, and a wounded man or two brought to the fore. Then the savage firing became less and less, and towards evening ceased entirely, the pursuers halting and making no pretense to follow any farther.

At night the fires of the white men were built. For hours the men were on the alert, but nothing occurred to occasion any alarm—not a red-skin was within a radius of a mile of them. Towards midnight all fear of pursuit had vanished, and even the sentinels lay down on their arms to sleep. Even in this careless position they were not attacked.

Most unfortunately, when the retreat had been resolved upon, a difference of opinion prevailed as to the best mode of effecting it.

The greater number thought it best to keep in a body, while a very small party deemed it safest to break off into detachments and make their way home in different directions.

Many attempted to do this, calculating that the Indians in a body would follow the main army. In this they were mistaken.

For the Indians paid little attention to the main body of the army, and pursued the small parties and wrought such effectual vengeance that very few of them escaped.

The only successful small party was that commanded by Colonel Williamson, composed of some forty men, who, late in the night of the retreat, broke through the Indian lines under a brisk fire and with some loss, and overtook and rejoined the main army the second day of the retreat.

For several days the Indians were spread over the whole country in pursuit of the straggling parties. They pursued them almost to the banks of the Ohio.

Colonel Crawford in the retreat had placed himself at the head, and hoped that the darkness would shield his command.

Dr. Knight, the companion of Crawford in his captivity, thus relates what followed:

"We had not got a quarter of a mile from the scene of action when I heard Colonel Crawford calling for his son John, his son-in-law Major Harrison, and Major Rise and William Crawford, his nephews, upon which I came up and told him I believed they were before us.

"He asked: 'Is that the doctor?'

"I told him it was.

"He then replied that they were not in front, and begged of me not to leave him; and I promised him I would not.

"We then waited, and continued calling for these men till the troops had passed us.

"The colonel told me his horse had almost given

out, that he could not keep up with the troops, and wished some of his best friends to remain with him; he then exclaimed against the militia for riding off in such an irregular manner, and leaving some of the wounded behind, contrary to his orders.

"Presently there came two men riding after us, one of them an old man, the other a lad. We inquired if they had seen any of the above persons, and they answered they had not.

"About daybreak Colonel Crawford's and the young man's horses gave out, and they left them.

"We pursued our journey eastward, and about two o'clock fell in with Captain Biggs, who had carried Lieutenant Ashley from the field of action dangerously wounded.

"We then went on about the space of an hour, when a heavy rain came up; we concluded it was best to encamp, as we were encumbered with the wounded officer.

"We then barked four or five trees, made an encampment and a fire, and remained all night.

"Next morning we again prosecuted our journey, and, having gone about three miles, found a deer which had been recently killed. The meat was sliced from the bones, and bundled up in the skin, with a tomahawk lying by it.

"We carried all with us, and, in advancing about one mile farther, discovered the smoke of a fire.

"We then gave the wounded officer into the charge of the young man, and desired him to stay behind, whilst the colonel, the captain, and myself walked up as cautiously as we could towards the fire.

"When we came to it, we concluded, from several circumstances, some of our people had encamped there the preceding night.

"We then went about roasting the venison, and when just about to march observed one of our men coming upon our tracks. He seemed at first very shy, but, having called to him, he came up and told us he was the person who had killed the deer; but upon hearing us come up he was afraid of Indians, hid in a thicket, and made off.

"Upon this, we gave him some bread and roasted venison, proceeded together upon our journey, and about two o'clock came upon the paths by which we had gone out.

"Captain Biggs and myself did not think it safe to keep the road, but the colonel said the Indians would not follow the troops farther than the plains, which we were then considerably past.

"As the wounded officer rode Captain Biggs's horse, I gave the colonel mine. The colonel and myself went about one hundred yards in front, the captain and the wounded officer in the centre, and the young man behind.

"After we had traveled about one mile and a half, several Indians started up within fifteen or twenty steps of the colonel and me. As we at first discovered only three, I immediately got behind a large black oak, made ready my piece and raised it up to take sight, when the colonel called to me twice not to fire; upon that one of the Indians ran up and took the colonel by the hand. The colonel then told me to put down my gun, which I did.

"At that instant one of them came up to me whom I had formerly seen very often, calling me doctor, and took me by the hand. They were Delaware Indians of the Wingenim tribe. Captain Biggs fired among them, but did no execution.

"They then told us to call those people and make them come there, else they would go and kill them. The colonel called, but the little party got off and escaped for the time.

"The colonel and I were then taken to the Indian camp, which was about half a mile from the place where we were captured. On Sunday evening five Delawares, who had posted themselves at some distance farther on the road, brought back to the camp where we lay the scalps of Captain Biggs and Lieutenant Ashley, together with an Indian scalp which Captain Biggs had taken in the field of action. They also brought in Biggs's horse and mine, and told us the other men had got away from them.

"Monday morning, the 10th of June, we were prepared to march to Sandusky, about thirty-three miles distant.

"They had eleven prisoners of us, and four scalps. The Indians were seventeen in number. Colonel Crawford was very desirous to see a certain Simon Girty, who lived among the Indians, and was on this account permitted to go to town the same night, with two warriors to guard him, having orders at the same time to pass by the place where the colonel had turned out his horse, that they might, if possible, find him. The rest of us were taken as far as the old town, which was within eight miles of the new.

"Tuesday morning, the 11th, Colonel Crawford was brought out to us on purpose to be marched in with the other prisoners. I asked the colonel if he had seen Mr. Girty. He told me he had, and that Girty had promised to do everything in his power for him, but that the Indians were very much enraged against the prisoners, particularly Captain Pipe, one of the chiefs. He likewise told me that Girty had informed him that his son-in-law, Colonel Harrison, and his nephew, William Crawford, were made prisoners by the Shawanese, but had been pardoned. This Captain Pipe had come from the towns about an hour before Colonel Crawford, and had painted all the prisoners' faces black. As he was painting me he told me I should go to the Shawanese towns and see my friends. When the colonel arrived, he painted him black also, told him he was glad to see him, and that he would have him shaved when he came to see his friends at the Wyandot town. When we marched, the colonel and I were kept between Pipe and Wyngenim, the two Delaware chiefs. The other nine prisoners were sent forward with a party of Indians.

"As we went along, we saw four of the prisoners lying by the path, tomahawked and scalped; some of them were at the distance of half a mile from each other. When we arrived within half a mile of the place where the colonel was executed, we overtook the five prisoners that remained alive; the Indians had caused them to sit down on the ground, as they did; also the colonel and myself, at some distance from them. I was then given in charge to an Indian fellow, to be taken to the Shawanese towns. In the place where we were now made to sit down were a number of squaws and boys, who fell upon the five prisoners and tomahawked them. There was a certain John McKinley among the prisoners, formerly an officer in the Thirteenth Virginia regiment, whose head an old squaw cut off, and the Indians kicked it about upon the ground. The young Indian fellows came often where the colonel and I were, and dashed the scalps in our faces. We were then conducted along towards the place where the colonel was afterwards executed. When we came within half a mile of it, Simon Girty met us, with several Indians, on horseback. He spoke to the colonel, but as I was about one hundred and fifty yards behind I could not hear what passed between them. Almost every Indian we met struck us either with sticks or their fists. Girty waited till I was brought up and then asked, Was that the doctor? I answered him, Yes, and went towards him and reached out my hand; but he bid me begone, and called me a cursed rascal; upon which the fellow who had me in charge pulled me along. When we came to the fire, the colonel was stripped, ordered to sit down by the fire, and then they beat him with sticks and their fists. Presently after, I was treated in the same manner. They then tied a rope to the foot of a post about fifteen feet high, bound the colonel's hands behind his back, and fastened the rope to a ligature between his wrists. The rope was long enough for him to sit down or to walk around the post once or twice, and return the same way. The colonel then called to Girty, and asked if they intended to burn him? Girty answered, Yes. Upon this, Captain Pipe made a speech to the Indians, consisting of about thirty or forty men and sixty or seventy squaws and boys.

"When the speech was finished, they all yelled a hideous and hearty assent to what he had said. The Indian men then took up their guns and shot powder into the colonel's body from his feet as far as his neck. I think not less than seventy loads were discharged upon his naked body. They then crowded about him and, to the best of my observation, cut off his ears. When the throng had dispersed a little, I saw the blood running from both sides of his head. The fire was about six or seven yards from the post to which the colonel was tied. It was made of small hickory poles burnt quite through in the middle, each end of the poles remaining about six feet in length. Three or four Indians by turns would take up individually one of these burning pieces of wood and apply it to his naked body, already burned black with powder. These tormentors presented themselves on every side of him, so that whichever way he ran around the pole he was met by the burning fagots. Some of the squaws took broad boards upon which they put a quantity of burning coals and hot embers and threw them on him, so that in a short time he had nothing but coals of fire and hot ashes to walk upon. In the midst of these extreme tortures he called upon Simon Girty, and begged of him to shoot him. Girty, by way of derision, answered that he had no gun, turning about to an Indian behind him and laughing heartily. Girty then came up to me and told me to prepare for death. He said, however, that I was not to die at that place, but would be burnt at the Shawanese towns. Colonel Crawford at this period of his suffering besought the Almighty to have mercy on his soul. He spoke very low, and bore his torments with the most manly fortitude. He continued in all the extremities of pain for an hour and three-quarters or two hours longer, as near as I can judge, when at last, being almost spent, he lay down on his face. They then scalped him, and repeatedly threw the scalp in my face, telling me that it was my great captain's. An old squaw got a board and took a parcel of coals and ashes and laid them on his back and head after he had been scalped. He then raised himself on his feet and began to walk around the post. They then put a burning stick to him as usual, but he seemed insensible to pain."

This is the doctor's narrative.

It may be added that Colonel Crawford's son-in-law and nephew were executed about the same time. John escaped. What became of the other members of his family cannot be satisfactorily ascertained.

Dr. Knight was doomed to be burned at a town fifty miles distant from Sandusky, and committed to the care of an Indian convoy. The second morning after their setting out, the gnats being very troublesome, Dr. Knight begged the Indian to unloose his bonds that he might assist him in making the fire to scatter the pests. Inasmuch as an Indian never fails to avail himself of help in the mere comforts of life, the doctor was soon freed and hard at work making up a fire with the Indian. While the savage was on his knees blowing the fire, the white man caught up a pole with which he struck the kneeling man upon the head with all his strength, hoping to knock him forward into the already fierce fire. But the stick broke, and the Indian, though sorely wounded, was not killed. He immediately sprang up and seized his gun, which the doctor grasped from him, but drew back the cock so violently that he broke the spring, rendering it useless as a firearm. Then the Indian ran off, yelling hideously, and the doctor made his way home, which took him twenty-one days to do, subsisting wholly on roots, and arriving at the station in an almost dying condition.

CHAPTER IX.

A PURSUIT AND AN ESCAPE.

THUS ended this most disastrous campaign. It was the last one that originated in this section of the country during the revolutionary contest of the Americans against Great Britain. It was undertaken with the very worst of views,—murder and plunder. It was conducted without proper means to encounter an enemy such as resisted the settlers. There was no subordination and discipline among the troops, and it ended in total discomfiture. Never on any occasion had the ferocious savages such ample revenge for the murder of their pacific friends.

Is the question asked: Why, with so small a force and such inadequate means, did the whites propose the campaign? The only answer is that most every one believed that the Moravian Indians having given offense to their belligerent warriors by their code of peace, there would be no friends to take up arms in their behalf.

On the scattered retreat of the troops which

followed Colonel Crawford's defeat a man named Mills, who had engaged in the unfortunate expedition, reached the Indian Spring, about nine miles from Wheeling, almost in sight of the settlements.

His horse being thoroughly fagged out, he left the beast here at the spring, and went on to Wheeling on foot.

Thence he went to Van Metre's fort. After a couple of days' rest here, he determined to go back after his horse, and started out.

He had not gone far on his way when a man started up from the long grass, a white man, but so jaded and worn and wild as to appear anything but a peaceably inclined settler.

"Who are you?" asked Mills, his hand on his gun-lock.

"A friend," answered the stranger, throwing up his hand to stay the action of the gun in Mills's hand.

"Do friends start up suddenly out of ambush?"

"Not usually. But who are you?"

"A friend."

"Do friends act so readily with their arms?"

"I thought you an Indian."

"As I thought you; in which latter case I meant death. And where do you go, friend?"

"For my horse at the Indian Spring, where I left him three or four days since."

"There is danger there, friend."

"I am used to danger. I was with Crawford."

"Yes. But the danger is different here; you travel alone through a hostile country. Let your beast go; you only expose yourself to unnecessary danger. I have a horse—I seldom use him; take him in welcome and spare your chance of life."

"How cowardly you advise me," laughed Mills. "You are one of those who stay at home and prate of danger to us who go to protect you."

"Home! I have no home."

"Do you live as Girty lives?"

"I have seen Girty, and I would like to be with the Indians as he is."

"You villain! do you dare say this to me? Do you dare avow a friendship with the Indians?"

"I have done no such thing. I have said I should like to be with the Indians as closely related as Girty is. So I would, but it would be because I might have the better chance to kill them."

"Who are you?"

"I was with Crawford too; I did my share in the work; would that it had been twenty-fold more!"

"Who are you?"

"Lewis Wetzel."

Mills looked at the harsh, weather-beaten stranger.

"Forgive me, I did not know you," he said, something in the other's face riveting his attention.

It was this something in Lewis Wetzel's face that attracted the rude settlers to him, but what it was they could not have told had they even had a thought of its meaning.

In these latter times, or in less wild places than he was, the habitual expression on the scout's face might have been denominated repression; repression of all the springs of life, a hushing of every instinct but the predominant one. The people were only attracted by the expression, and respected it without knowing it. So it was with Mills, who begged forgiveness and knew not why.

Together the two men now proceeded to the Indian Spring, for Wetzel would not allow Mills to go alone.

On the way one night they found an Indian, apparently astray from his tribe, sleeping beside a little fire, and farther from the fire rested a young dusky maiden.

The chief awoke on the approach of the two white men.

Wetzel's gun sighted him, when the girl arose from the ground with a shriek and threw herself upon the breast of her lover—for so he explained himself to be, and how he had run away from their tribe because of opposition to their marriage.

When Wetzel saw her devotion, he lowered his

gun, a tremor seizing his arm. "Go!" he said; "the woman has made me break my vow. Go! before I repent."

"Repent of what?" asked the Indian boldly, throwing the maiden from him.

"Of not killing you when I had the chance," answered Wetzel.

"It is the white man's big talk," sneered the Indian.

"Go!" commanded Wetzel, paying little attention to this insolence.

"It is the red man's land," said the Indian, "and the white man is the interloper. The white man fears the red man, say what he will."

Wetzel turned to the girl. "Get him away," he said.

She ran to her lover, entreating him. He answered her coldly, but pretended to put up his gun, which he had taken firmly in his hand.

Wetzel turned his back on the pair, and just then a bullet whistled close to his ear, the ungenerous Indian having fired his gun at the white man who spared his life. Wetzel turned like a wild beast.

"So much for my broken oath," he said, and shot the Indian down, and left the spot, with the girl wailing over the prostrate body of her lover.

The two men now went on to the spring, and

here they found Mills's horse, but it was tied to a tree.

Wetzel cried out: "Treachery! Beware!"

But Mills walked up to the tree to unfasten the animal, when instantly a discharge of guns followed, and he fell lifeless, pierced by a dozen bullets.

Wetzel, knowing that his only chance of escape was in instant flight, braced himself and with a plunge rushed through the line of astonished Indians who had now appeared on the scene and bounded off at the top of his speed.

He was followed by four fleet Indians, in rapid pursuit, and a hail of bullets. On, on he sped. His Indian pursuers yelped and whooped in proud exultation of soon having their victim.

For half a mile the chase was kept up, and then one of the savages had gotten so close that Wetzel was afraid he might fling his tomahawk with the usual unerring aim; but, instantly wheeling, he shot the red man dead in his tracks.

In his early youth Wetzel had acquired the habit of reloading his gun while at full run, and now this practice was his good friend. Keeping in advance of his pursuers for another half mile or so, a second Indian came close, and Wetzel turning to fire, the savage caught the end of his gun. The Indian tugged and wrenched; and met a strength that competed with his own. The other Indians were now in sight, coming recklessly on. By a powerful movement, the Indian, possessed of vast strength, brought Wetzel to his knee.

"White man die! White man burn!" said the savage. "Come, hurry up, chiefs, and see Wetzel die!"

Perhaps the astonishment of Wetzel at hearing his name in the mouth of his enemy gave him a new impulse, for by a last effort he freed his gun from the hands of the Indian, and, quickly thrusting the barrel to the side of the red neck, pulled the trigger, killing him instantly.

This seemed to astonish the other two Indians, for they had seen him discharge his gun with fell purpose before, and knew that he had not been allowed sufficient time since then to pause and reload his weapon.

"The long-knife is a devil!" shouted one of the braves, holding back.

"Kill the long-knife devil!" cried the other one; "the Manitou demands it."

But for an instant both of them seemed bewildered.

This trifling halt of astonishment gave Wetzel an advantage, and separated him by about two hundred steps from the Indians, and before they recovered their equanimity he was fleeing like an antelope over the plains, his trusty gun hugged closely to his breast by one hand, exhilaration over what he had done lending him a speed he had never possessed before, although in his time of youthful discipline, when he awaited a man's strength, he had practiced running, as well as other modes of Indian warfare.

As he sped along, he could hear far behind him the light thumps on the ground as the two Indians joined in pursuit of him, maddened into a like exhilaration with his own as they thought of his escape,—the man of whom their spies reported wonders, and whose oath was not unknown in more than one tribe.

On, and on they went; far away the Indian horses looked on for a minute at the flying men, and, tossing their manes, plunged aside; droves of turkeys spread their wings and moved—a black cloud—over the blue, cawing their note of trouble as they went.

On, and on, came the men, the white man first, the savages, like beasts of prey, resolved on blood. But the white man did not go as fast as at first: he was visibly slackening his pace. Was he giving out?

Leaping with immense strides, he yet managed to keep some distance ahead. Was his apparent weakness but a sham?

On, and on they went. Now the Indians were gaining on the white man. They could afford to send out a wild note of triumph towards the scout. Nearer and nearer they came to him. Slower and slower he went.

"If you halt now, we will not kill you," one of the braves called after the scout. Still he went on.

"If you let us take you alive, we will grant you many days' life," a brave now called out.

To take such a man prisoner and lead him into camp and there torture him and try his wonderful endurance would be a sight worthy the calling of all the scattered tribe together, a sight for the edification of old and young alike. They would far rather have him alive than dead. See how feebly he went! One brave urged on the other to run and grasp the white man.

Wetzel heard him say: "Do not throw your tomahawk unless he is too weak to stand much torture. Be sure and keep him without a wound till he is taken into camp."

"I shall be without a wound when I am taken into their camp, indeed," muttered Wetzel as he went along, his tottering gait surely deceiving his pursuers into the belief that he was making little progress and narrowing materially the distance between them.

"He holds up," said a brave, "and if his gun falls from his hand then he is weak enough to kill."

But such an accident did not occur: his gun remained in his hands, and although he used his arms strangely the gun did not fall to the ground. And indeed he was using his arms very strangely as he went. He was reloading his gun!

There were woods now close to him, and to this the white man directed his steps. Behind him he heard the whizzing of the feathers in the pursuing Indians' garments. Panting, his mouth open, his eyes starting from his head, almost spent, he yet spurred on, managing to near the woods as the foremost Indian sent aloof a long, loud shout of victory.

The woods were reached and entered, and just at that moment a tomahawk sped by the flying white man and buried itself up to the neck in a tree in front of him, immediately above his head, his bending his head to send home the bullet into his gun-barrel alone saving his life.

He was spent; his strength was gone. His teeth close shut together, his nostrils dilated, he yet feigned a greater weakness than was really his, and even stopped entirely once or twice in order to let his pursuers gain on him, and then he looked around him. As he looked around, the Indians disappeared. Then he would go on a little way, again to look around, only to find himself alone, the Indians having again disappeared.

This was repeated for perhaps half a dozen times, the Indians slipping behind trees every time he faced them, and regarding him from those fastnesses in awe as much as hate.

Nothing coming of these manœuvres, Wetzel took to the run again for a mile or two farther, hoping that his run would not be alone.

In this he was not disappointed, for in a little while he thought he heard the thud of feet on the ground back of him.

"I will not give them up," he muttered, and listened intently.

Yes, he was not mistaken: the Indians were pursuing him silently through the wood. At last the trees were not so close together, the path not quite so circuitous. The light became clearer, the ground less slippery. And there *were* sounds back of him: he was pursued by two pairs of moccasinned feet.

Then there before him was an open sunlit place, a space barren of herbage, with not a spear of the long grass so often a snare to the flying foot,—one of the open bare places that suddenly start before the eye of the trapper of the prairie, unaccountably denuded of life; one of the haunted spots of the Indian superstition that deals in natural phenomena and calls it supernatural magic. But, while in peace they avoided such places, war left them no preference.

Wetzel knew this; so towards this open space he ran. He reached it, and ran a little way. Then he slackened and turned, for no steps pursued him.

He wheeled around, but the foremost Indian was behind a tree in a wooded enclosure, peering out after the strange man.

The tree did not screen his body, however; so Wetzel fired and dangerously wounded him.

With a screech of terror the remaining Indian, who had also betaken himself to a sheltering tree, threw up his arms and took to his legs, yelling, as he went along the forest: "No catch dat man; him gun always loaded," and disappeared from sight.

With disappointed eyes Wetzel gazed after him, but was forced to be content with what damage he had already done.

"But there are only three; there should have been four," he said ruefully.

He turned away, and found that he staggered as he walked. It could not be all weakness that caused him to falter so. He had often run as far and as swiftly as this. Surely he was not wounded? No, the day's adventures had been too much joy—he was intoxicated as though by liquor. Wetzel always dwelt upon this adventure with peculiar vim, asserting that it was the first time he really knew joy.

But he made his way on, and in time came to Van Metre's, the scalps in his belt.

As he went into the clearing of the fort, a light step echoed his. Was it the Indian come back? A woman's hand was laid on his arm.

"You are a brave man, Lewis Wetzel," said the voice of Berta Rosencranz, and she pointed to the dangling scalps.

"Is it only you?" he said.

"Only me!" she echoed. "I hope I am something. But you are a brave man, though, Lewis Wetzel. I almost believe the story your mother tells about your being wrapped in a flag that Grizzie Heister brought to you when you were no age at all. Surely that flag must have entered your soul."

"Not that flag," he said, lighting up.

"Why not? I don't like all this nonsense about United States of America. This union of the colonies cannot possibly last. That flag——"

"That flag was wet with my mother's tears," he said.

"Your mother's tears! Dear knows you've caused your mother more tears than were ever shed on that pretty flag. Do you know you're breaking your mother's heart?—that it is broken already? She would so like you to stay home and—marry, I guess; most people marry, don't they? But what a very bold girl Grizzie Heister must have been, mustn't she? Don't you hate bold girls? I do. I wouldn't be a bold girl for anything. A bold girl would be sure to tell you that she liked you, wouldn't she? But I wouldn't tell you I liked you, although I do like you; now would I? I'd rather die first, wouldn't I? That's because I'm not a bold girl. Bold girls never die, do they? How you must hate that awful Heister girl, mustn't you? I guess she never had much of a bringing-up, had she? The idea of giving a little boy a flag! Isn't it dreadful? Indeed, I quite feel for poor Grizzie Heister because she was a bold girl. Now I like pretty, modest girls, not all the time throwing themselves at a man's head, don't you? But then Grizzie Heister was a miserably *old* girl, wasn't she? I hate *old* girls, don't you? Oh, Lewis Wetzel, whatever do you think!—Charley Madison wants to marry me! He's a nice fellow; you know very well he is. And such a kind fellow to women. What would you do if you were me?—would you say yes or no? I wish you would advise me, will you?"

"Yes, marry him," said Wetzel, taking her hand from his arm where it yet rested.

But she burst into a passion of tears.

"Oh, how can you, how can you!" she sobbed.

"What have I done?" he asked.

"Everything," she retorted, with the peevishness of a woman who is asked what causes her tears.

"I have done nothing that I know of. You caught me as I came in."

"I didn't catch you."

"And you asked my advice about your marrying a man."

"Oh, you ought to be ashamed of yourself for calling him a man! He's not a man, thank you, Lewis Wetzel. He's as good as you are. A mere man, indeed! I've a good mind to tell him what you said about him." And Berta flounced away, Wetzel gazing after her.

He could not understand it at all, and wondered why Berta always seemed to like to ask him queer questions which almost any one else could answer apparently far more to her satisfaction than he could.

The next time he met her it was he who made the advance.

"Berta," he said, "I am sorry we do not understand each other."

"We do," she said unctuously, and brightening unaccountably.

"Then I am very glad," he rejoined, turning aside, happy that he had not offended her. But her voice arrested him:

"Don't go," she said, "for I am mistaken. No, we do not understand each other at all."

"I thought not, and I am very sorry."

"If you're very sorry that you don't understand a person, then you'd better understand a person," said Berta logically.

"Then how shall I go about it?" he asked.

"Why understand 'em," she returned.

He looked at her for explanation. She was very pretty, and her eyes sparkled and her mouth smiled. He wondered that nobody had asked Berta to go and be married.

"Thank you, Berta," he said, "that's very nice advice. Now do you know what I think when I look at you?"

"No. Tell me what you think when you look at me, Lewis Wetzel. Do I look nice when you look at me?"

"Very."

"Well, what do you think when you look at me?"

"That——"

"What?"

"That you look nice."

"Really?"

"Really. And I think something else, Berta, even though I don't understand you."

"Something else nice?"

"Yes, Berta, even though I don't understand you, I——"

"But you do understand me, and it is very mean not to understand people. No, no, you don't understand me, either; but you ought to."

"I suppose so. But sometimes we don't do all that we ought to do in the world, little Berta."

"Don't we? Well, we ought to. Why don't we?"

"Because we cannot. And so it is no fault of yours or mine, either, that I cannot quite understand you. But whenever I look at you and think——"

"And think I look nice?"

"Yes. Whenever I look at you and think——"

"You said that before. Why don't you say something else. You can't think all the time that you think I look nice."

"Yes, I can."

"How silly! What do you do it for?"

"I can't help it."

"Oh, Lewis Wetzel," cried Berta, "you ought to be ashamed of yourself, indeed you ought to." She went and put her hand on his arm. "And now tell me what else you think when you look at me and think I look real nice. May I guess?"

"Yes."

"Is it about me?"

"Of course."

"Is it about you too?"

"I don't understand," he said, a puzzled expression in his face.

Berta lost all patience then.

"For goodness' sake," she pouted, "why are you so stupid?"

"I can't help it."

"You don't try to. Here I am, ready to help you to try, and you won't let me. If I was a man, I'd understand everything."

"There are some things that even a man is better without understanding."

"You mean me, Lewis Wetzel."

"I don't know what you mean," he said, more puzzled than ever.

"Well, never mind," she cried, "only tell me what you think when you think——"

"I always wonder why some real nice fellow don't come along and marry you, Berta."

She looked at him for a second and seemed thunderstruck; then, bursting into tears, she struck at him, ran past him with her apron to her eyes, and left him standing there, lost in amazement.

"I do *not* understand Berta," he said abstractedly.

CHAPTER X.

AN INDIAN WAYLAID.

AGAIN, shortly after this Indian escapade and his subsequent meeting with the pretty Berta, Lewis Wetzel disappeared from the midst of those who knew him, and was only heard of now and then as having been seen in the forest by some hardy hunter, going on his human quest and granting little talk to the chance friends he encountered.

"The Injuns are not thick enough here for him," was the opinion of the men at Wheeling.

"Berta Rosencranz wants to be too thick with him," was the opinion of the women.

"He is too thick-headed," was Berta's own opinion, and she turned up her little nose at the thought of his stupidity.

For Berta could pick and choose, and more than one delightful man had suddenly betaken himself to a season of solitary wandering after having pressed his suit and been ignominiously rejected by Berta Rosencranz.

Yet the opinions of all these people as to the

cause of Wetzel's periodical disappearances were scarcely correct. His was a restless, chafing nature; there was a constant want for something without a name, and unattainable, that urged him on from time to time to go away from humanity and try to seek whatever it was he desired so acutely in the dusky forests, in communion with the most secret harbors of nature. At a later age, and with modifications, this restless, wistful nature would have been determined as that of a poet or a scientist—the one as much as the other so far removed from the dissecting ken of practical life.

Any one walking on a busy city street, if he has any power of sight apart from mere physical vision, will assuredly be struck by a dozen faces in an hour —faces that are but a mask of something behind and beyond them—faces which he is assured tell little of what the wearers of them are, saving one solitary phase of the entire life.

If such an observer be a rhymer, he will go home and make some melancholy verses, without quite knowing what inspires them. If he is a practical man, he will have the "blues" for a little while, without knowing why. Lewis Wetzel's face upon a busy street might have caused verses and been responsible for the "blues."

Wetzel's face spoke of a hush, and little else, to a

casual observer. Men coming out of prison cells after a lengthened incarceration have much of the look in their faces—the old passions and thoughts have not died out, but one concentrated idea has left its stamp on the countenance which it will take, perhaps, years of mingling with the world and the world's people wholly to eradicate.

The prison cell is as much a world as the wild nature around the scout.

> "Stone walls do not a prison make,
> Nor iron bars a cage,"

was sung long ago with full understanding of this principle.

Yet it was not all communing with nature out there in the dimness of ages-old trees. There were scenes there which were discordant with the beauty of the place, and cries of pain that startled many a singing bird and hushed its hymn of thanks or turned it into chirps of terror. Indians were in those forests, and Lewis Wetzel was never so much at ease and free from his irksome restlessness as when he was on the trail of a red-skin.

The vengeance he wreaked in these places was quietly done, and little or no record has come down to us of the two years of hermit-dwelling in the woods until circumstances brought him to the front again. His absence in a little while failed to elicit comment: he was admired for his bravery—but who missed him?

His mother had her friends, and had pleasure in women's gossip, and no longer wished to regain her high estate of a brave woman. His sisters had their friends, and were blooming out of girlhood, with young women's dreams and hopes. His brothers had as much as they could do in looking after themselves, as brothers even now often have when any trouble is anticipated if they try to find out too much about their relatives. He had never had many bosom friends, had never courted friendship. So he was missed very little.

At length, in the autumn of 1785, he once more appeared in the haunts of the settlers, a strange, taciturn man, loaded down with Indian scalps. He had spoken to few men in the years of his absence, and his tongue seemed too accustomed to silence to be loosed now.

He went quietly around the places he had formerly known, looking kindly on all whom he chanced to meet. Again the children and dogs were his friends. Often he was seen surrounded by little ones, who took the most familiar liberties with him.

A pretty woman once saw him in the woods

covered entirely with flowers, while a party of little children danced around him in wild delight, dragging his gun and powder-horn after them.

"Such a man!" said the pretty woman, hurrying away, and not disturbing the sport.

"Who is there?" asked Wetzel, raising himself on one arm, for he had heard the movement of the woman going through the leaves.

The children paused for a minute and looked up.

"Oh, it's only Berta," said they, and Wetzel sank back upon the flowers again.

Again this same pretty woman saw him beating a man for ill-treating a dog and tossing its little blind pups into the water. She waited until she saw how the battle went and that Wetzel severely punished the other man.

"Such a man!" she said as before. But she gathered her skirts close and dodged behind trees so that he might not see her; and when the beaten man presented himself among the people she was the hardest calumniator of the men who ill-treated dumb animals, and told him to his face that his treatment had not been half severe enough.

But Wetzel had not returned to his old haunts for ease and rest. The occasion of his coming now was Major Doughty's expedition down the Ohio to the mouth of the Muskingum, to build Fort Harmar.

The completion of this work appears to have been entrusted to General Harmar himself, who had been appointed commander-in-chief of the forces on the northwestern frontier for the year 1785. Shortly after assuming the command and proceeding to the fort, he employed a number of white men to go with a flag to the nearest Indian tribes to prevail on the warriors to come to the fort and there conclude a treaty of peace.

As General Harmar was known to be an honorable man, the invitation was not disregarded, and a large force of Indians encamped on the Muskingum River a few miles above its mouth.

General Harmar then issued his proclamation, giving notice that a cessation of hostilities and a laying down of arms was mutually agreed upon between the red men and the whites until a strong effort for a treaty of peace had been concluded. But as treaties of peace with the Indians had been so frequently and flagrantly violated, very little faith was placed in the stability of such agreements by the shrewder frontiermen, notwithstanding that they were as often the aggressors as the Indians themselves.

Half the backwoodsmen of the times had been born in forts, and had been reared, so to speak, in a state of siege. The Indian war had continued so unbroken for such a length of time, and was, moreover, so bloody and outrageous, that they believed war with the savages was the normal state of affairs, and would continue just so long as an Indian remained to prove treacherous and to attack his prey in the most cowardly and secret manner. Their experience and their inability to believe in anything partaking of the Indian nature made it impossible to place confidence in the stability of treaties with the Indians. Lewis Wetzel, hearing of this proposed treaty, came to the fort.

General Harmar was anxiously engaged in his endeavors to effect peace,—a peace which the scout thought scandalous, but which he had no power or voice to set aside, and he deemed that as the Indians must be incessantly passing and repassing between their camp and the fort there would be a fair opportunity of adding a few scalps to his many. For days he loitered around the fort. General Harmar knew that he meant vengeance, and that he alone might yet make the peace abortive. He commanded that Wetzel should be brought before him.

"He must be caught first," said a settler.

"He shall be!" angrily exclaimed the general.

"Shall be?" quietly concluded the settler.

The general looked at the man. There was

something in the impassive face of the frontierman that suggested to the officer that Lewis Wetzel, if he had no bosom friends who took his griefs as their own, yet was not without aid if he chose to avail himself of it.

"General," said another frontierman to the commandant, "don't you have too much to say to Lewis Wetzel."

"I do not intend to have my projects for peace set aside because of one murderous man."

"Murderous! That's a hard word, general. Lewis Wetzel never committed murder."

"Do you mean to say that he never killed an Indian?"

"Do you call that murder?"

"What else is it?"

"His father was murdered; he only kills his father's murderers. But, peace or no peace, Lewis Wetzel had better be left alone."

"Why?"

"Well, you see the people kind o' dote on him, and if there's a hair of his head hurt—blessed if I know what mightn't happen."

"Nothing shall happen."

"We'll see."

"We will."

But the general awoke to the consciousness that

Wetzel was not merely a renegade, as many Indian scouts were regarded. The people understood the feeling that actuated him, and fully sympathized with him.

So Wetzel loitered about Fort Harmar, and he often chanced upon a settler or two without understanding why so many frontiermen had nothing more to do than he had.

General Harmar understood a little better, and knew that these settlers loitering in the steps of Wetzel were a guard to defend the scout from the incursions of the military.

"I cannot understand," said the scout once to a chance acquaintance, "why you men love idleness so. I have been here for days; it is a busy season, or ought to be; and yet each day, wherever I walk, I always come across a strong, hearty man or two who go slinking on, seeming so lazy as not even to bestow a second look on me who cross their path."

"Well," said his acquaintance, "it do seem queer, don't it?"

"You yourself," continued Wetzel, "have you nothing to do to-day?"

"Who? Me? Lor' bless you, Wetzel, I'm not goin' to my grave doubled up like old Daddy Eberly, till I really believe we'll have to bury him in a barrel—he's that round. He worked too hard, and work doubled him up. No, sir; I haven't got the first thing to do. And, sir, if you choose, you can see me any day you walk around, sir, and it's none of your business, sir, neither is it any of mine."

Wetzel walked away from the man, who was grinning and clearly making fun of his interlocutor.

"It is none of my business," the scout said to himself. "The man was right, my business is not with idle men; it is with busy devils."

One day as he rested on a slope of ground overlooking the fort, his eyes turned towards a squad of men going through a rude form of drill, Wetzel was startled by a voice saying:

"Not so bad, eh, partner?"

He looked up. Beside him stood a tall, thin, begrimed man, looking intently over towards the drilling men at the fort.

"Guess you don't know me," he said after awhile, his eyes still fixed upon the fort. "Guess you have forgot old friends."

"Are you Veach Dickerson?" asked Wetzel, remembering a man as reckless as himself and filled with as bitter a hatred for the Indians

"You've got it," said Dickerson. "And now tell me what brings you here?"

Wetzel imparted to him his plan.

"I'm with you," said the other, as the scout concluded; "I'm your man."

Wetzel never cared particularly for a partner in his battles, arguing that it was from no common love of bloodshed that he acted as he did, but that his old injury called aloud to him at all times, demanded revenge, and would not allow him to rest inactive. But that injury was no other man's; he held jealously to it as his own alone, and that no one else on earth had a right to avenge his slaughtered father—his own hand only must wither and grow tired before the spilled blood of his father would be fitly and sufficiently atoned for.

"Do the varmints at the fort keep you from beginning now?" asked Dickerson, impatient to begin the work of destruction.

"No," answered Wetzel; but few Indians have come up yet."

"There's danger to you, though," said Dickerson.

"It would be murder if no danger attended what I do."

"While now?" questioned Dickerson, not quite apt at this reasoning.

"Now it is only carrying out the Bible precept, 'an eye for an eye, a tooth for a tooth,'" said Wetzel.

Dickerson looked at him.

"Don't that same Bible say a little something, here and there, about forgiving our enemies?" asked he.

"Yes, forgive our enemies when they come to us contrite and asking for mercy. Not when they creep silently over the ground in our tracks; come to us in the night with murder in their minds; wait for us in quiet places, cruel, sharp knives in their hands; study day after day how they can best injure us, and carry in their minds a hatred for us only made greater and more deadly from feeding on the imagined cause. The Bible don't say one word about forgiving such an enemy. Such an enemy crucifies forgiveness, pierces the heart of forgiveness, and bathes the parching lips of forgiveness with vinegar and gall. No, no, no; I have read all about that for years, when I have been alone. And then, more,—how can a mere *Injun* be an enemy?"

"The last part is true," assented Dickerson, convinced. "And now come on."

They set off without any further delay, and soon arrived at the desired point, and sat down in ambush in the long grass near the path leading from the fort to the camp, and waited grim as fate. They could hear the men in the fort laughing, and over from the Indian camp came the loud squeal of a pig which the savages were killing. Birds flew up from the grass, their mouths filled with woolly roots and mosses for their little nests. Wetzel's eye followed these birds, which meant home and love and mated happiness. Did the man hiding in the grass, and filled with intent of doing harm, yearn for some of the peace which even little birds could have, and which was denied him? Did careless birds carry no deadly life-long hatred in their little songful breasts? But birds had no souls, no intelligence, were not responsible; if their fathers or mothers were killed, they were not called upon to avenge the murder, but went singing on as ever.

"If we only had a jug of spirits along," laughed Dickerson, breaking in upon his companion's reverie.

"What for?" asked Wetzel, regarding him coldly.

"Why, we should enjoy the whole thing more," said Dickerson.

"Enjoy!" repeated Wetzel, harshly, "did you say enjoy! How can you think of such a word as enjoy! Does the Lord enjoy the smiting of his base and perverted children? Did he enjoy the sending forth of the children of Israel?—the killing of Pharaoh and his host? What pleasure is there in avenging our wrongs? It is our duty."

"If you don't take any pleasure in all this, you'd better be by yourself," said Dickerson, offended at the dictatorial tone of his companion.

"I did not ask you to come," returned Wetzel.

"Maybe you'll ask me to go?"

"You can go or stay; I regulate no man's actions.

This is not my land; it is as much yours as mine. You are not my enemy, and I would like to be your friend. But I am not here for pleasure."

"I can't understand you, Wetzel," said Dickerson, laughing lightly and seating himself upon the ground again.

"Now, every one knows, Wetzel," went on Dickerson, crumbling a flake of loose earth between his fingers, "that you'd grind the Injuns into Injun-meal, as fine as this mud in my hand. And why would you do this? Simply because it pleases you to do it. Nobody interferes with you here; you do just as it pleases you to do, and if you do what it pleases you to do, don't you call that pleasure? I do. You do it for fun, and fun you have. We all say of nights, when we gather 'round a fire, or smoke in the moonlight, 'I wonder where Wetzel is? Up to some fun, be sure o' that.' That's what we say, Wetzel; and among so many of us somebody is sure to be right. The only trouble about it is, that you make too much of a secret of it. Why can't you always have one of us along with you? We hate the red cusses as much as you do, and we'd like a little o' the fun too. For you've had more time than we've had, and you've studied up the thing more, and can tell just where the fun comes in and when it is coming. But no, you take it all quietly, and don't act cheerful and share your fun with your friends. You're not doing right, Wetzel; that's what it is,—you are not doing right by your friends. So none of us can understand you."

A pained expression shot across the face of the scout. Did anybody understand him?

But the man at his side was only as the others. Wetzel said a few words to him kindly and to prove that there was no harshness in his thought.

Dickerson did not answer, but lay at full length contemplating the other's face, so set and cold, as he waited in the tall grass, the sun glinting down and making his long hair shine like great shafts of ebony.

And thus they waited on, silent and almost motionless, as the hours went by, and there was no approaching step near them. They were almost like statues, their guns in their hands, their eyes peering through the grass, their ears on the alert for the slightest indications of the approach of a moccasin.

They were so silent and motionless, that a shy-eyed deer came and looked at them, cropped a few spears of grass near by, and then leisurely trotted off to join its companions, possibly to report the discovery of a new species of plant shaped like men with guns, but which did not possess even vegetable motion.

Shortly before sundown, and when they least expected it, a dull thud smote their ears.

"Hist!" said Wetzel, breaking the silence, "a chief on horseback, coming at full speed. Up with you, and hail him."

They were on their feet, and called to the hurrying red-skin.

But, owing to the clatter of the horse's feet, he may not have heard them. At any rate, he did not heed them, but galloped on, sweeping by them with a grand flourish, never vouchsafing to cast his eyes in their direction.

"He will accept of no quarter," said Wetzel; "he will not heed us."

"Then he is an enemy," cried Dickerson.

They raised their rifles; there were a couple of sharp crackles in the bright air, a bird or two flew up, a couple of deer whizzed by, the flying horse of the Indian threw up its head.

But the Indian did not fall from his saddle, going on as unconcerned as ever.

"How could both of us miss him?" grumbled Dickerson.

They could see the camp of the Indians, and they thought there was a sort of alarm there. The escaped Indian was riding on rapidly, and from the camp issued mounted savages, all directing their course towards their attacked brother.

"Do you see that?" asked Dickerson.

"It is time for us to go," returned Wetzel.

For as the alarm would very soon be spread among the vast number of assembled red-skins that one of their number had been waylaid and fired upon, the white men knew of the scurrying of the country after the shooters, and began an immediate retreat.

Wetzel's friends had known of his going to watch for the Indians from around Fort Harmar, and they awaited him and his companion in camp, and eagerly clustered about the two.

"And what luck, what luck?" they questioned.

"Luck!" repeated Wetzel.

"How many Injun's scalps?" was the question. "That's luck, isn't it?"

"Then we had bad luck, cursed luck," he replied.

"This is the first time you ever was played false by an Injun," said the man who held him in talk. "I always say that the Injuns ain't more to be depended on in death than in life. They do all they can to prevent a white man doing of his duty, and then pretend they want peace, and are willing to do anything to have it. What do they waste good powder and balls of the white man for, eh?"

"Yes, we shot at a fellow on horseback, but he rode on scratching his back as if he had been stung by a yellow-jacket," said Dickerson, gloomily.

But that night into the camp came a jaded horse with a dead Indian on its back. He had been shot through the hips, and had bled to death on his horse's back.

It was soon rumored that Wetzel was the slayer. Fort Harmar was outraged.

"And this is how my efforts at peace are regarded," said General Harmar. "The murderer shall be taken, and an example be made of him."

Accordingly, Captain Kingsbury and a picked company of men were directed to proceed to the Mingo Bottom, and take Wetzel alive or dead,—the precaution of a large number of troops detailed being necessary from the desperate character the scout seemed to have acquired.

But it was a useless and wholly impotent order General Harmar had given.

"A company of mere men could as easily have drawn Beelzebub out of the bottomless pit, as take Lewis Wetzel from the Mingo Bottom settlement," says the chronicle of the times.

On the very day that Captain Kingsbury and his men arrived at the Bottom, there was a shooting-match there, and Lewis Wetzel had been prevailed upon to show his dexterity with the rifle.

A heap of slaughtered pigeons beside him attested that he had delighted his entertainers to the best of his ability; and he was on the point of reloading his piece when Captain Kingsbury was seen coming up the river.

His object was at once conjectured.

Without acquainting Wetzel of the fact, for his back was towards the river, and he was quietly firing, it was resolved to ambush the captain's barge, and kill him and all his company.

"What else can be done?" they said, in extenuation, "for Wetzel shall not be taken."

But, happily, Captain McMahan was present, and he went to Wetzel and told him the state of affairs, and prevailed on him to use his influence in persuading his admirers to suspend the attack, while he (McMahan) would go down to the shore and await Kingsbury, and, perhaps, by representing matters in their proper light, induce him to return without landing.

"I am, then, to persuade my friends by this argument that I look upon myself as a man guilty of murder?" said Wetzel, smiling.

"You alone can prevent an indiscriminate slaughter of innocent men who only come here by command of a superior officer," was the reply of McMahan.

"At least I may tell them that it is for their own good not to attack those who are coming for me?" asked Wetzel.

"You can say whatever you please; but you know the consequences to your friends if these men are attacked."

Wetzel immediately went to his friends and argued with them, almost failing at times to convince them that it was fool-hardiness that prompted their attack on the men sent from the fort to arrest him, and that such an attack would be the worse for their interest as well as his own. At length he persuaded them that it was not the best way for them to assist him.

"Well, we'll promise to suspend operations—for the present," said one admirer.

"But you mustn't keep us too long waiting," said another.

With this reluctant proviso, Wetzel came to McMahan.

"I have them in check for the present," he said, but I cannot tell how long they will obey my wishes. Do all you can to prevent them from landing, and I will stay here and endeavor to turn the matter into a burlesque, and the troops may receive only laughter, which will not prove fatal to any of them."

"I shall report this to your favor," said McMahan.

"I want no report, favorable or unfavorable to me, to go to General Harmar," returned Wetzel. "I do what I am doing to save my friends. You speak as though you, too, accused me of crime."

"Did you not kill the Indian?"

"Whether I did or not, that is not a crime—not a murder. But go! you do not understand—no one does. Go! hurry to your friends; and I will stay with mine."

Hurriedly mounting his horse, McMahan thundered down the embankment to the river.

Kingsbury and his men were slowly toiling up the river, the roots of trees and the debris there making the journey peculiarly troublesome. The men on board were grumbling, and complaining that all this trouble should have been taken merely for the sake of capturing one simple frontierman.

"If this is army discipline," said a regular at the bow, "it's the queerest *I* ever heard of. A big party of men like us to go and capture a single man that never makes a pretense of hiding himself. You might suppose he'd set the world on fire, and the Old Boy had sent for him to punish him for doing things without authority from down below. Instead of setting the world on fire, here he is a simple, stupid enough sort of fellow, who would rather go alone with his gun, than join us and go in a squad. Pretty discipline that takes a crowd to capture one single, simple frontierman."

"A murderer," said Captain Kingsbury, who overheard the complaint.

"It will take more than General Harmar to prove to the settlers so much as that," answered a man.

"Well, the general's orders have got to be obeyed," said the captain, "and I will not leave the Bottom till I have Lewis Wetzel."

"Then you'll never leave it," growled a man, "and the prospects are that we shall not, either. Does that look hopeful?"

He pointed over to the shore towards which they were pulling.

McMahan had dismounted, and stood anxiously gesticulating to those on board. Behind and above him was a solid group of determined men restlessly chafing under the promise they had made Wetzel that they would not stir from where they were, nor approach the water any closer for a quarter of an hour. This was as much as he could get them to promise. He had tried to turn the affair into a joke, and had failed. It might seem mightily amusing to have a few militia men to come to the Bottom to tell the settlers what their duty was. But it was an insult to their manhood to be told that they were expected to stand by quietly and consent to see one of their number taken, merely for having shot down an Indian, who would have shot him down without scruple if he had got the first chance. General Harmar was not the commander-in-chief of the settlers, let him remember that.

Had General Harmar come in person just then, all the respect due to military authority might have been overthrown by the indignation which spoke from every face. General Harmar was nothing more than a man, and were they not all men also? And what did they owe General Harmar that he should think he had the authority to command respect of his orders? He had done more harm than good, anyhow—had made the Indians more impertinent than ever, if that were possible; and now he said that that same impertinence must be respected besides all the old flagrant behavior of the Indians. Murmurs were heard on every side.

"I can't stand in one position all day, even to please Wetzel," said a man, nervously handling the trigger of his gun.

"And who is Wetzel, any more than Harmar, to make us obey him?" asked another.

They lost sight of everything but the sense of the slight put upon themselves.

"But be quiet! be quiet!" said an older man, and possibly a cooler one, "he only bargained for minutes. It takes sixty o' that sort to make an hour.

Just you wait till our minutes are up! Then if them men in that boat won't have a pretty long hour, just tell me my name ought to be Ananias, and I won't tell you you lie. Be quiet! be quiet! There's plenty more minutes in the world, and some other men shall think it's better to stand in one position all their life than to change too often—as them men in that boat 'll surely say afore I'm through with 'em. Be quiet! be quiet!—and do your duty by yourselves."

"Be quiet! be quiet!" echoed another man, and the complaints were hushed for the time being.

Every moment's enforced quiet, however, made the men more outraged at the slight put upon their intelligence.

"Just as if General Harmar knew more about the Indians than we do," they argued.

Captain Kingsbury was now near the bank of the river.

"Shall we let them land after all?" asked a settler.

"Where is Wetzel?" asked the one addressed, cautiously looking around.

"Here!" said Wetzel, who heard it all, and now came forward.

The men remained silent.

Captain Kingsbury was now within speaking distance of the shore. The settlers could scarcely restrain themselves, and scowled at Wetzel.

"A pretty state of affairs," said one, to hang a man for shooting an Indian that kills his white man every day.

" Will they hang Wetzel?"

"That's the punishment for murder—and that's what they accuse him of."

"They'll never hang a settler for a cut-throat Indian as long as I'm around."

" Nor while I am."

" Was Wetzel's father nothing? Why didn't they hang the Indians that murdered him?"

Wetzel saw that his authority was weakening with every word they spoke, and he looked anxiously towards the slowly advancing militia.

He never for a moment harbored the intention of giving himself up as a murderer, but he *would* protect his friends.

Major McMahan, down on the river's bank, was as nervous as he over the possible result of this expedition. He threw up his arms when the boat was yet a good way off, and signaled Captain Kingsbury not to come any nearer.

" On !" said Kingsbury, seeing the men ship their oars.

" But the major signals us to stop," said a man.

" On !" commanded Captain Kingsbury. " Major McMahan is not commanding this boat."

The oars splashed into the water again, and sparkled in the light like silver. The boat grated on the shore.

"Halt!" rang out the voice of Major McMahan.

Those on the shore saw the commander of the boat pause for the first time when that word rang out with doubtful meaning.

The men on the boat had their guns in their hands, looking up to that grim, silent company of settlers high on the shore, not stirring so much as a foot now, nor whispering a word, but each waiting anxiously until the few minutes elapsed which should absolve them from their promise to the man these others had come to take against the principles of the settlers' warfare. The settlers on their part could see the anxious looks of Major McMahan as he directed Captain Kingsbury's eyes inland.

They could see that a confab was under way.

For the major was informing Captain Kingsbury of the force and fury of the people, and assured him, that did he attempt to seize Wetzel, he would have all the settlers in all parts of the country upon him, and that then nothing could save him and his troops from massacre.

"But my orders?" remonstrated the captain.

"Orders or no orders, sir," said McMahan, "you either turn back, or take the consequences."

"Am I and these men under me to be thwarted by one man?"

"By a thousand men, you mean. Lewis Wetzel himself has little power with the men who would avenge him. They love the principle more than they do the man."

The captain turned his eyes inland; he could see the crowds of men collected closely together and glaring out towards him, repressed excitement plainly discernible in their enforced attention.

One man stood apart, leaning on his rifle, his eyes directed with the others in the direction of the would-be captors.

"That is your man," said Major McMahan, pointing out the solitary figure.

"Am I to be so near him, and yet not take him?" frowned Captain Kingsbury, looking towards the man leaning on his rifle.

"Can you take him with such odds as I have mentioned?" asked McMahan. "And hurry! hurry! He has forced the men to respect your authority—inasmuch as they will not attack you unless you attack him. His authority is at an end, and doubtless in a few minutes it will be too late. Hurry! hurry!"

There was but one thing to do; that Captain Kingsbury conceded.

Fearing for the safety of the men under him, he immediately gave orders to turn about, and the next minute the barge floated on, eagerly helped along by every man inside who had seen the hills and the men there.

There was a frantic huzza from the crowd of settlers. The fifteen minutes' grace were up. They ran pell-mell down to the river side, some going into the water and offering to swim after the barge; others gathered handsful of river mud with which they bespattered the receding troops; and others again dug bits of rock with their hands and hurled them after the barge. They danced on the shore, reviling Captain Kingsbury for a coward and a poltroon, well knowing that such was not the case, but angered now that Major McMahan had forced them into inactivity.

"Where is McMahan?" some one cried.

"Where is McMahan?" cried all.

But the major had known what was coming, and was not in view.

In the midst of the excitement a man cried out:

"And it was not Wetzel's bullet that killed the Indian; and Wetzel knew it, and would not lay the blame on me. You all know me, Veach Dickerson. I swear that we both aimed at the Indian; but my bullet struck him. I swear this, and I swear that

Wetzel knows it. But who will believe it? Wetzel will not say he missed fire, and who will believe his aim was ever at fault?"

Whether this story of Dickerson is true or not, and whether he did not thus try to draw the blame from the scout, knowing his prominence, and feeling assured that this was not to be the last they should hear about the dead Indian, is not in the province of the present narrator to say.

But it was sufficient for the time to turn the crowd from the protection of the principle to the adoration and protection of the man. They now declared that they were glad they had obeyed the scout, and let Captain Kingsbury off; and that were the captain and his troops here now they would be treated as lambs, which, considering that mutton is frequently slain in the shape of lamb, is but equivocal.

Then they turned on Dickerson.

"Why didn't you own up, then?" they asked, "and not let an innocent man take the blame?"

"If Wetzel wanted me to be accused wouldn't he have denied the killing?" argued Dickerson.

Thus was the authority of the scout with these men, that they willingly believed any tale which exalted him and proved that while they obeyed a certain indefinable something about him, that something was an innate and simple nobility that never fails of partisans in a simple and rude community.

Well might Captain Kingsbury, in the now far-off barge, feel that he had cause to be thankful that he had taken Major McMahan's prudent advice when he looked and saw that river bank alive with wild and audacious men.

The troops were gathered about him, looking back with him.

"There's a solitary figure, behind all the rest, and it has not moved since I've looked at it," said a man.

Captain Kingsbury turned his eyes in the direction indicated, and saw, alone and still leaning on his gun, the man he had come to arrest, but who had escaped him.

Further and further floated the barge, and the men on the shore were dispersing one way and another, and a bend in the river hid them entirely from view.

But still those on the barge could see that solitary figure looking in their direction, motionless as a statue, as though he was nothing in common with those around him, but in their midst was an alien to their inmost feelings while he was the motive power of their principles.

CHAPTER XI.

CAPTURE AND ESCAPE.

THE settlers by this retreating movement of Captain Kingsbury from the object of his quest so easily decided, considered the affair as finally adjusted. Many of them came to the conclusion that the whole proceeding was only instituted to scare them into quiescence, so that no more Indians might fall, pending the establishment of a code of peace. But, one and all, they determined that the general had seen the folly of his orders, and had come to the conclusion that he had business more in his line than attempting to impeach the good conduct of one of their number for the simple every-day occurrence of making wild game of a villainous Indian.

"Boys, I'll tell you how it is," said a strapping fellow, jambing his hat over his eyes, and mounting upon a stump. "Boys, I'll tell you how it is, Harmar he's ashamed of hisself—that's how it is; he's doggoned ashamed of hisself. He's seen the error of his ways and turned over a new leaf. Why what's the good o' Harmar talkin'? If orders had come for him to fight the red-devils 'stead o' protectin' 'em, wouldn't he done it as soon one way as t'other? I haven't no patience in a man like Harmar."

"But orders is orders," interrupted a friend.

"Orders! I'd just like to see the orders that'd make me go and hold a Injun chief up to my buzzom and call him 'dearie,' and chuck him under the chin."

"Gin'ral Harmar didn't hold no Injun chief to his buzzom and chuck him under the chin, as I ever heered tell on," said a literal man.

"Who said he did?" asked the orator angrily. "What I said was that I wouldn't do it, orders or no orders."

"Well, I'd just like to give a Injun chief a good tight squeeze myself," said another.

"Shut up, boys!" said the orator, "and hear me out."

"We'd ruther hear you in; you're out now—out o' your reckonin'."

"What I mean, boys, is that Harmar wants to skeer us; and we don't skeer. He's so ashamed o' hisself that he'll take Wetzel's part the very fust time he gets into any trouble. Just mark my words if that ain't so."

"Yes," they all assented, "the general was ashamed of himself for trying to intimidate a lot of peaceable men simply because a murderous Indian had gone the way of all Indian flesh, and could not blame any disease for the taking off. Yes, surely, General Harmar meant to show a different line of conduct in the future."

But in this the settlers erred; the affair was by no means at an end, and, from what they considered such a trifle to make so much bother about, the whole principle of the scout system was destined to become involved, and a trial of strength instituted as to which was the ruling power—the military determined to establish peace between the white and red men, or the settlers, equally determined from long experience, that such a peace was fallacious just so long as the Indians claimed the land and stock which the white man had cultivated by strenuous exertion, and with untold difficulty.

For General Harmar, having had familiar acquaintance with the insubordination of the frontier, and having been a frequent witness of the small respect entertained for military discipline, decided to make a test case of this matter; and after the return of Captain Kingsbury, and his report of the reception of the general's orders, to press those orders to the fullest, in the settlement of this flagrant breach, and to prove to the utmost the relative strengths of the settlers and the military.

The military, however, demurred, and some of them flatly refused to obey any orders that made them the enemies of the settlers, their old friends. Others, again, openly deserted, and went over to the other side, declaring that the general usurped his authority, and that his better mode would be to establish peace, now that the frontiermen admired him somewhat for his respect for their principles. But those who knew General Harmar best, knew that this could not be; that no general of the army would brook such insolence from men who rebelled against established authority.

"This man Wetzel shall be my prisoner," he said, "if it takes my life and the life of my army to accomplish the capture."

Therefore orders were issued that a new expedition was to be forthwith undertaken for the apprehension and detention of the white man who had shot the Indian near Fort Harmar.

As Wetzel, filled with his old unrest, was never very long stationary in any one place, but ranged at will along the river from Fort Pitt to the falls of the Ohio, and was always a welcome guest and perfectly at home wherever he chose to go, a little while after the frustrated attempt to seize him by Captain Kingsbury, he made one of his usual excursions.

He got into his canoe with the intention of proceeding down the Ohio to Kentucky.

But having a friend named Carr who had lately settled on the island near Fort Harmar, he determined to pay this friend a visit, and here he stopped, with a view of remaining over night.

But by some means, which were never explained, General Harmar was advised of his presence on the island, a fugitive from justice coming directly into the teeth of the law without a particle of fear. It was too much for the commander. A guard was selected, and with much difficulty, for they expected a warm reception; besides, they may have been a little in sympathy with Wetzel, and felt the shame of a party of well-cared-for men surrounding and capturing another man who, without home or means, was simply carrying out a line of war which had hitherto been regarded as perfectly legitimate, and had been instituted from stern necessity by the men who first came to the wilds in advance of their more timid brethren, who came after danger was over to prove to those who had come in advance that their mode of procedure had been entirely wrong, and that it must be upset and begun all over again.

However, the guard was sent across the island in the night time, and was guided to Carr's house.

It was but a small, rude cabin, hastily put together by the young man, whose bride, it is said, used to direct his labors, sitting on a log, and telling him how to construct the house most convenient to her. It is also told, that after he had gotten it pretty well under way, she discovered that the chimney was not in the place she liked it best, so he tore the entire structure down and built it all up again, this time taking care of the chimney. When it was finished, she said:

"Now that chimney was all right in the first place; but I wanted to see what kind of a husband you would make."

But this had been some time ago, and the house the troops approached was finished, chimney and all. All was darkness and silence here; moreover, none of the occupants suspected any advent of military authority. The men outside waited a moment in the darkness and silence, and then the captain in charge knocked on the rude door.

"Open, in the name of the law!" he cried.

A woman inside screamed.

"We're killed! we're killed! we're killed!" cried the woman within, and kept up a scream of prodigious intensity.

The men outside were awed; some were for breaking open the door.

"She's upset the babby," said a man.

"Silence!" commanded the officer in charge.

Just at that moment the startling scream subsided as suddenly as it had broken upon the stillness of the night.

"Babby's upset the mother," said a man.

"Silence!" commanded the officer in charge.

There was whispering inside for a minute, and then that was hushed.

Again silence came.

"Open, in the name of the law!" cried the officer a second time.

"Injun law, or white law?" asked a man's voice from the inside.

Clearly a suspicion existed inside as to who the visitors were, and time was wanted.

"Who are you?" asked the voice from within again.

"Friends to friends of law and order," was the reply.

There was a fumbling inside, and entreaties in a woman's voice and assurances in a man's.

Then the door was opened by Carr himself, with a lantern in one hand and a rifle in the other.

He was immediately disarmed and held by the regulars.

"Is this friendly violence?" he asked indignantly,

while his wife wept on his breast. "You come to my house in the night like a party of marauders; you demand admittance to my house without telling me who you are; you disarm me when I would protect myself from enemies who could not come more deceitfully than you do; you hold me a prisoner without saying of what I am accused. Keep where you are, wife!" turning to her; "if these men so much as lay a finger on you, run to the stove and throw a live coal on the powder barrel."

She stood from him, but not a man laid a finger upon her, and she smiled as she saw them give her a wide berth, for the stove was beside her.

"We are after our prisoner," was the explanation offered for the imposed indignity, "and we must not be put to more trouble than is necessary in our quest."

"There are none of your prisoners here," returned Carr in a loud voice.

"Lewis Wetzel is here," replied the captain.

The woman, for some time silent, now rent the air with cries, clearly to apprize a third party of the proximity of danger.

"Is Wetzel here?" asked the captain, confused by the heart-rending cries.

"He is not your prisoner, and never will be. Treason! treason! treason!" shouted Carr, his wife's voice ascending the gamut till she reached an ear-piercing note, which she held to tenaciously.

"Enter, men, and do your duty," commanded the officer hurriedly, snatching the lantern from one of the men and leading the way.

Guided by the dim lantern, they found in an inner room the man they sought, and who had not been wakened by all the noise around him. Worn out by fatigue and privation, he slept, the lantern light along his face failing to disturb him, only showing the lines and weather-marks there.

"Secure him!" whispered the captain.

The men actually bound him hand and foot without awakening him.

They then shook him, and he arose in bewilderment, but soon understood the situation, and tried to free himself from his bonds, but unsuccessfully.

"Cowards!" he said. "A score to one sleeping man!"

Without a word of reply, he was hurried from the house, the wife of Carr still keeping up her vocal endeavors, and her husband, whose gun was carried off, crying after the troops:

"The settlers shall know this! The settlers shall know this, and then look out! Keep up a good heart, Wetzel, and don't let them treat you ill. Die for the principle, Wetzel, but don't live at their mercy."

Wetzel was hurried on to a boat in waiting; then he was rowed over to the guard-house.

Here the jailor proceeded to load him with irons. He protested strenuously against such treatment.

"Am I a malefactor, to be thus ignominiously chained?" he asked indignantly, thrusting the man from him. For to a man like him this treatment was worse than death itself.

"You are accused of murdering an Indian," was the reply vouchsafed his protest.

"Murdering!" he repeated bitterly. "Do you know what you say?—what that word conveys? Then I am to be treated as a mere cut-throat murderer?"

"You had better ask the general," said an officer present, who plainly entered into the feelings of the scout; "we are only doing what we are instructed to do, Wetzel."

"Then take me to General Harmar."

"That is impossible, just now."

"I can see him, though?"

"You can make the request."

"Then go to him, and tell him his brave men, who protect murdering Indians, have this night captured a sleeping white man, who, being now awake, and destined to sleep no more where military authority protects the people, requests to speak with him."

"You cannot expect General Harmar to obey in those words."

"They are the only words from me. I am not used to deceive in words."

One of the men was despatched with the message to the general.

This haughty request naturally only made Wetzel appear more rebellious in the eyes of the commander, whose mission was to effect a subsidence of frontier disturbances, which added materially to the cares of an already overburdened country.

The general heard the request of the scout, delivered in the self-same words, without a word of indignant reply, or even a frown.

For General Harmar did not bear any ill-will towards the scout as being Wetzel, but towards the scouts as a system which must be subjugated to more pacific authority. He regarded Wetzel as a very brave man, he said; and, being no coward himself, he could understand the feeling that prompted the protesting request to have an interview with him.

He resolved to treat the scout with consideration. He came to the guard-house early the day following the capture, and, disdaining a guard, went into the close place.

"Good-morning, General Harmar," said Wetzel,

starting up from a reverie he had insensibly fallen into. "Do you see these irons? Are these by your instructions?"

"We could not quite trust you."

"You see I am your prisoner?"

"I see, and I wish it were a less brave man," replied the general.

"You know that I shot at the Indian——"

"You confess it?"

"Of course. And what is proposed for my sentence?"

"You know the punishment of a crime like yours."

"Such a crime never had a punishment laid out before this."

"You know the punishment of men who kill other men?"

"It is to be killed by yet other men, exactly. It has always been in my mind—this punishment. These Indians killed my father, and I avenge my father's blood. Oh, yes, I understand that."

"But there is another name given to this careless killing of men."

"You mean the actuation of it. I know it has been called insanity in me. I have killed upwards of a couple of scores of Indians, but I cannot say that I am insane. If a snake stings you, do you not kill it? The men I have killed were only such as would kill me, and who tried to do so. If I do not feel guilty, I am not guilty. I stand the chance of being killed by Indians at any time. They stand the chance of meeting the same fate at my hands. We are in so much equal. Well?"

"There is yet another name than insanity given to the man who kills his fellow-man, no matter what the provocation."

"I do not understand you."

"There is such a thing as murder!"

"General Harmar, you surely cannot mean that I shall be punished as a murderer!" cried Wetzel, recoiling at the word. "No, no, General Harmar, that cannot be your meaning! I am no cowardly murderer; I do not come upon my foes for the sake of plunder or the pleasure of a vengeance or wrong committed against my own rights. I do but avenge my father and his rights. I have fought, and always do fight, the red-skins, with the odds against me of their cunning and ferociousness. They are against me; I against them. No, no, you must not hang me. Give me up to the Indians whom you think I have wronged; let them be my executioners in their own way, but do not hang me. Hear me! hear me! Do not turn away from me. Give me up to these Indians here in your own fort; tell them they may do with me what they choose; place them all in a circle, with their scalping knives and tomahawks in their hands, and tell them how I fired on one of their number near the fort, and how I openly confess to having destroyed a hundred of their brethren,—and then give me a tomahawk, and place me in the midst of them, and let me and the Indians fight it out the best way that we can. But hang me!—no, no! my father's blood must never bring his son to the gallows—my murdered father's blood! It cried aloud to heaven for vengeance, and could I hear it unmoved? Think had it been your father, torn from you who loved him so; think if you had stumbled across his mangled body, seen in the light of your burning home,—how would you have felt? Think if you saw in every Indian the one who made all this ruin; would you have let him go unpunished? Would you have seen the fairness in being condemned to the halter for doing as I have done? Anything but that, man; anything but that!"

To this passionate appeal, spoken as it was with all the energy of outraged sensibility, General Harmar had nothing to say, but turned aside for a minute. Then he faced the prisoner, his face stern once more.

"Lewis Wetzel," he said, "I own to your wrongs, and the provocation of spirit which actuates you to avenge them. Perhaps, were I in your place, my acts would be condemned as yours are, in the light of reasonable law. But I am an officer appointed by the law by which we must all be held in check or else we make a hell of earth. And as that same law does not in one iota authorize me to make a compromise, I cannot grant your request," and the general hurried from the room.

The two days succeeding this were filled with torture to Wetzel, whose manhood suffered from the stigma proposed to be attached to it.

He plotted and contrived his escape.

He recognized the honor of General Harmar's obeying the law, but he scorned the law itself for a false, bad thing, not taking cases like his into consideration, and turning a deaf ear to his provocation.

At the end of two days he was calmer, and seemed to have made up his mind to submit. He again sent for the general.

"I submit to your interpretation of the law, general," he said, "but there is a leniency which rests with you individually."

"Anything that I can do, consistent with my sense of duty, I am willing to attempt," returned the general.

"I have never been confined, then, general, and I shall die, if I have not room to walk about."

"Strike off the fetters about his feet," commanded the general, and an officer obeyed.

"Thank you, general," said Wetzel.

But his handcuffs were not removed.

He was allowed to walk about at the mouth of the Muskingum, but the men were told to keep a close watch on him.

As soon as they were outside the fort gate, Wetzel ran and jumped like a child, apparently filled with delight because of his liberty.

The men laughed at him, and he seemed to appreciate their laughing, and endeavored further to amuse them.

He would start and run a few yards, as though about to try an escape; then he would turn around and join the guards again.

The next time he ran further, and then stopped. In this way, each time he ran it was a little further from the guards before he stopped and returned. At length, he called forth all his strength, activity, and cunning, and resolved on freedom or death at the hands of the soldiers, but never death on the scaffold from the common hangman.

He gave a sudden spring forward, and dashed off with the speed of the wind for his beloved sheltering woods.

His movement was so quick, so wholly unexpected,

that his watchers were taken by complete surprise. Laughingly they expected every moment to see him turn around and run towards them. Some of them clapped their hands at this child's-play, so inconsistent with Wetzel's ordinary mood. He had now put about one hundred yards between himself and the men, when the latter began to realize the situation.

"He is escaping! he is escaping!" they cried.

Their voices only spurred the hurrying man the faster.

"Fire!" came the word of command.

Bullets whistled about the fugitive, one of them crashing upon the manacles that held his wrists, as he raised his arms above his head to make a spring forward.

He heard the rush of men after him, and he spurred on towards the dense wood straight ahead of him, where hiding-places awaited him, even with his arms bound out-speeding his pursuers.

On, on, and he reached the friendly darkness of the familiar forest, and was swallowed up and absorbed by the dense foliage.

Being so fully acquainted with that part of the country, he made his way to a thicket, three or four miles from the fort, which promised a safe covert. In the midst of this thicket he came across an immense tree, one of the patriarchs of the old forest, which had fallen across a log, where the surrounding brush was very thick and close.

Under this friendly tree he managed to squeeze his body, without disturbing the leaves about him.

Here he was comparatively safe from discovery, for the brush was so thick that detection seemed next to impossible, unless his pursuers had the cunning of Indians and examined everything suspiciously.

"But I will never leave this shelter alive in the hands of hangmen," he said.

This was his firm determination. He would far rather die by an Indian's hand. In his cramped and painful position, more than ever did he realize the predicament he was in. And yet he decided that anything was better than to have left an Indian unscathed when it was in his power to inflict well-merited punishment.

"But a murderer!" he thought indignantly. "How dare they use such a word to me! Would Isaac have been murdered had his father sacrificed him at the command of God? 'Honor thy father,' God commands me; and I honor him in avenging him. And to be hanged for doing this! No, I will never give myself up to the hangman!"

CHAPTER XII.

FREE.

AS soon as General Harmar knew of the escape, he started the soldiers in pursuit.

"Let the Indians go, too," he said. "This man has wantonly betrayed my confidence in him."

The general had lost confidence in the bravery of the man who abused kindness. How could he be expected to enter into Wetzel's feelings? He saw only that it was strength opposed to strength, and he resolved that Wetzel, the Indian scout, should not laugh at the soldier.

But in the forest the man who had abused the soldier's confidence lay hid, determined, and expectant of death every minute.

Death stared him in the face, and he was not afraid.

"Why should I be afraid?" he thought. "I have but done what I know to be right in the sight of One who governs both life and death."

But he would not risk his life ruthlessly; he must keep life at all hazards so long as he might. There was no bravery in forcing death upon himself. Death had often stared him in the face before, and once, when he was starving, when he had kept himself apart from his friends while he waited for a man's strength, he had eaten clay to withstand the pangs of hunger, as he had more than once seen the Indians do, to allow the distended muscles of the stomach, that awaited food, to go on with their work, and allow him time to search for something more appetizing than earth.

And to think of a man wearing an honorable uniform to come after him, as General Harmar did, knowing so well the principle he was violating! His face burned with indignation as he thought. And he himself had been so willing to assist the military when it had been the pride of the military to shoot Indians. He could not understand, any more than the other settlers could understand. He only knew that he and the men like him were being assailed; he most of all, because his provocation had been greater, and he had asserted his rights. He pitied the civilization that called his offense a crime.

No, he would sell his life dearly. He had not lain in his place of concealment very long, before he heard the noise of pursuers. With his knowledge of the sounds of wild life, he distinguished the difference between the coming steps.

"I did not think that General Harmar was so cowardly as to take Indians into his confidence to carry out the laws which should make the earth more than a hell," he muttered.

The sounds of approaching men smote upon his ear, coming nearer and nearer.

The soldiers kept to the more open wood, looking cautiously about them.

But the Indians separated from the whites, and, plunging into the heart of the wood, tried the manœuvres of savage life.

In the first place, there being many empty tree trunks there, they lighted heaps of leaves and thrust them into the hollow trunks to smoke out any concealed human being. They trampled upon heaps of innocent wood-debris for the same purpose of detection. They found mouths of hiding-places which in all probability had never been before known, and their instinct appeared to lead them correctly to places of possible retreat which man had never used. They were plainly disgusted with their failure to discover him they sought, and became ill-natured and exacting of each other, and some even accused others of being cowards, and afraid to capture the white man if they even knew where he was hiding.

There were more trees overturned than the one

Wetzel used, and in the outskirt of the wood these were more plentiful, and they did not escape the attention of the vigilant men who, adepts in slyness and cunning, deemed their enemies their equals in these qualities. But their search was unavailing, and their tempers were not sweetened by the contemplation of defeat.

Yet the patience of the men who waited months, and even years, to get an enemy into their clutches, was not of the timbre to give way under early defeat and discomfiture. They went into squads and reconnoitered, but without success.

Then two of them strayed from their red brothers, and, entering into the depths of the brush, prodded around there. "No white man yet," Wetzel heard them complain.

These two becoming tired of their fruitless search looked about them, and seeing an overturned tree, went and threw themselves among its branches and swung as in a hammock.

They could not hear the heart that throbbed wildly under that tree. To be taken by these depraved Indians was the worst ignominy of all to the hiding man. He dared not move a muscle, and yet how he longed to plunge a knife into the base hearts of the red-skins who lay directly above him, and called him a coward for hiding, as he plainly made out as they talked on in their braggadocio manner. At last the two Indians arose from their perch and went on with the search.

Wetzel could hear them talking and cursing as they prodded about in the bush. Then their voices grew indistinct, more distant, and only the noise their clubs made in beating the brush could be heard. Then that died away, and all was quiet. The squirrels leaped in and out among the branches of the fallen tree, and that was all.

The danger for the present was over.

The day wore away and night came down, and there was no sound in the thicket which told of man.

Not until the stars were many in the heaven did Wetzel creep out from beneath the log, and stretch his cramped limbs and stand upright. He went a little way from the log and looked about him. The moon silvered the trunks of the trees, and cut a shining path whichever way he turned towards the spaces where the trees were thinner than in the place where he stood. But what should he do? His hands were yet confined by iron cuffs, and he knew of no place on this side of the Ohio where he dared apply for assistance.

He remembered that a man from Wheeling, one Charley Madison, had lately put up a cabin on the

Virginia side of the Ohio. He determined that he was the man who would assist him. But to cross the river was the difficulty! He could not make a raft with bound and fettered hands. He could scarcely trust himself to swim in his present disabled condition.

He left the thicket, and directed his course to the Ohio by a circuitous route, which, in time, brought him to a lonely spot four miles below the fort.

Here a piece of good luck awaited him; by the light of the moon which made everything visible as the sun, he could see that not far from the opposite shore a man was fishing.

He looked anxiously at this man. At length he recognized him as Isaac Wiseman, an inveterate fisherman, whom he had often helped to mend nets.

Could he rely on this man?—might there not already be a tempting reward for his apprehension, which should make many a poor man see the scout only as an escaped murderer, which justice, as represented by the law, plainly had a right to?

But it was all or nothing to him, and he had resolved never to be hanged.

Not daring to call to the fisherman and test his allegiance, for he suspected his pursuers were everywhere around, particularly as now the Indians were called in as officers of the law, he made a gentle splashing in the water, then waved his hat with his manacled hand, to attract the attention of the man.

The fisherman in his canoe appeared not at all astonished, and this awakened the suspicions of Wetzel. The canoe paddled over towards the shore, its occupant lightly humming the refrain of a song. In a few minutes the canoe touched land.

"I am fishing," said Wiseman sententiously, without waiting to be accosted.

"Do you know who I am?" asked Wetzel, bending his eyes upon him.

The other shook his head.

"I am fishing," he repeated.

Wetzel hung back.

"Was it Peter, who called himself a fisher of men?" asked Wiseman, looking at him. "Get in! get in! I heard of the escape of a man from the fort, so I bethought me the night was fine for fish, which the noise at the fort might drive down this way for a little quiet nibble. So, says I, 'Isaac,' I says, 'you'd better go a-fishing.' So I go a-fishing. Don't you see? But I don't know you—never saw you before. Get in!"

In another minute they were paddling silently, but very rapidly, over the Ohio in the moonlight.

"For," went on Wiseman, bending his eyes on the line that flowed in the wake of the boat, "when a man goes a-fishing, there is no telling what he may catch. Once I got a nibble, and it was a man-fish escaped from the British, who doubtless wanted him for supper. They came for him. Says I, 'I go a-fishing, that is all I do.' So they cursed my stupidity and went on. But at the same time, the man-fish was in the bottom of my boat, covered over with a blanket, which I always have with me in case the fish should become cold. And, now, here we go!"

So he talked with a nasal sadness, as he paddled the canoe across the stream.

Once on the Virginia shore, Wetzel had little to fear, for his well-wishers were numerous there, and would have shed their blood in his defense.

Wiseman let him go without a word, and Wetzel could hear him singing as he hurried over the ground, the fisherman spreading his nets without the slightest trace of discomposure.

Wetzel succeeded in finding Madison's cabin which he had helped to erect, and cautiously aroused the friendly occupant.

"Not a word, Charley," he said, as his friend tumbled out of the cabin, rifle in hand, to ask the meaning of this intrusion, "you see how I am loaded down. All I want you to do, is to strike off my irons, friend, and immediately."

These settlers, perhaps, had learned from the Indian code of politeness that it is scarcely in good form to ask unnecessary questions of a sudden guest, and surely questions were unnecessary in this case.

So, hurrying into his cabin, Madison soon returned with a hammer and a small anvil.

"On with your arms," he said, indicating a space on the anvil, and stepping aside that the moon might fully illuminate the delicate operation. A couple of sharp, well-directed strokes, and—"Off with your armlets," said Madison, concluding his speech.

"And now, good-bye!" said Wetzel, seizing the hand of his liberator.

"But you will stay over night," urged the other. "See, you are weak, even now."

"But it may bring you into danger."

"Cuss the danger! Here you are, and here you stay."

When he had eaten and felt refreshed, Wetzel apprised his friend of the circumstances of his case.

Then he laid him down to rest. In the early morning he prepared for departure.

He had said farewell, when Madison called out to him:

"But you haven't asked me why I've built this cabin."

"I suppose it's because you wanted to do it. I thought that from the first."

"Oh, no; that's not it. I'm going to be married."

"I wish you happiness."

"But you haven't asked me who she is."

"I'm not very inquisitive."

"Then I'll tell you; it's Berta Rosencranz. Such a dance as she has led me; such a dance as she's led me these three years. I did think that she cared for somebody else; but last week she told me all men were cowards but me, and that she never saw such a world for cowards. She even said you were the biggest coward of all."

"All the same, I wish you and her happiness. Good-bye!"

For Wetzel was in a hurry to get down the river and on to Kentucky, where he should feel safe from the grasp of General Harmar.

It was not, however, until years had elapsed, and General Harmar had returned to Philadelphia, that it was safe for Wiseman and Madison to avow their assistance of Wetzel, such was the weakness of civil authority and the absolute supremacy of military rule on the frontier.

At a bend in the river Wetzel came, after a hurried and cautious walk, upon Wiseman in his canoe.

"I'm a-fishing," said he. "I thought it just possible the noise Madison and his hammer and anvil made would drive the fish down this way for a quiet nibble. So, says I, 'Isaac,' says I, 'now's your chance.' So here I am, and get in."

But the angler got out as the scout got in.

"It's an unlucky canoe," explained Wiseman, "for the fish never stay hooked. I'll make you a present of it; it may bring you better luck; besides, you've a long journey to go, and the canoe wouldn't carry two well. And here's a blanket and a rifle and some fodder. I'm a-fishing—that's the reason I happen to have so much about me. Catch! here's the fodder. There's the rifle and the blanket."

"Blankets are to warm your fish, I suppose?" smiled Wetzel.

"Precisely," answered the other; "you and I have no idea how cold the bottom of a boat is after you've lived for years in the warm water. And now hurry on. The brush opposite bloomed with eyes all of last night."

Thanking his friend, Wetzel paddled on, and the disciple of Walton, satisfied with his catch, strolled on humming.

Subsequently to Wetzel's escape, General Harmar removed his headquarters to Fort Washington, Cincinnati. One of his first official acts in this new place was to issue a proclamation offering a considerable reward for the arrest and delivery at the fort of " the body of one Lewis Wetzel, an Indian scout, well known to the frontier."

"Though I scarcely expect to get him; for I doubt if there is a man daring enough to attempt such a service," said the general, speaking to a companion.

" Or base enough," was the rejoinder.

So the scout was free again, and only that poor reward for his apprehension shadowed his path.

CHAPTER XIII.

THE HUNDRED DOLLARS REWARD.

AGAIN there is a silence of some time before we hear of Lewis Wetzel in the company of other men. His time was busied in the usual way of solitary vigil, and as he never boasted of his achievements, nor, indeed, thought very much of them, it was only after a long continuance of loneliness that he sought out the habitations of men, when the incentive to his vengeance seemed to grow less in the peaceful habitudes of the forest and the close communion with nature.

But a party of savages having, in the spring of 1787 (De Haas says 1786), crossed the Ohio at what was called the Mingo Bottom, three miles below the present Steubenville, and began their depredations, the people took alarm.

The savages killed an entire family of whites, but retreating immediately, for some unexplained cause, they effected their escape with impunity.

This inroad took the settlers by surprise, the Indians not having crossed the Ohio in that neighborhood for the previous eighteen months.

The people were in a wholly unprotected state, and filled with the direst apprehension.

A subscription was immediately drawn up, headed by those in the easiest circumstances, for the main purpose of stimulating the young and active to habits of vigilance, which pledged a reward of a hundred dollars to the scout who would first bring in an Indian scalp.

This offering of a reward for scalps proves how futile had been the efforts of General Harmar to impress his ideas upon the settlers thus liable to outrageous attacks from the Indians.

It seemed that the young men had only waited for a stimulus, and now this reward was the needed stimulus, though the desire to wreak vengeance on the foe was the main-spring. And whatever the pacific intentions of the general may have engrafted into some minds, those intentions were nothing, alongside of what the settlers had to excite them in a contrary direction.

For two or three days after the attack, some relatives of the family massacred came into the settlement, calling aloud for help in their hour of trial.

There were tales of misery told by these survivors of the massacre that made strong men weak as they were related. Those who listened grew strong in wrath as they heard, and made their vows of vengeance before the recital of the outrages were finished by the narrators.

They looked at one another, and they looked at the horror-stricken faces of the few people remaining of a flourishing little settlement, who had come to them with their wrongs, telling for prompt sympathy the story of what they had undergone.

"We will aid you," was said to them.

"Aid us to get our revenge," was the speedy rejoinder.

"What is peace to these red-skins?" they asked. "It is only that the whites lay down their arms and submit to murders like this. Did it take the army of us white men to drive the settlers back to the first principles of the forest—that is, to own to the rights of the Indians to our lands and stock? Must we calmly sit down here like so many whipped children, and say that this family deserved the treatment they received, and that they were carrying out the spirit of the law in receiving murder at the hands of the savages; while, had they turned on the savages and killed *them*, they would have been guilty of a flagrant breach of the code set down by General Harmar, and folks of his stamp. Who will avenge this murdered family, and show the white soldier how little he knows of Indian warfare?"

Fifty voices declared that fifty men were then and

there willing and anxious to take up arms and vindicate their rights, and that their number would increase hourly.

But this enthusiasm meant only killing without mercy, and that was not what the older and cooler-headed had intended. The reward should stand as it had at first been fixed, but some order must be maintained and some show of discipline organize the company that might be deputed to go in search of the depredators.

It was a long time before the feverish settlers could see in this determination to maintain order anything else than an upholding of the army code of peace. But it gradually settled down into some show of authority on the part of the projectors of the expedition, from whose pockets the reward was to come,—though it would be ungenerous to hint that the money alone actuated any one of the poorer settlers to undertake an expedition that promised death to more than one of their number.

Our friend, Major McMahan, was then deputed to raise a company of twenty men only. In a half-hour his ranks were filled, and a host of disappointed ones were clamorous to have the number increased, volunteering not to touch the hundred dollars should any of them be so fortunate as to earn it. But Major McMahan was inflexible, and refused to add one more man to his ranks, well knowing the trouble of many such reckless men, to whom subordination meant nothing, when they once sighted the enemy.

The day at last came when the little party were to set out on the search, and a crowd of settlers, their wives and children, were collected in the early morning to see them off.

When the men were drawn up in line, twenty-one men were counted.

"How is this?" inquired the major.

"Wrong count," shouted a by-stander.

"Right count," shouted another.

The men were told off again, and it was twenty-one.

"It's Nancy, whose sweetheart is going, and she's dressed herself to follow him," cried a woman.

Nancy, a blushing woman with her apron to her eyes, stepped forward and disavowed any such intention, though her sweetheart was going, and as brave a man as any man there dare be, let any man, or woman either, contradict her to their peril.

"It's dirty Dick," cried another one of the loungers.

A man, covered with dust, here strode out from the ranks.

"I could come no faster than I did," he said; "let me go."

"You look as though you sadly stood in want of a hundred dollars," returned Major McMahan, failing to recognize the unkempt, wild-looking, long-haired man.

The stranger only glared at him, going back to the ranks.

"Not so fast, my friend," said the major, "not so fast."

"Let him go," shouted half a dozen voices.

"Don't let him go," screamed a female voice.

"Let him go," screamed another female voice, Nancy's.

"He makes more than twenty," answered the first female voice, spitefully.

"Mind your business, and don't attempt arithmetic, Mrs. Madison," cried Nancy; "and don't go to saying a second time that I'd dress up like a man and follow my sweetheart."

"You would—you know you would."

"I would, if I was like you, that followed *one* man I know, till he had to clear out."

"Hurrah for Nancy!" shouted some.

"Hurrah for Berta Madison," shouted others.

In the midst of this distraction, Major McMahan turned to the stranger.

"Who are you?" he asked.

"I am Lewis Wetzel, Major McMahan," was the reply.

"The company is twenty-one!" cried the major, in a voice that silenced belligerent man and woman.

"That's not fair," cried a man who had not been accepted in the ranks. "Why should a stranger have the preference over us?"

"A stranger!" sneered Nancy; "where's your eyes, Bob Thomas? That is Lewis Wetzel; I knew him from the first. So did Mrs. Madison—that's why she said he had no right to go."

"Why, I thought they were sweethearts once?"

"Booby! she hates him. What do you know about sweethearts? She couldn't get him! That's what!"

"Forward!" cried the major, giving the word of command, and the little party tramped off, cheered out of the settlement by their friends.

On the perilous expedition the little company set out forthwith, and soon crossing the Ohio, discovered an Indian trail, which they followed till they came to the Muskingum River.

Advance guards were sent out, who proceeded cautiously to inspect the locality.

They had not gone far before they discovered a party of Indians around a newly-set-up lodge, on the bank of the river, and far superior in numbers to the advancing white men.

Hurriedly retracing their steps, the guard reported

to Major McMahan the condition of affairs, and he, thoughtful of the safety of his party, retreated to the top of a hill, where they might consult as to future operations.

"But the Indians have not discovered us," said a voice from the ranks.

"But there is a chance of their doing so at any minute," said the major.

He then entered into conference with the more experienced men.

The conclusion of the conference was that a hasty retreat was all that was left the white party.

There was grumbling from the youngest and most ambitious of the little troop; for, besides the glory attached to the successful operations of the command, the reward of a hundred dollars was not to be despised, even by a brave man, as a hundred dollars went a little further in those days of necessities without luxuries.

"I want the first scalp," said a young, stalwart fellow, "for I mean to be married in the fall."

"You may have your own scalp off by that time," replied a companion.

"But I mean to try to keep it on, and try how an Injun feels without one. And even if it goes, Nancy will know I tried for the money we want for housekeeping things."

While the party were in close confab as to whether prudence consisted in going or staying, Lewis Wetzel carelessly sat upon a mossy log, his gun laid across his lap, his tomahawk in his hand. He paid no attention whatever to the council; he had not come to talk.

"They will send us home again," said a man to him.

"Will they?" he asked, and turned his back on his informant.

As soon as the resolution to retreat was adopted, the party set about obeying the command.

All except Lewis Wetzel. He still sat upon the mossy log, his gun in his lap, his tomahawk in his hand.

His companions called to him, and he paid no attention to them.

The party set out, and had gone a few yards, when Major McMahan, thinking the man asleep, came back himself, and ordered him to go along with the rest.

Lewis Wetzel turned his face up to the major, without arising from the log.

"I shall stay for what I came," he answered quietly. "Go, major; you take back the twenty men you had before I interloped."

Arguments were unavailing; he was said to be so

stubborn in the one idea of his life that he never submitted to any control or advice which threatened to thwart him.

And as military discipline dealt not with men of his stamp, Major McMahan and his party were compelled to leave him, a solitary being, in the midst of the thick forest, surrounded by vigilant enemies ever on the alert.

As soon as he was assured the men had left him, and he no longer heard the snapping of twigs as they crushed the sapplings to the ground, he arose picked up his gun, and struck off into another part of the country, looking about him. He kept moving along swiftly through the underbrush, but aloof from the larger streams, where he could see great parties of the Indians encamped, and he gritted his teeth as he saw them rollicking and at ease.

He prowled through the woods with a noiseless tread, and the eye of the eagle; he traversed the ground all that day and the next, when towards evening he discovered smoke curling up from among the bushes.

He crept softly forward in this direction, nearer and nearer still, till he came full upon the fire, and found two blankets and a small copper camping kettle.

This was then the camp of but two Indians!

He exulted at the thought.

He concealed himself in the thick brush, but in such a position that he could readily see the number, and watch the movements of the campers.

Pretty soon one of the Indians came in and stirred up the fire, and brought forth a huge piece of venison, and, stripping the tough hide away from the flesh, began roasting it. Then, while he was attending to this culinary business, the other Indian came in with a grunt of satisfaction, as he sniffed the ascending fumes of the deer-flesh in the glowing fire.

Two bright eyes among the bushes were looking intently on, but the chiefs noticed them not.

Perfectly assured of their safety and freedom from intrusion, they began ravenously on their supper, eating with a gusto that was tantalizing to the white scout in the bushes, who was almost famishing.

Then, supper finished, the Indians began crooning songs, drinking from flasks the "fire-water" of the whites, and telling comic stories, bursting into peals of hearty laughter.

Nearer and yet nearer crept the white man in the bushes; nearer and nearer he came, noiseless, but with the fullest of intents, nearer yet to the now waning fire, till he was close enough to have touched one of the men, and could easily have snatched the meat from the fire, of which the Indians had now enough, and were allowing the remainder to burn to a cinder.

The wolves around, attracted by the scent, were howling, and birds of prey fluttering in the branches.

The liquor they had taken seemed to make the savages fiercer, for they dropped from their mirthfulness and songs, and began a low war-song, speaking of vengeance on the whites, and torture to the first scout they would get into their clutches.

Grasping his weapons, Wetzel looked on, and saw and heard all. Yet he bided his time.

About ten o'clock one of the Indians, throwing a heap of wood on the fire in order to keep it bright, and prevent an inroad of the wolves, wrapped his blanket around him, shouldered his rifle, and taking a chunk of fire in his hand, left the camp, doubtless with the intention of going to watch a deer lick— the fire and smoke of the torch in his hand to keep off the gnats and mosquitoes.

This absence of one of the Indians was a severe vexation to the watching white man, who now went back a little way, but who still hoped that the absent red-skin might return to camp ere day.

In this he was forced to bear a disappointment.

Night waned, and chirping birds proclaimed the approach of day, but the Indian had not returned.

Cursing his luck, Wetzel went on to the camp-fire, chopping at a wolf who attacked him.

He found the remaining Indian fast asleep, lying on his side and snoring loudly. Wetzel drew forth his formidable knife, and, nerving his arm, sent it with all his force through the unconscious savage's heart.

There was a short quiver, a convulsive movement, then all was still, and life had sped through the forest thickness, past the prowling animals, past the singing birds, up to the Maker of life to be judged and awarded according to its earthly usefulness.

Wetzel looked down on the still, bronzed face, upon the brawny limbs and tough muscles, and wondered why so much superb strength had been given a creature who used it in slothfulness and pleasure.

He grasped a little of the charred remains of the venison on the fire with which he satisfied the pangs of growing hunger. He then scalped the dead Indian and slung the gory braid of hair to his belt. Stamping out the remains of the fire, he strode along, apostrophizing the lurking wolves as he went.

"Go," he said, "your meal awaits you," and pointed towards the extinct camp-fire and the prostrate body of the dead brave.

He strode through the forest, he walked day and night without food, and reached the Mingo Bottom only one day after his unsuccessful companions.

"What luck?" they asked him.

"I want Major McMahan," was his response.

"But what luck?"

"Where is Major McMahan?"

"At least tell us your luck."

"I have had no luck. And now where is Major McMahan?"

"He is not here. What is your hurry, man? Why can't you rest here with us and tell us all that happened you after we left you?"

"I want Major McMahan. I have no time to rest. I must away again as soon as I have seen him."

He went from them, and paced up and down on a long slender piece of sward. For hours he waited to see the major. He was not impatient, and time was of little account to him when he had to put up with delay of this kind. For he meant to see the major, and the major alone, as he owed him some sort of excuse for refusing to obey his orders in the woods and marching along home with the other men.

The major was seen approaching. Wetzel went forward to him, throwing the scalp of the Indian upon the ground before him.

"You have earned the reward," said Major McMahan.

"What reward? I want no reward of money. My reward was in getting this."

"But, man, you will surely claim the hundred dollars?"

"What good will it do me?"

"It will replenish your store of necessities. Your clothes are ragged, your gun is broken, your blanket torn—surely you think of your comfort?"

"Comfort! Am I a Judas? Do I accept blood-money?"

The men who heard him turned away, some of them smiling at the crazy scout, as they called him.

And this was the man who had been accused of murder!

"I only wish the chance was mine," grumbled one of them.

"What would you do with the money?" asked Wetzel, quick as a flash, turning to him.

"I'm going to be married soon, and I'd buy housekeeping things for Nancy."

"Is that all?"

Wetzel turned away gruffly, and went and sat down upon the ground.

That evening, when the men were disporting themselves, he presented himself to Major McMahan.

"Well, Wetzel?" began the major.

"I have come to claim the hundred dollars," returned the scout.

"I thought you'd regret that nonsense of yours," smiled the major. "And you are perfectly right in claiming it. You earned it, and men wealthy enough to give it are the originators of the reward, and a poor man like you has every right to come forward and claim it. I am glad you've got over the notion of blood-money. It is rather late in the day for you to become squeamish, Wetzel."

"Yes, it is rather late in the day," mused Wetzel.

In the month of June, there was a simple wedding in the Bottom. When the bride had been kissed, and stood, all blushes, among the dames and damsels, a boy ran in, and went up to her.

"Get out," cried an indignant wife; "where's your manners, dirty Dick?—going up to a lass in white with those filthy paws of yours."

"It's something for her," demurred dirty Dick to this treatment.

"It's some ugly thing you've caught in the woods for a present for her, I'll be bound. But get away, do, you and your present. What will she want of it, alongside of the beautiful chain Major McMahan sent her?"

"Oh, Mrs. Madison, let him come to me. Indeed, Dick, I'm thankful for your offering, whatever it is," said the bride.

"It taint mine," he said sulkily, "and she wouldn't give me time to say so. It was given to me by a long-haired man, who made for the woods. He said I wasn't to give it into any hands but yours."

"Don't take it," screamed the wife, who had hitherto kept the boy off; "it's some poison Indian thing that your old jilted lover sends you."

"I never had a jilted lover, Mrs. Madison," began the bride.

"Oh, la! didn't you? Why I had twenty; there was Lewis Wetzel, and——"

But she was interrupted by a cry of surprise from the rosy bride, who had taken from the boy a scrap of crumpled paper, upon which was written, in rude, uncouth characters: "For Nancy, to buy housekeeping things with." While inside was a hundred dollars sewed up in a leaf.

Who the donor was no one knew, and as Dick's description of the man varied with the importance that now attached itself to him, they were not able to ascribe it to any one in particular, although the popularly-accepted opinion was, that the President had sent it, and did not desire it to be generally known.

But Nancy's bridegroom had another idea, which he did not make generally known.

CHAPTER XIV.

THE TURKEY-CRY.

ABOUT this time, Wetzel made one of his periodical visits to Wheeling; and after vainly trying to discover the whereabouts of his brothers, who had moved further West, he went to his sisters, who were yet in the fort, and remained for a short time with them.

"This day I am ninety years of age," writes old Eberly in the last pages of his manuscript, "and as I was moving from the fort, richly pleased that the mercy of God had lett me remain here while so manny of the younger have gone before me, a man came upp to me and helped me down a hill. For I bee proper feeble now, though hoping to bee strong again by next Spring, as the cool air never goes well with the rheumatiz. The man was Lowis Wetzel, the sonne of John that was killed by injuns years ago. Lowis is a quiet man, and when I blessed him for helping of me hee said hee might bee olde himself some day, and hoped a younger man might bee by to help him. Hee is properly wrong in calling me olde. I bee as young as the youngest. But hee is well-intentioned, though ferce to look upon, and not overly careful of his manners inne calling of peple olde."

Wetzel was well received by the people during this visit, and he might have had a merry enough time, had he been so minded. For his assistance in time of need was not soon to be forgotten, and just now men like himself were rather scarce in the settlements, a more studious set having taken their place. Men other than mere plodders and diggers and delvers were coming to the land of promise, white-faced men from desks, sickly men from hospitals, worn-out men from the shambles of pleasure where dissipation calls itself enjoyment, and is not disowned until the body and brain fail of their best functions, and life itself palls upon life vitiated.

Then the more cultivated and wealthier classes in the Eastern States had itching palms to possess in fee-simple the wild rolling lands of the West. These latter sent colonists from the work-shop and loom, and claimed the land thus settled on by their employees, which the employees were at liberty within a stated time of forsaking for land of their own, when they could keep themselves without calling upon the resources of the wealthier men.

Mechanical industries were springing up, too, and in some of the older settlements the little work-shop and the single loom made humming music in the air that had never before been broken by the peaceful sound.

To work land was not the only thing thought of; there were men here who did not possess physical strength enough to do that. There was a report in Wheeling that a dress-maker was coming out with her husband, and women were wondering if the fashions had changed within the last five years, and if they would be ashamed of themselves after the arrival of the dress-maker. The changes and thicker settlements drove the Indian further away, but made him more revengeful and crafty. This was the state of affairs when it was told that Lewis Wetzel had come to see his sisters and people. Strangers had him pointed out to them.

In this visit to his sisters, Wetzel did not mention his mother's name, and it was only on the eve of his departure that one of his sisters dared say, timidly:

"I am sorry mother is not here to see you. Surely you know she was never strong after father's death, and we had quite a time to get her over her nervous spells. She often speaks of you and the other boys, but she thinks it rather hard she should be left alone without a son in her old days. She needs some one to console her——"

"She has some one now, I have heard," he interrupted.

"She has gone up the river for a spell, to visit——"

"Her husband's people. Yes, I understand," he interrupted again. "But I did not come to see her; she is nothing to me—I have no mother. She forgot my father, and has a new husband now."

For John Wetzel's widow had married.

"She was lonely."

"Had she not her children?"

"She had grown weak and querulous."

"And married her husband in consideration of her weakness and querulousness? Let it be so. My mother was a strong woman who helped to make a home for her children in the wilderness. She died with my father. She is better without me—she has a husband to take care of her. I could never like her husband, so I will not wait to see him. Good-bye, my sisters!"

"But, indeed, he is not a foolish man. He is even now trying to find out the cause of the turkey-call, and has left mother with his family while he is away."

"Turkey-call?"

"You know what I mean; the call that annoys us so just now."

"Good-bye!" was all the brother said.

But he went about the place inquiring into the nature of any disturbances in and around Wheeling. He also found out that his mother's husband was a sensible, practical man.

"Then why did he marry my mother?" he questioned himself.

He was glad that good reports had been left behind them by his brothers, for he took an interest in all the affairs of his family, though his line of action and self-ostracism from them and their apparent interest might seem to prove a denial of the fact. But was not the ridding of the country of a pest taking the interest of his family into consideration?

Now this fatal decoy of the turkey-call had for a long time proved disastrous to the frontier.

The painful cry of birds in distress had flown through the air, and the most superstitious of the people thought it a harbinger of some evil about to befall the land so lately rebellious against the king, and shuddered as they listened. But the more practical souls had determined to bring the mystery to earth, and on several occasions men from the fort at Wheeling had gone across the hills in their quest, and on more than one occasion the men had never returned.

When Wetzel's sister told him that his mother's husband had determined to try to solve the mystery, he, too, undertook to get at the bottom of the mysterious cries. For these cries would come up from the earth; down from the cloudless sky; in the midst of gatherings of people; when wives alone in their homes attended to their household duties; at night when half the place slept. At all times, in all places the cries were heard; now far off, now near at hand, wailing and distressing in the extreme. Prognostications of all manner of evil were not wanting among the people, and the very failure of some of the investigating men to come back again argued in the nervous minds the supernatural quality of the gruesome sounds.

A young wife deposed that at noon, when rocking her sickly babe in its cradle, suddenly from the cradle came the sad bird's cry of grief. That night the child died.

An old woman, long bedridden, awoke in the night, and in the far-off hill saw a fitful "death light," as she termed it, from which the distressing cry floated over to her with dreadful warning. When she had power to call some one to her bedside, the light had disappeared and the usual darkness of the hills at midnight reigned in its stead, while no longer came the cry of the bird in trouble.

Every one heard the cry, and Wetzel had fifty stories told him in as many minutes, and all tending to the supernatural. Some of the younger women grew hysterical in their recitals, and asked him what he knew about witchcraft.

So the scout spent day after day making inquiries about the mysterious cry, and listening with all avidity to the many stories concerning it. Not that he doubted he knew the full meaning of the sad cries, but a higher principle than mere curiosity prompted him.

With long strides he left the fort, and sought the hills one day in the midst of the narration of a new story. Night came down upon him, and he sought a tree, climbed it, and in a crotch of it passed the night.

All night long, at intervals, came the plaintive cries; now far off and faint, again at his very feet, all about him.

He even heard the brush beneath him agitated as though by the passage of some mysterious agent.

The cries, too, seemed to hush the snarling hunger-moans of the wolf and coyote, and, borne upon the wind, it alone reached his ears insufferably sad and gruesome. Then would come the soft rustling of the bushes beneath him, and, though he strained his eyes and peered down around him, he could make out nothing. At last the moon came out and silvered a track across the brush. Through this track, which he watched with keen scrutiny, once in the heart of the night he saw a dark body of many links, or a chain of bodies, pass noiselessly up towards the crest of the hill before him, the cries seeming to float about the path of silver, and down to the habitations of the pioneers at Wheeling. Turning his eyes towards the white settlement, he could see lights moving about in the houses, as the worried people, unable to sleep, wandered here and there seeking an answer to the cries.

"I am glad my mother's husband is more practical," he said.

At the first break of day the sounds had ceased, and he descended from his perch and reconnoitered the brush beneath. Yes, the place was trodden here and there. He got down on his knees and examined the crushed grass.

"It is as I suspected," he said.

He followed these marks in the wounded brush, and they took him high above the level. He mounted to at least sixty feet above the water on the east side of Creek Hill, and there the marks ended. Here he found the mouth of a capacious cavern, running he knew not how far underground, the entrance almost completely obscured by a heavy growth of vines and foliage.

In the very heart of this wild growth he ensconced himself, pulling the leaves all about him, and entirely burying himself, and here he waited.

He waited all the morning and ascertained nothing. Once he thought the vines were shaken as though somebody or something issued from the cavern's mouth, but he was hidden and could see little that was beneath a man's stature that might go from or into the cave. And there was no sound.

All the afternoon he waited there, with his old tireless vigilance, which was never exerted but for the one reason—to hunt his hated foes. Late in the afternoon a high, shrill turkey-cry cleaved the silence, then another, and another, till it seemed that a whole brood of birds were in the direst agony.

The cries came from the cavern! Cautiously raising his body until his head was on a line with the tallest grass, and he could see about him, he looked towards the cavern. But all was motionless there, the heavy bushes before the entrance were moveless in the stilly air. Still he kept his eyes fixed on the spot, assured that he had not fixed on that place in vain.

He was rewarded for his patience.

Presently the tangled vines at the mouth of the cave were agitated a little. What was coming forth—a gruesome object to strike terror to the heart of the human watcher?

"I never feared live devils; I never intend to fear dead ones," said this watcher, who watched and waited.

The vines became still again. Then they were agitated once more, and from amidst their green leaves reached forth a human hand.

"Not a dead devil," commented the faithful watcher.

Directly after the hand had appeared and thrust aside the many vines, another sort of flower took its place, for the twisted tuft of an Indian warrior slowly arose in the mouth of the cavern, and below that a villainous face daubed with war-paint looked cautiously about, to right and left. Then, twisting his mouth into a long horn-like shape, the red-skin sent forth the shrill, prolonged, and peculiarly distressing, moaning cry, and immediately afterwards disappeared, as though he had indeed been endowed with spiritual power to appear and disappear instantaneously.

"No, not a dead devil," said the watcher, almost positive that in that cavern he had detected, in the momentary glance he had had of it, the dead body of a white settler—doubtless one of those who had recently come here to investigate the nature of the supernatural phenomenon.

This, then, alone, was the lure which had proved so fatal to those who had come to ascertain its import. From that point so elevated the concealed savage had long commanded an extensive view of the surrounding country, and more especially of the hill-front upon the opposite side, and the incautious soldier or embarrassed settler coming straight down towards the river, looking out first one way then the other for the struggling bird, quickly met his death.

Lewis Wetzel had suspected the truth, his long and intimate study and hatred had inducted him into many secrets not well known by the more peaceful and kindly-intentioned people around. He recollected the wolf-cries around his father's cabin years ago—he recollected the bear in the bushes beside his father's cabin!

Even now, after the Indian's head had disappeared, Wetzel looked towards the side country, and saw a little party of three or four white men coming on gazing into the bushes and searching.

The silence, around his height from the level, enabled him to hear almost every word the men on the opposite declivity said.

"It was around here," said one.

"Do you think it was a bird, or a spirit?" asked another.

"No doubt of it," responded the first speaker, "that it is a spirit."

"That must be my mother's husband," said Lewis Wetzel grimly. "My father would never have spoken thus."

"But if I had thought it was a spirit I would not have come after it with a rifle," said the third of the little party, speaking now for the first time,—" nor had I thought it was a turkey, either. My son is not an Indian murderer, but this is an Indian ruse!"

"Your son! You mean Lewis Wetzel?" inquired one of them.

"Yes, my son. Did I not marry John Wetzel's widow—their mother?"

Wetzel turned his attention towards the mouth of the cavern determinedly, his gun cocked, anxiously waiting.

He had not long to wait.

Up rose from the tangled mass of pretty vines the barrel of a gun, then the tufted head of the red-skin. And then again, and for the last time, the sad note that had created such consternation sounded through the air—for the last time, for, unseen and taking a fine aim at the polished head, Wetzel had raised his rifle to his shoulder.

There was a sharp, quick report, as the Indian raised his own gun at the three men below, a curl of pale smoke, and the turkey-cry was silenced forever.

"A dead devil," said Wetzel, as the strained vines sprang back over the form that fell in their midst.

Standing upright, and looking down towards the opposite hills, he saw the hurrying forms of the three men coming his way.

"It was a rifle-shot," said the foremost of the three, "and it surely means something."

"Might it not be a decoy to get us up there?" asked the more prudential one, pausing for a second—the man who claimed the scout for a son.

Then all three paused.

"Even if it is, though," went on the last speaker, "we might as well look into it. Have we all got our knives? Had you taken my advice when we started out you would have brought your rifles. But, no, you were all so positive that the whole proceeding was supernatural."

"We have not found out yet what it is," answered one of the two.

"Only worldly powder makes the blue ring we saw up yonder. Decoy or no decoy, come on, if you are not afraid!"

They then plunged forward.

"He is no coward," muttered the man on the opposite hill, standing out from the furze, and deliberating what he should do next.

He turned and rapidly beat down the vines that choked the entrance to the cave, so that the body of the slain Indian was exposed to full view. And what his slight glimpse into the cave in the first instance had suggested to him was verified—for the body of a settler lay a yard from that of the Indian.

"They will understand," said Wetzel, looking vindictively on the fallen red-skin.

He turned his eyes upon the approaching white men. Again he hesitated, went a little way, then returned.

"Can I, or can I not?" he asked himself.

He could see the husband of John Wetzel's widow breaking his way through the obstructing stubble, a manly looking man, the only wonder being what he had seen to admire in the weak and peevish wife.

"Never mind," communed the scout with himself. "I do not know him—I *cannot* know him. He may not be a coward, but he cannot take the place of my father—with me. But my mother shall not be a widow at the hands of the red-skins a second time. Poor mother!"

Grasping his rifle, and casting an envious glance

towards the yet intact scalp of the originator of the turkey-cries, he plunged through the long grass, seeking a place in which to hide from the approaching strangers, more especially the one man; and at last, when their voices came nearer to him, he hid in the grass, and saw three men laboriously mounting the hill to the cavern.

He saw them start when they saw the Indian.

"This explains it all," he heard one of them say.

"But who fired the shot?" asked the second man.

The third man was busily turning over the dead Indian. He now raised something aloft in the air, between his thumb and finger.

"Here is one of Lewis Wetzel's bullets," he said. "It went straight through the red-skin's head."

Wetzel, hearing this, struck off, and made his way out without discovery. He had saved the life of his mother's husband, as he had tried to do. More than that he had not intended. Yet in saving the life of the second husband he had once more avenged the death of the first. This idea crossed his mind as he hurried away.

"How strange that chance should make me the instrument in this instance," he said. "Why should I not let the men who murdered my father keep his place sacred by removing the usurper of it? Why should I strive to help my mother to forget her loss, and every day see in the new husband traits of excellence the dead one never possessed? It must be because my father loved my mother and toiled for her happiness—he would not like her to be distressed and dreary. Ah, well! let her be happy with her husband—if she can. As for me—I have my duty to perform, and I must be a stranger to all else."

It is said that he never saw his mother's second husband after that.

CHAPTER XV.

A CHANCE FOR AN ARREST.

BUT General Harmar's pursuit of Wetzel for the killing of the Indian had in no wise ceased, although the scout had long since dropped out of his mind any concern of the matter.

The officers under Harmar had standing orders to arrest "the murderer of the pacific Indian" whenever and wherever they might find him.

It was even suggested that a reward be offered for the arrest, but to this the commandant turned a deaf ear; he knew too well that a reward would only make the settlers more indignant and more persevering to thwart justice; while secrecy would eventually throw the game into his hands, and the excitement aroused by the arrest would be more of a negative than a positive order.

It would appear now that Wetzel, after his taking it in his own hands to put a stop to the turkey-cries, went leisurely down the Ohio River towards the Kanawha.

Here he roved about for a little while in the

fastnesses of his beloved woods. Apropos of this love of the woods, he is reported to have once said, "I cannot breathe in the open air. I require the leaves of trees to break and filter it before it enters my lungs."

As he went along one day, he met a white man, who eyed him.

"Are you Lewis Wetzel?" inquired the stranger.

"That is my name," replied the scout.

The stranger turned on his heel and abruptly left him. The scout gazed after him, hailed him, but received no reply whatever, the stranger only hurrying the faster when he heard the detaining voice back of him. This man traveled day and night till he came to the station of the military. He informed them of Wetzel's vicinity, instructed them how to get there, and then asked for the reward.

He was told there was none, and was ignominiously hustled from the camp by the troops who despised the cowardly informer, as much as they desired to capture the scout—for it was mortifying that a single man should thwart the vigilance of the entire army. Yet for all the information, they did not know where, exactly, to place hands on the scout; for he might be here to-day, but not even himself could tell where to-morrow would find him.

Wetzel, in the meantime, had taken to the Ohio again, and floated leisurely down, often for days at a time lying on the broad of his back, letting the boat go whither it would, and gazing up to the clouds which were always a wonder to him.

At last, one day, he sighted Point Pleasant, and landed there.

Following his usual humor when he had no Indians to engage his deadly attention, he ranged the little town for a few days, looking at the sights and filled with admiration.

His old friends, dogs and little children, used to tag around at his heels, and in a few days he was well known, and people used to stop and gaze after the wild-looking man with a string of animals and boys and girls following happily in his footsteps.

"A strange man," they would say.

It is related of him that a woman with a sick child cried aloud in the night that she was all alone and that her child was dying

Wetzel, passing along outside, called up to the window that if she wanted assistance to say so. She wanted the doctor, and there was no one to go for him. The scout brought the doctor, and stayed besides and quieted the child all night, making the mother go and lie down and get some rest. Men hearing of it smiled and thought " a screw is loose in him." Women thought it brave in him.

"He is a hero!" said a pale little school-mistress who had braved everything and come out here to establish a hall of learning; "he is a hero! I am neither pretty nor attractive, and yet the man never meets me with a pail of water but he takes it from me without a word and carries it for me. I require heaps of water, and, oddly enough, I always go to the stream about the time he comes along."

"You never used so much water before he came," said a woman friend, cynically.

"No. Isn't it odd?" returned the little school-mistress, with the ghost of a bloom in her thin cheeks.

"Very odd," said her friend, who had not the heart to go any further into the new demand for water. So women thought of him—the frailer the woman, the stronger her admiration for manly strength.

He whittled toys for the children, made them bows and arrows, and often he had a row of urchins surrounding and hemming him in, as he worked and listened tenderly to their prattle. They would ask him if he had any little children of his own; and if he had ever been a little child like them; and if he would not like to be as they were; and if when big men like he died they went up to the stars and were taught to be happy, just as little children who died were? They would seem to pity him, and fondled him caressingly. They climbed over him, pulled and platted his hair, and committed all the reckless depredations of young children.

And he was a man whose hands were deeply imbrued in human blood!

Was he a guilty man? He could not have been the harsh man that some of his detractors have declared him. Here, too, he did chores for the women—mended their broken furniture, fixed a gate, even patched shoes, for so had he learned to be of use on all occasions.

Yet it was not for long that he remained, here or at any place, no matter how frequent might be his visits; for, always restless and ill at ease, he might retire at night promising all manner of things for the morrow; but in the morning, before his entertainers were awake, he would be gone; and no matter how much the children might cry, they might not see him again for months, though the possibility existed that it might be but weeks—no one could tell when. "A strange man," was the verdict as usual.

Lieutenant Kingsbury, attached to General Harmar's command, happened to be at the mouth of the Kanawha at the time of one of Wetzel's periodical visits, and, while scouting about, ran against the scout one day while the latter was carrying a child across a muddy puddle.

Wetzel saw Kingsbury first, before the latter recognized the approaching man, and guessed at an arrest. He kissed the little child in his arms, and gently set it down on the ground.

"There," he said, "now run away, little one, run home to mother, and wait till I come back with my big pocket full of nice nuts. Run fast, now; let me see how fast you can run."

The child took to its heels, and soon ran out of danger, its innocent laugh becoming fainter and fainter as it went further away. Wetzel then turned to Lieutenant Kingsbury (who had halted likewise), silently leaving it to the lieutenant to decide on the mode of procedure, feeling himself prepared and ready for whatever might happen, but as resolved as ever that he did not deserve hanging.

He could not have been detained by a better man; for Kingsbury was too brave a man himself to entertain anything but good feeling towards a spirit like Wetzel's, and would not attempt to injure him, even if it were safe to do so.

He turned frowning to the scout.

"Why are you always getting yourself in danger?" he asked sternly.

"Am I in danger now?" asked Wetzel.

"Look here," said the lieutenant argumentatively, "why are you making me disobey orders? I deserve court-martialing, do you know that? If I were anybody but myself I should call myself a coward. I never saw a fellow like you; you won't give peaceably-inclined people a chance to rest. You know very well that the orders of General Harmar are stringent, and that he is a disciplinarian. And you have no right to upset all his plans, as you have done for a long time. Pshaw, Wetzel, I am almost ashamed of you! If I were you I'd turn monk, and quit the world. It would be a great benefit to—the Indians. Is there an Indian monastery anywhere around? Go there! Why are you always in danger?"

"Am I in danger now," asked Wetzel in return for this harangue.

"You know you are. Are there not standing orders to arrest you?"

"Do you intend to do it?"

"Would you have me held for dereliction of duty?"

"Does your duty begin and end in General Harmar's orders?"

Frowning like a thunder-gust, Lieutenant Kingsbury ended this conversation, which had been a mass of interrogations from first to last, by saying merely, "get out of my sight, Indian killer," and brushed past the man he should have taken had he felt that his duty lay entirely in the standing order of his superior officer.

Wetzel turned away, too, and perhaps as much to save the brave lieutenant any further awkwardness as to preserve his own equanimity, went directly to the bank of the river where his canoe was fastened, pulled up the stake, got into the frail bark, and paddled off in the direction of Limestone, which he had long intended to visit.

CHAPTER XVI.

THE INDIAN GIRL.

AT Limestone and Washington, the county town, Wetzel now established his headquarters.

Here he took part in hunting-parties, and showed the wonderful dexterity he had acquired with his gun. He helped in the fields of grain, and in the forest felled and sawed the wood for winter firesides that would never warm him.

He also went out with other scouts in search of predatory Indians.

While many of the scouts took the Indians indiscriminately, Wetzel deprecated the making captive of women.

"Not a woman," he would say, "for our mothers are women!"

"Our fathers are men, too," was the argument held out to him.

"And as men, can defend themselves," he replied. "But men to attack and capture women! That is not for me—for you."

So many a squaw owed her impunity from

capture and harsh treatment to the man who would gladly have killed her male relatives before her very eyes while shielding her from any harm whatever.

There was one squaw, a young girl of fifteen, bright-eyed and winsome, who, witnessing the shooting of her three brothers and her father, was taken prisoner by a party of whites and brought into the camp in the woods where the scouts were assembled.

Some of the younger men complimented the girl on her prepossessing appearance, and she turned away, abashed at their rude and openly-expressed admiration.

"Let us make a vivandière of her, such as the French have," suggested a careless young fellow.

"Let the girl go," commanded a stern voice.

"Who spoke in that tone?" demanded the young fellow, leaping to his feet in anger.

Wetzel came to him and put his hand on his shoulder:

"I spoke, lad," he said. "The girl must go. Have you sisters? If you have, think of their position in an Indian camp."

"Their position in such a place should make me detain this girl from revenge."

"It should make you liberate her for very pity," said the scout quietly, going over to the girl who looked on open-eyed.

"Go, child," he said, "your people's camp is waiting for you."

She buried her face in her hands and broke into piteous weeping, nor could she be quieted for a long time, the men gathering around her in perturbation, and lost in sympathy, where a few minutes ago they had been cruel and callous.

When at last she dried her tears, she peeped through her fingers at the men. Then she smiled, showing her beautiful teeth.

Then she threw her hands from her face, and radiant and her eyes sparkling like stars from very happiness, she ran and caught Wetzel's hand in both of hers, and covered it with kisses, and stood silently beside him, looking earnestly in his face.

And here a new difficulty arose: she refused to be separated from the man who had given her freedom.

"Indian girl got no father, no brothers; she like white brave; she go with him."

"But the white brave cannot take you," said Wetzel kindly, as he spoke to all children.

"Pooh!" said the Indian girl with sovereign contempt; "Indian girl don't want to be took—she take herself. She know every path; she follow after white brave."

She came calmly and placed her hand in Wetzel's.

"But what am I to do with her?" asked the scout in despair.

The other men enjoyed the situation.

At length he took the girl with him, and they wandered through the forest till they came in sight of an encampment of some of her people. Then, pretending that he desired a parley with them, he prevailed upon her to go before him as an ambassadress of the mission.

She sprang lightly forward, glad to do his behest; and when he saw her safe within the line of Indian pickets, he dived through the brush and made for foreign parts.

In the camp that night, however, the girl presented herself again.

"What am I to do with her?" asked one of the young men derisively.

Wetzel said:

"Do you think this girl was allowed to come because she wanted to? She is either a decoy, or else her people cast her off, now that her father and brothers are no more."

"Her people cast her off because she loves a white man," said a voice out of the darkness, and the crack of an Indian rifle was heard, and the girl with a moan fell lifeless at the very feet of Wetzel.

Whether the bullet had been intended for the scout or her could only be guessed at.

But the camp was in an uproar, and the men filed off, seeking for the murderer.

The search was unavailing, and by midnight the party were collected in camp once more, and a grave was dug for the poor child.

Wetzel composed her limbs decently, and wrapped her in his blanket. They laid her in the gloomy, narrow trench they had dug, and the cry of gathering wolves was the funeral hymn. The men prepared to throw on the earth, when Wetzel stopped them.

"We commit this body to the earth from whence it came," he said in a low voice. "And as from the earth spring up flowers and healthful things for man's life, so may this immortal soul arise to the seat of mercy, a flower, a fruit in the sight of God. Amen!"

Then he motioned for the men to proceed, and soon the earth was piled high upon the young breast whose life had been so suddenly cut off by the ruthless bullet of one of her own people.

The camp-fire was moved on to the grave to protect it from the wolves; and piling wood on it, and waiting until the flames were high and fierce, the party of white men moved silently away from the spot, and made their camp further off, and where the flame on the grave could only be seen like a thin golden vapor.

In the early morning Wetzel went alone to the grave and saw the white ashes of what had been a fierce fire the night before. Long he stood there lost in contemplation. Then he roused himself, and looking furtively around, and finding no one near him, he went and pulled some crimson blossoms, that made an adjoining bush like a living flame, and threw them upon the ashes, until the ground seemed carpeted by sunset. The girl had been killed as he might have killed his own sister had she chosen an Indian for her protector. What was the difference? For the first time in his life he paused in asking himself the question—what was the difference between the soul of an Indian and a white man?

CHAPTER XVII.

TRIAL AND ACQUITTAL.

THERE were seasons of inactivity, too, when the scouts wanted a variety of amusement.

"Amusement!" echoed Wetzel, to whom the rumors of discontent in camp came more than once, which discontent he could not comprehend. "Amusement!"

"Oh, it is all very well for you," cried one, who noted the intonation of his voice; "you never seem to care for anything but loneliness and Indians. We don't overly like loneliness, and we don't want to spend our entire lives in murder."

"Murder!" was the word echoed now, and other scouts came between the two.

"Now, look here, Wetzel," said one, "you must own yourself that you're not always downright lively —your company manners are not quite cheerful. What's the use of going through the world like a quart of blackberries? Why can't you make one of us, and try to see a little fun? Do you know how many times you have laughed in your life?"

"I hope you give me credit for bearing no ill-will towards you—towards any man in the world?" said Wetzel.

"How about Indians?" laughed his companion.

"Indians are fiends."

"No, Wetzel, we know you have in you the making of a good fellow; but why don't you make the good fellow? Come, now, for once in a while see if you can't be happy with us."

"Happy!"

"Well, whatever stands for happiness in you. Will you try?"

"I will do what I can, friend."

To satisfy and gratify the—to him—careless souls so bent on a different line of *amusement* than that one which partook of more perils than any others, there were shooting-matches, foot-racing, and wrestling with the hunters, or any chance comer who desired to contest. The settlers heard of these games, and came in to see them.

"Why don't Wetzel try?" asked one. "Can't he do anything but fire off a gun?"

So to please them Wetzel tried and conquered.

His enormous strength found few competitors and no rivals. His prowess with the rifle was well known, and hardly any would take part against him in shooting. His speed of foot was marvelous, and his endurance something that created a species of awe in the hunters, themselves no mean runners. His wrestling soon left him without an antagonist. And this was how he contributed to their amusement.

And thus, though he conquered, and conquered so easily, he made no enemies, and those he worsted most admired him most. For once, when he had hurt a man in wrestling with him, he constituted himself the man's nurse, and tended him assiduously and carefully as a woman. He entered into the sports with no bragging tendencies, and only consented to take part after much pressing and when a refusal would have created ill-feeling. Such a man is bound to make few enemies. In fact, he has been represented by those who knew him at this period as being a general favorite, no less for his personal qualities than for his services.

Now, constituting a part of the amusements, there was called a shooting-match at Maysville, and after long coaxing Wetzel consented to take a part in the contest.

The day came and brought its crowds, and the competitors of the scout were resolved to have their revenge.

But the usual luck attended him, for he would not shoot ill; he entered solemnly into everything he attempted and with the full intention to do his best. The match being so unequal, and finding at what a disadvantage he placed his rivals, Wetzel at length offered to withdraw.

The opposition to his intention was not overpoweringly strong; and waiting a little while to look on, so as not again to be accused of a lack of congeniality and good feeling, he slipped unperceived from the noisy party, and made his way to an adjoining tavern and had a pot of cider placed before him.

Into this place others soon after straggled, for when Wetzel stopped shooting the interest to many was over. Then his rivals sauntered in, discontented and not overly pleased with the man over there in the corner silently drinking his cider and paying little or no attention to any one.

"It was the fault of my powder," declared one.

"My shot were too light," said another.

"That gun of mine has got to be looked over," cried a third.

"Give in, boys," laughed an old man, "and blame the right cause of your failure."

"You mean Wetzel," said two or three at once, looking darkly over towards his corner.

"I mean yourselves," laughed the old man.

All the same they eyed Wetzel grudgingly.

In the midst of the talk, which now became general and noisy, one voice pitted against another, and all against every one, and when some were blaming Wetzel for taking part at all and so easily putting them all out of countenance, there came the ring of a sword pounding on the door lintel. There entered a lieutenant of the regular army, who was on his way down the Ohio to Fort Washington.

"Welcome, lieutenant," cried some of the men; "and here's to you!"

"Thanks, thanks, good fellows all," responded the lieutenant, "and here's at yourselves! I only stopped because I heard your loud voices, and I knew there was a chance here of getting a generous nip of real cider. I see by indications that some of you have been having sport of some sort."

"Only a shooting-match, and that wasn't a match, after all," responded one of the discomfited heroes.

"How is that?" asked the new-comer.

"Well, one of us is too good a shot for the others, and he won't shoot bad to please us."

The lieutenant laughed.

"You could hardly expect him to come down from the pedestal," he said. "I am only sorry that I came too late to be a witness of all this. Can't we have a little match now?"

"Not if Wetzel takes part," replied the man.

"Wetzel!" repeated the lieutenant. "So he was the champion? No wonder you were all beaten. I have heard of him."

"Oh, you've heard of him? I hope a good many have heard of him?"

"Tell us something new," cried the same old man who had once before spoken. "You're sure you've heard of Wetzel, eh?"

The lieutenant laughed good-humoredly, and paid for a stoup of cider all around.

"Won't the man in the corner have some?" he asked, nodding his head in that direction.

"If the man in the corner wants some, the man in the corner can say so," returned a discomfited hero, not quite over his bad shot.

But the man in the corner did not say so, and the others drank their cider without his company.

The lieutenant ordered a little more, looking over to the man in the corner, anxious that he should drink. Then the lieutenant paid the reckoning, and moved towards the door.

"Well, as we cannot have a match, I'll go down to my boat. Good-day to you!"

"Stay a little longer, lieutenant; maybe we'll get up the match. Only wait awhile."

But the lieutenant had hurried out.

"What made him act so strangely?"

"He was afraid of Wetzel," said one; "did you see how he eyed him?"

"More likely he was afraid of being asked to pay for more cider for us."

"Not troubled with politeness, anyhow; he didn't even tell us his name."

But Lieutenant Lawler had hurried down to his boat.

"A file of men immediately!" he cried.

The men came to shore with all speed.

"To the tavern," he ordered, "and seize the man Wetzel there. Go hurriedly, seize him at once, and hurry him down to the boat, before there is a chance of an interference. We must take him by surprise."

They went forward, and reached the tavern.

"That is your man," cried Lieutenant Lawler, indicating Wetzel, who was sitting at a table in the corner, playing a game of checkers with his host's little son.

The company in the room, taken by the surprising boldness of the proceeding, gazed on with open-mouthed wonder.

A party of the soldiers rushed upon the scout, pinioned his arms, hustled him from the tavern, and ran him down to the boat and pushed from shore before those left behind in the tavern had recovered from their astonishment.

It was only when the boat was far down the river that those on board saw the tavern door suddenly fly open, and a host of wild, indignant men hurry down to the river side, gesticulating and yelling after the receding boat, and vowing vengeance with voices that made those who heard them involuntarily grasp their rifles. But a rescue was all too late, and the men on the shore grew smaller and more indistinct while the boat rowed on and on with its prisoner safely bound.

That same night Lieutenant Lawler delivered Wetzel to General Harmar in Cincinnati.

"So, Wetzel, we meet again," said the general. "You will not again have the chance to reward my clemency so vilely. Your irons will be doubly strong this time, and you must become used to a lack of exercise."

There was the trial and subsequent condemnation, for Wetzel never denied shooting the Indian at Marietta; he would have disdained to do so.

"Speak, Lewis Wetzel," was said to him during the trial. "Are you guilty or not guilty?"

Wetzel folded his arms and faced his accusers.

"Guilty of what?" he asked.

"Of murdering a fellow-being in cold blood, without provocation."

"I killed an Indian—that is my crime," said Wetzel.

Certain well-disposed people clearly saw that it was their mission in life to endeavor to impress such a reckless man with the true meaning of murder. These came to him and talked to him, and left with the idea that if they had not edified him, at least they had not been unedified themselves. They spoke to him as though they were speaking to a child, as so many good-intentioned make the mistake of imagining that a great criminal should not be allowed to explain himself, but that they should explain themselves, and try to make him understand that he is a most hardened wretch; and, as the laws of the land grant him little mercy here, the Higher Law can scarcely be expected to do much for him in lenient treatment hereafter.

The criminal has his story to tell, and that story more often than not justifies him in the commission of his act—in his own eyes. The crime he knows, as well as do his accusers; but he alone knows the sting of the provocation, and, while the act is a stigma, the facts leading to it are the excuse. Criminals to be made to comprehend that something more than man's law and order have been overthrown by a flagrant act, must feel that eyes as benignant as those turned upon the thief dying on the cross are reading their hearts and guaging the possibilities of their souls. For crime, in the eyes of him who commits it, surely has not the horror which it holds for us when we calm and cool ones read of its commission.

This will be explained when we realize that it would have been impossible, in his then frame of mind, for Lewis Wetzel to have seen murder in the killing of the Indian at Marietta; he could bring evidence after evidence, based upon biblical precedent, to place his act within the pale of Divine commandment.

Judas was a murderer in his sight,—the basest, most unscrupulous he could imagine,—nothing more; for Judas never knew that he plotted the murder of his Lord—he would have known that Divinity could not suffer at the hands of man, even if man could be so insane as to imagine such a thing, which Judas could not. Herodias was a murderess, because something more than mere revenge for insult actuated her; her guilt cursed her, and made her see in murder mere retaliation, not revenge. But Goliath had not been murdered, nor had Samson murdered his tormentors. Therefore it was a needless and thankless task these good-intentioned people had taken upon themselves when they tried to teach him that the killing of an Indian was the act of a Judas.

He was thought to be hardened and lost to conscience—abandoned to the devil and his works. He was sentenced to death by hanging.

But General Harmar, although well acquainted with the routine of military service, was somewhat destitute of the practical sense of it, which is always indispensable in frontier settlements in which such severe measures as were exercised in Wetzel's case are more likely to rouse the settlers to revolt than to intimidate them, and he soon found that the country around him was up in arms and determined to resist him.

For the story of Wetzel's capture and proposed punishment for the mere fault of shooting an Indian had spread through the various settlements like wild-fire, kindling the ever ready passions of the frontiermen to a pitch of fury. "He shall never die," they said. "We will rescue him or die ourselves. The principle we laid down must be maintained. And after all this time to go and capture the man! It would appear that the army has had nothing to do but plot to waylay one white man, while the ravages of the Indians are not repressed, and peace is preached to us who must submit, and we are told that to disobey a soldier is to disobey the law of the land."

Meetings were held, and indignant protests made. People straggled in from all sides "to see justice done." There was but one voice in the matter—the scout must go free. "Not that he is Wetzel," they persisted so in saying that no one believed them, "but because our principle is involved. The man shall not hang. We will see who has the strongest arm—this military man who comes ignorantly among us and presumes to teach us our duties towards a miscreant race who murder and pillage us with impunity, or we who own the land and who have gained it inch by inch from just such foul thieves as this savage that Wetzel killed for us."

Petitions for the release of Wetzel came pouring in upon General Harmar from all quarters and from all classes of society.

At first he paid little or no attention to them.

"They are the protests of indignant friends," he said, "which are natural in any case of a criminal sentenced to death."

But it was not Lewis Wetzel who called forth all of the protests so much as the principle involved, came the after-report.

If a man was to be hanged for killing an Indian, then would society go to the dogs, and no man's property would be assured to him either by law or justice. No, Wetzel represented themselves; his fate represented the retention or the slipping away of all the property which had become theirs by dint of struggle and untold difficulties.

There was little else thought of, little else talked of. While the settlers determined that Wetzel should not suffer for the execution of an Indian thief, their farms were probably more devastated by red-skins than they ever had been before. For nothing was guarded now, and cattle and garden-stuff might go until after this difficulty was adjusted.

But an Indian dared not show himself around while the ire was unabated. The troublesome affair became known to the savages, and there was not one met with during all the time of Wetzel's incarceration; but they worked their depredations silently in the night, and woe to the Indian that a scout would have come across just then.

"And yet it is but a test case," said an old hunter, who had been in the court room as a juryman once, and who, therefore, was considered quite an authority on legal points.

"A test case!" echoed a handsome virago, her arms akimbo. "Call it a test case, do you? I'd like to make a test case. Here, somebody go and bring me in an Injun, and I'll pretty soon make a test case of him. Hang Lewis Wetzel, will they?—the man that mended my tubs without being asked, and never said a word about it! Never! I wish I had my ten fingers in General Harmar's eyes, wouldn't he see stars! Hang Lewis Wetzel, will they?"

At length the settlements all along the Ohio, and those even of the back counties, began to embody in military array to release the prisoner by force of arms. And many of these indignant people were women and even little children. These many stern faces meant something which military law had scarcely ever encountered.

Representations were made to Judge Symmes which induced him to issue a writ of *habeas corpus* in the case.

"Who will go security for Lewis Wetzel's good behavior?" was asked in court.

"Good behavior!" cried a woman, "why you must be a fool. There isn't a better mannered man in the country than Lewis Wetzel. You don't know what politeness is."

"Order in the court!"

When order had been restored, the question was again put as to who would be security for the scout.

A party of hunters, who had attended the trial from first to last, now came forward with big bags of money in their hands.

"We're his bondsmen," said one.

"Yes, we're his bondsmen," repeated the others in chorus.

"Have you any property?"

"Here it is," holding out the bags.

"But I mean *landed* property."

"Bless the man's sweet eyes! Just as if gold wasn't landed property!—just as if gold wasn't safer than land in these Indian settlements. Now, judge, just you look here! Landed property, do you say? Do you mean *land?* Perhaps, then, you'd like us to go out and dig up a whole prairie and bring it into this here court and give it to you as a security for Wetzel's decent conduct hereafter—is that your meaning, judge? We don't quite get the hang of these here court proceedings, but if that's your meaning, just out with it, and if we can't lodge a whole prairie here, we'll bring you the stock of one, —grass, bisons, wolves, and Injuns,—and you can keep them all as long as you want to—'specially the Injuns. Say, now, look here! this good, honest gold will have to do, judge. And bless the Injun we come across on our way out; they'll remember this day. Take the gold, judge?"

"The prisoner is acquitted!"

With shouts and wild hallooing, Wetzel was lifted out of the rude dock, and borne aloft on the shoulders of half a dozen brawny men, and taken out into the open air.

Such shouting, such festivity! A chance-comer might have supposed that Alexander or some mythical conqueror had come to life again. The principle was preserved intact, and Wetzel represented the entire country.

He was borne in triumph to Columbia, where he was feasted and fêted. The place bore the appearance of a fair, and the festivities lasted two days. And not an Indian was to be seen, nor a camp-fire smoke in the sky.

And while the Indians had the good sense to remain in covert, it was equally good that Lieutenant Lawler's duties did not lead him down that way.

"Let him come!" said the lady of the courthouse.

Wetzel is thus described at this period, August, 1789:

Twenty-six years of age, about five feet, nine inches high. Full-breasted, very broad across the shoulders, arms very large, skin dark, face heavily pitted with small-pox His hair when combed out reached to the calves of his legs. His eyes were very black, and when he was excited they sparkled with such vindictiveness for his enemies that few cared to provoke him to wrath, although he was very forbearing. He was quiet and kindly of voice. His morals were never impeached.

CHAPTER XVIII.

THE INDIAN CAMP.

FROM all records and tales which have come down to us, it appears that Wetzel had now his regular seasons for hunting Indians, as other men around him were accustomed to hunt for deer and buffalo, and to shoot them down wheresoever he might chance upon them, with as little compunction as he would have shot a deer or a panther. He knew the seasons when his advantage of attacking his prey would best reward his search. Before this time he had, of course, studied the habits of the red man, but hate made him understand their very intentions, it would seem, and he appeared to scent them long before any one else knew of their advent into his vicinity.

His predilection was known to every one, and often, when his fine aim would have been desirable in a lick of deer, some one of the hunters would say:

"There is no use asking Wetzel to waste powder on a mere deer. He has other and more worthless game to track."

For his recent liberation did not elate him, nor did the warning of his incarceration weigh very heavily on him. He went about his self-imposed task as though he had gone through no experience that any time had threatened him with disaster. He harbored no ill-will towards his captors or his judges.

"They only did their duty as they understood it," he said, "and as I do mine."

So he only waited until the fall of the leaf to set out on one of his old expeditions. For days before going he prepared his implements, the little children playing around him, and then one morning he was missed.

He had set off alone the night before on an Indian hunt. At this time of the year the Indians were generally scattered in small parties around their hunting-grounds, making their lazy provisions for the winter's subsistence. For the renewed vigilance of the settlers had made the red-skins more wary, and they ventured less within the enclosures of the farmers, fearful of hidden rifles and scientifically wielded tomahawks. Their spies had seen and reported the liberation of Wetzel, and they divined what they had to expect now that the scout was held on his good behavior, and what they might look for at the hands of his friends who guaranteed in court that he would behave himself in the most praiseworthy manner.

Wetzel going out in the night proceeded in his little canoe to a point some where on the Muskingum River. Here he paused, attracted by a soft movement in the bushes hedging the river. He divined that this was the vicinity for him. He laid all night in his canoe watching for morning to show him more.

"I scent them," he said.

He put aside now the recent celebrations over his regained liberty with a species of disgust.

"Why did I let them feed me, when there was work for me to do here?" he said, and quite hated what he called his weakness in having submitted to the wishes of his admirers and letting them do with him as they pleased.

At the first break of morning light he landed, and, securing his canoe and hiding it in the bushes, he proceeded to reconnoiter.

He had not proceeded far when he perceived a thin thread of smoke arising and blurring the sky.

He followed that thread of smoke! Nearer and nearer he came to the place from which it emanated. Then he could hear the low guttural tones peculiar to the Indian voice, and he crept forward through the under-brush, and, sooner than he expected, he sighted within a short distance of him an Indian camp where four braves had fixed their quarters for a hunt.

They were gathered about the fire now, early as it was, and were lazily complaining that they could not sleep any more, having gone to rest at an earlier hour than usual the night before.

They were great, strapping fellows, and their murderous faces argued ill for the foe attacked without the fullest provision for defensive warfare. But they were not on the war-path now, but were amicably inclined,—towards themselves,—and were only waiting till *afternoon* when they should be sufficiently rested to go for a stroll through the adjacent plantation, as they could take their ease and rest when nothing important claimed their attention.

Wetzel, lying in the bushes, leaned forward to catch the intent of their conversation, and to try to find out if their camp meant depredation of a white settler or merely a pleasure jaunt.

That it was the latter he soon understood, and regarded the men eagerly—his was a *pleasure* jaunt also. The Indians were so wholly unsuspicious of any enemies prowling about them so late in the season that they had neglected the precaution of out-posts, and were completely off their guard, keeping neither watch nor sentinel.

Wetzel at first hesitated as to the propriety of attacking such an uncompromising number. But after a little spell of cogitation he concluded to trust to his usual good fortune, and so he began to meditate on his mode of making an attack. He concluded that their first sleep was the best time for him to begin the work of death. He sat down and watched them there, stern as fate, and as relentless.

The afternoon came on, and the sun filled the wood with resinous perfumes. The braves got up from their recumbent positions, stretched and yawned, and sauntered off through the thicket.

Wetzel, too, glided further off from the camp to rest awhile. He thought that about midnight their senses would be most wrapped in stupor, and that that would be the proper time for him to enter their camp.

He determined to walk to the camp with his rifle in one hand and his tomahawk in the other. Should any of them happen to be awake at the time, he could shoot one, and then run off in the darkness of the night, assured of a hiding-place in the friendly forest, and thus he could make his escape. Should they all be asleep, he would make the onslaught with his trusty aids—his scalping-knife and tomahawk.

Day passed away, and darkness came. A lost

mocking-bird filled the wood with plaintive, broken melody of unrest and grief for the passing summer. Other songsters answered here and there, and the place was like a harbor of innocent yearning. Like a disturbing spirit to ruin all this innocence, through the darkness came the scout, silent and sure, towards the open spot where reposed his sleeping victims. The light from their fire soon shone upon the glistening autumn leaves, lighting them up with new radiance. It showed a path directly to the men beside it. It crackled its warning voice, but did not awake them; it sent its flame jets across their dusky faces, but did not disturb them; it sent its smoke across their nostrils, but still they slept. The fire, their only friend at night in places where wild animal foes abounded, could not deter the human foe, but lighted him on his way.

That human foe was now standing amid the illumination. He saw around the fire the heavy-blanketed enemies,—four sleeping forms, helpless as babes in the partial death of sleep.

For a minute or so Wetzel regarded them. Was he admiring their splendid physique, their calm, even, unobstructed breathing, that told of freedom from all bodily ills, and a wholesome lack of fear? Was he thinking that possibly there were dusky women in far-off, silent lodges tenderly dreaming of these men, seeing in their sleep the possible dangers they might encounter, and fearing for their safety now that the white man was equal to them in cunning? Was he thinking that possibly little children were waiting for these men, and at every sound in the morrow's air running in expectation of meeting them and being raised aloft in strong, caressing arms?

While looking down on those sleeping forms, he was thinking of the best mode of attacking them!

He set his rifle against a tree, determining to use only his knife and tomahawk, as these promised surer aid if used properly by a well-strung arm whose sinews were not relaxed by dissipation.

He leaned forward, cool and self-possessed, the fire-sparks striking and stinging his face. He stood thus for a second. Then he raised aloft the tomahawk, sent it whizzing down to the head nearest him, and then raised it, reeking, and the death had begun.

With hideous yells, he aimed the tomahawk at the second Indian's head; and for a second time there was a dull thud, and fresh red added to the terrible instrument of death. Then the third Indian was rising, confused and confounded at the unexpected attack, but with two blows he was stretched lifeless beside his companions. The remaining Indian dashed a blanket over the fire that showed him to his foe, and Wetzel made a rush forward to him.

But he was too late; the brave had escaped without his blanket, and was speeding through the brush, and the fire was smouldering and muttering.

Wetzel pursued him for some distance, but he did not succeed in coming up to him. He then returned to the camp, scalped the three Indians, pulled up stakes, and made for the white settlements.

What ghosts must have affrighted him as he went through those gloomy woods in the heart of the night had he stopped to imagine such a possibility! The spirits of the Indians who had fallen by his hand might have made a strong company of accusers to point at him with their fingers, asking him for their lives which he had so wantonly deprived them of while they were in the full glory and lustiness of early manhood! And he might have answered such dread spirits:

"My father's life was worth far more than all of these!—and where is that?"

So he made his way onward, gained his canoe, and went down the river.

When he came into the settlement after this expedition, he was asked what sort of luck he had had.

"Not very good," he said. "I treed four Indians, and one got away from me. I have taken but three scalps, after all my pains and fatigues."

"Well, luck can't always go along without some disappointment," was the consoling reply, "and you must hope for better things next time."

"Oh, I don't complain—I don't complain," said Wetzel, and fastened his canoe to a pole by the river, and told some adventurous children not to venture there, as the water was deep.

CHAPTER XIX.

THE HUT IN THE STORM.

WETZEL knew that the Indian who had escaped him would make it hot work for him to avoid the many braves sent out to avenge the other three.

He knew that, while he sported with little children in the settlements, councils were called in the distant woods, and the peace-pipe buried and war-paint donned, and all for him. For one of the Indians he had killed had been a "big brave," and his scalp was adorned by a circlet of brilliantly-dyed feathers, while the leggings he had worn were deftly wrought with beads and horse-hair, and his blanket jingled with the bits of bright glass and metal and stone that fringed it.

Reports came that an Indian or two had been seen in the woods very near to the heart of the settlement. Men going to look into the truth of the report returned with a denial—nothing was there. But Wetzel was not so positive of denial, though he remained silent.

Often has he been well assured in his mind that

while he slept, a sleeping town around him, red men paced patiently and tirelessly before his house, tried the handle of his door, looked in at his window; that when he walked through the place a red man paced near by him, taking step for step with him, and that, for all he knew, the rifle and tomahawk were often raised on him, only to fall back again because of the approach of some one whose coming augured death to the would-be dealer of death; that only the superior numbers of the settlers prevented an open attack on the whole settlement. For the Indians no longer mustered in large enough numbers, nor so far inland, to attack by any preconcerted movement a place inhabited by even a score of white settlers.

So the holding-out qualities of the whites had reduced the Indians to a sort of subjection; and the red man in his lodge could only point abroad and tell his children that once upon a time his fathers owned and held, without any question of their title to the ground, all that sweep of land between them and the setting sun, all those herds of horses and cattle, all those fields of grain and fruits; while now no red man dared claim an ell of land, the horse he rode was begrudged him, and supposed to belong to some white adventurer from whom it had been feloniously purloined, and that only the grave promised a last resting-place, where no longer the body would be tortured by hunger and the mind with constant apprehension. No red man could understand why all this had come to pass, and no red man at this distant day can understand and feel assured that it is just and right. The white man's logic must ever fall powerless upon the ear of the red man, who once possessed the land upon which the white logician has built his house, and who invites the red man thither to listen to reasons why the house and land are the white man's and not the Indian's.

Wetzel, after his last adventure, rested a little while inactive. He, in common with the settlers, was beginning to understand that the Indians no longer possessed that unique simplicity of character which should let them trade their possessions of inestimable value for a bunch of beads or a bottle of fire-water. They began to comprehend that the Indians had become systematized, and that they had learned, in a perverted form, the value of the white man's right and wrong. The settler was now compelled to be wary at all times in all places, for Indians were even now presenting claims, for damages done, to the white courts in different provinces. In the Eastern States there were arising philanthropists to look after the interests of the

Indians, and who, leaving theology to its professors, undertook to look after the worldly interests of "our oppressed and native population." The romance of Indian life afar off attracted the attention of readers and thinkers, and the wrongs of an indigenous race were looked upon as the wrongs of individual Indians who had degenerated from the noble red man, by intermixture with the less principled whites, and a misunderstanding of the meaning of civilization, into the veriest cut-throats and blackguards on the face of the earth.

The settlers knew the Indians as they found them, and had no theory of their merits and demerits beyond a doubt of every word they asseverated to be truth and every moral they professed to have.

These friendly disposed whites afar off made the evil-intentioned savages more bold and unprincipled than they had been before. They arose from what those whites called *oppression*, and were slyer and more cruel than ever.

No white man could tell Lewis Wetzel more about Indians than he already knew; he had tested the romance when he was a child, and the reality had not been difficult to learn.

So on his next scout he used a little more precaution, and resolved to be more on the alert till the excitement among the Indians attendant upon his last attack on their people should have subsided. But he met few or none of the red-skins for a long time on this new scout. And this time he had undertaken the adventure as much to find out the intentions of the Indians upon the whites as anything else—to ascertain how far the sympathy for the savages had awakened in their untutored breasts a fierce revolt against all hitherto accepted restriction of their privileges. But he could not come across a lodge, his foes had all apparently left the neighborhood and gone further West, and the doubts and apprehensions at the white settlements must therefore be without any foundation. He resolved to learn if his opinion on this head were correct, and then he would go back and take the welcome news to the settlers.

Now during this search there came a wretched night of storm and rain. Those who have never experienced a storm such as the wilds of Virginia suffered can form but a faint conception of what is meant by only rain and wind. At last, drenched to the skin and chilled, Wetzel came across a half-destroyed cabin, and crept into it for shelter. He groped his way to the loft, as being less draughty, and threw himself down to sleep.

How long he slept he knew not. The howling wind and the deluge of rain could not wake him.

But suddenly there seemed to cross his brain a vivid flash of light. It was not lightning; it was not white enough for that, even if it had been the season for it. Then another flash came, and stayed longer than the first.

He opened his eyes, and saw the flames coming up the entrance to the loft. He heard voices below.

"He came here," said one voice in the Indian tongue; "he was near here all day long."

"He is not here now," grumbled another, "or he would have taken shelter here. Curse him!"

"He does not mind the weather," said the first speaker.

"Neither do we," was the answer, "but this rain is such as I never saw before."

Wetzel, in the loft, crept forward to the entrance, and looked down through the flame. Below were six Indians, who had taken possession of the hut, lighted a blazing fire, and were busily preparing their supper.

"But this light will attract his attention," said one of the Indians.

"Good!" said another; "let it attract him. See, this hut has a loft; let us go there, and wait till he comes along, and, thoroughly wet and tired to death, seeing the place empty, enters."

Wetzel, in the loft above, drew his keen knife,

determined that did they put this project into execution, and attempt to enter the loft, he would fight for his life till the last drop of blood in his veins was expended.

"But we will eat our supper first," one of the Indians now said, "and then we will talk of it."

They gorged themselves with the meat they had cooked, and then began a loose, disjointed talk.

Wetzel knew their characteristics too well to feel that he was in any immediate danger of an attack that night. And sure enough, in the middle of a long preamble, one of the Indians turned over and fell asleep on the floor.

"What a fool to sleep," said one of his companions, "when there is so much to do."

"What is there to do?" asked a third, rubbing his eyes and gaping.

"Why, is not Wetzel to be caught? Then, with his scalp, we will go on to the white settlement, lie in wait, as he did at Fort Harmar, and one by one we will pick off the white cowards, steal their women and children, and teach them what it is to set a man free after he has murdered so many of our braves."

"Humph!" grunted the chorus, but did not appear very much impressed.

The fire was warm and grateful, and supper had

been very tasteful. They relapsed into silence. Then there came a stretching out of one of them, and a second one slept. A few minutes more, and another, the third, followed the example of the other two, and only three remained awake.

"Shall we roast Wetzel?" asked one of these.

Wetzel leaned down from the loft to catch the answer.

"We will half-roast him," was the reply.

"We will then skin him, perhaps?"

"We will treat him as half-roasted Crawford was treated by Captain Pipe."

"Good!" came the grunting reply; "we have much to remain awake for."

"Good!" said the other two.

A minute's silence was enough to allow of a fourth brave sliding forward into the warm ashes of the fire fast asleep.

Only two were left awake, sitting bunched up about the flame, their backs towards the entrance to the loft.

"I had a dream last night," began one of them in a low monotonous voice; "I dreamed I was in the happy hunting-ground, my lodge filled with white-faced squaws, each with coal-black eyes and a cheek red as the bison's blood."

"Good!" grunted the other. "I often have that

dream. I, too, dreamed last night that a snake stung me on the heel, and it turned to a coal of fire when I trampled on it with my bare feet. I had put my foot in the flame in my sleep."

"Ugh!"

They bundled themselves up closer, their eyes sleepily fixed on the fire, and rocked their bodies slowly to and fro.

Noiselessly Wetzel lowered himself from the loft, his eyes fixed upon the two, his long, keen knife between his teeth.

They did not perceive him; they had ceased rocking their bodies—they were asleep.

Noiselessly the scout crawled over the prostrate forms on the floor, and so gained the door-way and the wrack of the storm. Once one of the sleeping Indians moved, and the scout thought he was discovered. He paused for an instant to ascertain if this were the fact. But the savage only turned in his sleep, and was now snoring. Wetzel gained the door-way.

"Must I go sneaking away? Must I let these men who are seeking my life go on with their brutal quest?" he asked himself. "No, I cannot do that. And then the dreams of those two!"

He hid himself behind a log at some little distance from the door, and resolved to wait all night there.

The storm was at its height, and terrified animals came and sniffed at his hiding-place jealous of his safety. A wolf came up to him and whined piteously in his ear, then turned and plunged into the vortex of water that flowed roaring across the land below. The light from the ruined cabin showed the water like ruby wine, and Wetzel could see the draggled wolf struggling in the eddies that bore him on, yelping his death-cry, and buffeting the water with his fast diminishing strength.

All night this storm raged, the like of which had rarely been experienced there. And soaked in water, but holding his rifle and ammunition close up to his skin to protect them from the weather, Wetzel waited until day-break. In the morning the storm had passed away, leaving ruin and devastation in its track. Huge trees were overturned, countless birds lay dead and strewn upon the ground. The ruined cabin looked as though it were upon an island, the water had so sloughed deep passage-ways on all sides of it. The wonder was that the ramshackle place had held out. But so it is; forest trees which task all a man's strength and ingenuity to uproot and tear apart succumb to the fury of the storm which tears them apart into fibrous masses. But the handiwork of frail man who could not move the tree, still dominated by that feeble strength and giant ingenuity, withstands hurricane and natural phenomena against which all else is powerless and futile.

In the early dawn the East was blooming into color, and the earth was glad and bright after the overthrow of the night before. But the storm had not washed out man's handiwork, any more than it had washed out from his heart the spirit of crime and the aching for revenge—any more than that storm that settled about that lonely Figure on the Cross and made the earth black with sudden night failed to wipe away the spirit that had placed the Crucified One there and did not tremble for the enormous crime.

In the early morning, from that dismantled cabin in the ruined place, stepped forth the tall form of a savage. He stretched up both his arms, yawned ecstatically, and seemed to take in a deep inspiration of the invigorating air.

The next instant there was the sharp snap of a rifle, the Indian fell heavily to the ground, and with the smoking gun in his hand, Wetzel was darting through the sodden wood, secure from pursuit.

"I could not leave them *all*," he said.

For hours, in all bodily distress, had he lain there to accomplish this one task—to send a soul to its reckoning unasked by its Maker.

His own would have gone had he been caught, and this, in his eyes, and in the eyes of people belonging to a late generation, was sufficient to exonerate him from any accusation of guilt. That he might have escaped, was not the thing; his enemy and he could not live on the same earth at the same time; the wide world is not wide enough for the man who knows that among the millions of men around him is one who seeks to strip him of his life, and who never forgets, in all the distractions which that wide world and its millions of other men hold out to him, that he will not have sufficient room until there is one man less, and he can go through the million miles, among the million men, conscious that there is no chance of coming face to face with the only one whose living is a reproach to him and the crying evil of his times.

CHAPTER XX.

THE STORY OF THE LOVERS.

EVERYWHERE that Lewis Wetzel now went the story of his arrest and detention seemed to have preceded him, and made him one of the foremost men of the rude places where he had not been known before. The principle of the settlers in common was the principle of every man in particular; and Wetzel had vindicated that principle, and he alone. And so was Wetzel elevated to a height of heroism which was as irksome to himself as it was extravagant in its premises.

The vast number of scalps he had taken proved his invincible courage, as well as his prowess in war; the persecutions and sufferings by which he had been pursued by General Harmar secured for him the sympathy of the frontiermen. The higher he was esteemed, the lower sank the character of General Harmar with the fiery spirits of the frontier.

Had General Harmar possessed a tithe of the courage, skill, and indomitable energy of Wetzel, the gallant soldiers under his command in the memorable and disastrous campaign against the Miamis might have shared a different fate.

The estimation in which the scout was held, however, may, to the casual reader, appear to be the admiration of a wild set of men for one wilder than themselves. The heroism of the man may seem to disappear under the almost unnatural ferociousness of his enmity, and it may be adjudged that, in wreaking an almost insane revenge, the better parts of manly nature were blunted and obscured, and that religion, the most noble characteristic of a noble character, had little share in his being.

That he was not without religion is plainly proved, I think; that is, that his religion partook more of that which the Old Testament inculcates,—that of stern determination that a criminal must suffer for his crime. And yet he was loved by little children, and the simplicity of his helpfulness was such that other men looked upon him as a tower of strength, and scarcely knew what, besides his recklessness, drew them towards him.

The contradictions in his character may prove the kind of religion his was. His boyhood had been dwarfed, the only being he ever truly loved had been torn from him and murdered before his eyes at a time of his life when he was most impressionable, and might as easily be swayed by wrong as by right.

Looking dispassionately upon a life like his, at this wide separation from it and its living causes for impulse and at this time of ease and safety, the wonder seems to consist in the fact that from that boy grew up a man with the honorable intentions of Lewis Wetzel—that he did not, by reason of his love and its overthrow, sink below the level and become an outlaw in the truest sense of the word.

Instead of which, are there many who will call him a bad man? "By their fruits ye shall know them." The fruits in Lewis Wetzel's case were not perfect, being of human origin; but from those fruits came surer protection to the settlers, and turned the eyes of the country upon white man and Indian alike, arguing better treatment for both; for the settlers were not treated as they had a right to expect, and which the urgency of their cases demanded. They were settling an almost irreclaimable country, and no means but their own personal exertions were given them, and even these exertions were some times cramped by unmeaning authority in high places.

Shortly after his return from Kentucky, a relative of Lewis Wetzel, living on Dunkard Creek, came to the settlement where the scout was and invited him to go home with him on a visit.

The man was not used to houses, nor did he love them any more, and the ties of blood seemed weak in him, in his care for communities. But this was a relative of his father, so he accepted the invitation. They made their way on foot, hunting as they went. Wetzel had been silent one day for a long time. At last he said, as they rested on a log:

"Simon, I doubt if I shall go all the way with you, my lad."

",What, Wetzel," cried the young fellow, "and after all my preparation for you? Do you know I have gathered all these birds purposely for you?"

"For me?"

"Yes, I want you to see how Tilly can cook."

"Tilly! Who is that?" asked Wetzel.

"Was there ever such a man!" cried the young man. "Here I have been talking of Tilly, Tilly, Tilly, and nothing but Tilly, all the way, and you do not know who she is. Did you not know it was a young woman?"

"Old women can be named Tilly, too, I suppose."

"But young men won't talk quite so much about old Tillies as I have been talking. Can't you guess who she is?"

"Maybe your sister. Maybe you told me you had a sister!"

"Maybe somebody else's sister. Upon my word, Wetzel, you are a regular Indian in your refusal to ask questions. It is not such an easy matter for a man who meets another man for the first time—and you are almost a stranger to me—to tell him that he is going to be married. Yes, Tilly will be my wife. I wanted to surprise you when you saw her; such a beauty as she is. I suppose you know a beautiful woman when you see one?"

"Oh, I don't know."

"Don't know! Then you are a heathen!"

"Nay, Simon," said Wetzel in a softened voice, for he was always in sympathy with tender minded men, "there has been too much said about my being a heathen. I am only anything rather than a heathen—I am only a weak man like other men, like you; and like other men, strong physically, my bodily excellence often makes me seem mentally deficient. People too often associate religion with weakness. Whatever my beliefs or disbeliefs may be, I am never a heathen. Perhaps those with the strongest faith are not always those who speak oftenest of it."

"But you take so little interest in men and their doings."

"It may be, and it may not be. I take little interest in my own doings. I am impelled forward to do the work of my life, and I do it; some power within me urges me on; what it is I know not. I only know that the power is there, and that I cannot gainsay it. There are so many things that urge us against even our own convictions; so I am sure you will not judge me harshly here. And now tell me about the young woman—Tilly. When shall you be married? How can I help you and her? Have you a house to take her in?"

"Now, that's something like," cried the young fellow. "If there's anything I despise it is to talk on and on about the woman I love, and have people look and act as though she were just like other women. No woman with a lover is just like other women. Two married women are precisely alike, as all men are precisely alike. But a young woman who loves a man for the first time is unlike anything on the earth, though there be millions of young women that are in the same pickle with herself. The pickle is the same, the young women are not. Don't you see?"

"If I fail to see, it is not your fault, Simon; and maybe I appreciate pickles better than I do women. And yet a women to me is something sacred. And once there was a time when I could have——. But go on, go on."

So in the green wood, with a soft accompaniment of bird-songs and whispering leaves, there was heard a lengthy dissertation on the excellences of the young woman to whose house the lover was bearing his cousin, the scout.

With patience and attention Wetzel listened, being careful to comment and ask questions that brought wordy answers, and altogether redeemed himself in the eyes of his companion.

Then, the tale over for the time, they proceeded onward, shooting a few more birds further to test the culinary accomplishments of the lady under discussion.

When they were but one day's journey from her home, the lover was all impatience to go forward. No more stopping to talk, no more stopping for more birds; they must go onward, and rapidly. Wetzel, yielding to the importunities of his companion, struck out with him. Towards sundown they neared a clearing. Wetzel's eyes were fixed on the ground.

"What do you see, Wetzel," asked the young man.

"Nothing of much account," was the answer. "Have we much further to go?"

"Only a short distance," cried the enraptured lover, "and then you will see such a sight. A little cottage overhung with vines, a bird in a cage at the door, a snow-white curtain floating from the window, and at the gate, waiting for me, a brown-eyed girl, shading her eyes with her hands, and searching the hills for her lover. A hundred more steps, and we will be out of the woods, and then you will see it all."

But Wetzel's eyes were still anxiously fixed on the ground. He did not raise them till they were out of the woods, and then a wild shriek from the lover caused him to look up.

Where was the vine-hung cottage, with its birdcage and snowy curtain? Where was the brown-eyed girl facing the sunset? There was nothing but a pile of smoking ruins!

The lover had fallen to the ground. Wetzel likewise fell to the ground, but only to examine the trail that had attracted his eyes so long in the woods. He arose again, and shook the prostrate man to his feet.

"Be a man," he said sternly.

"A man!" echoed the other, turning stony eyes upon the scout, "I will be a devil. I will search these Indians to their lair and never rest till——"

"You have recovered your bride. Don't be too rash in your threats. It may not be so bad as you think. There have not been Indians alone here; this trail proves that three Indians and one white man took away the captive."

"Then there is a little hope."

"Not from the white man. Come, we will go, there is nothing to keep us here."

"Nothing," groaned the young man, "and yet it was everything."

Placing himself under the control of Wetzel, the two strode on, hoping to come up to the enemy before they had crossed the Ohio; the yet smoking ruins proving the capture to have taken place that same day. But it was found, after proceeding a short distance, that the savages had carefully obliterated their trail.

"That is the cursed spite of the red devils," cried the young man.

"Rather it is the work of the white man," said Wetzel. "But do not despair; a villainous white man is no match for one who knows the Indians' cunning. Come, I have a plan. Follow me, and keep up a brave hope."

He spoke more hopefully, perhaps, than he felt, but he feared for the sanity of his companion, and he resolved to save *him* if he could, although the young girl might never be recovered. He also knew that the depredators would make for the river by the most expeditious route, and, therefore, he disregarded the trail and pushed on to intercept them at the crossing-place.

"Oh, my dear could never go so far," groaned the lover.

"She could if she were forced to do so," calmly said Wetzel.

"Who would dare to force her?" asked the lover, on fire on the instant.

"That is right," commented Wetzel. "Only keep up that spirit and quit driveling and you may be of some service to the woman whom you think and almost constantly say you love."

"The woman I *say* I love!"

"Yes; I only have your word for it, you have not demonstrated the fact."

Then, without waiting for another word, he pushed on. After an hour or so of hard travel they struck a path which the deer had made, and which their sagacity had taught them to carry over knolls in order to avoid the long curves of ravines.

Thus the pursuers had an unexpected advantage over the wretches they pursued. Wetzel followed the deer-path because he knew that it would eventually prove to lead in almost a direct line to the point for which he was aiming. Night came down in all its starlit beauty; but the very beauty of it seemed to lead one of the men to the confines of despair.

"Such nights we were always on the porch in front of the house," he mourned.

"And you shall be again," said Wetzel. "And now eat this," and he offered some food from his pocket.

"Eat at such a time as this!" cried the other, spurning the morsel.

"Then don't do it, and have no strength left for the preservation of the woman you love."

The young man took the food and ate it, and together they spurred onward, until about midnight, when a heavy cloud obscured the heavens, and they could follow the path no longer.

"We shall have to rest until the morning," said Wetzel.

"Oh, my dear, my dear!" returned the lover. "Will it ever be morning again for you and me?"

The night was passed in miserable watching, not a word on either side. With the first break of day Wetzel looked at his companion, and noted a change in him. There was a new determination in his face, a look of dignity which the stars last night had not seen there.

A rosy pencil of light, tingeing the tops of the highest trees, seemed to point the way to them like a finger from heaven. The young man fell on his knees and prayed, and Wetzel bowed his head. The young man arose and came to him.

"I have seldom prayed," he said calmly, "but my

dear told me she always did when she was in any difficulty or danger. I know that wherever she was last night she was thinking of me and praying for me; wherever she is at this moment her eyes are raised above, and she is asking for divine guidance and support. I prayed all last night that I might be in communion with her, that my words might meet hers in their flight to heaven, and be assisted by hers to reach the throne of mercy. Now let us go on."

Wetzel, still with bowed head, pressed the hand of his friend, and then the two resumed the chase.

After descending from the elevated ridge along which they had been passing for an hour or two, they found themselves in a deep and quiet valley, which looked as though human steps had never before pressed its virgin soil.

Traveling a short distance, they discovered fresh footsteps in the soil. But the eyes of love saw more than this; the lover it was who now fell to his knees and regarded the tracks, crying gladly:

"She has been here, she has been here! Here is the mark of a little shoe with nail-heads around the little heel."

He leaned down and kissed the print of the little shoe in the leafy soil. Hour after hour the pursuit was kept up, now tracing the trail across hills, through valleys, and often detecting it where the wily captors had taken to the beds of streams. Late in the afternoon they found themselves coming nearer to the Ohio, and shortly after dark discovered, as they struck the river, the camp of the enemy upon the opposite side, and just below the mouth of the Captina.

"Can you swim?" asked Wetzel, turning to his companion.

But the young men was already in the water, plunging boldly out for the opposite shore.

Wetzel sprang in after him, and they soon reached the point of their destination.

They reconnoitered the position of the camp, and discovered, they thought, the locality of the captive. Wetzel proposed waiting till daylight before making an attack.

"Wait!" cried the lover, "what can the word mean to her in the hands of those red devils?"

"I don't fear for her safety with the red cusses as much as I do with the white man. A white man on friendly terms with these marauding Indians is worse than a devil; he is a depraved saint," returned Wetzel.

"But I cannot wait until day."

"You must. You have got to be as wary as your enemy. Make an attempt to-night, and the chances are that the first load you fire you will disperse the red-skins, and find your lady love———"

"Yes."

"A corpse! If the Indians would not murder her, the white man with them will."

Shuddering, the lover acceded to the scout's suggestion.

Another sleepless night ushered in a hopeful morning.

At early dawn the savages were up preparing to leave, when Wetzel said:

"Take good aim at the white man, he is your worst enemy. I will look out for my beloved Indians."

Before the words were out of his lips the young fellow was sighting his enemy.

"Careful, careful," cautioned Wetzel, "don't for the life of you miss him. For your lady-love let your shot be. Now!"

They fired at the same moment, and each brought down his man.

But here the lover threw down his gun, rushed forward, and was met by the frightened creature he sought, while the two remaining Indians took to the woods.

Wetzel, with a frown on his face, stepped apart from the two lovers—for what had he to do with these things?

"I have no time for love—I dare not have," he muttered, "or I should fail of my intention and become gentle."

He threw out his arm towards a settlement of whites within half a mile, and called to the rapturous young man:

"That is your way; go seek it."

"But, Wetzel, come here," was the glad cry in reply.

Wetzel, keeping his head averted, answered:

"My way lies in another direction. Farewell!" and he strode into the wood after the two fleeing Indians.

He reloaded his gun, and, failing in his search, fired his rifle at random to draw the Indians from their retreat. The ruse succeeded, and they rushed from their covert of trees and made after him with uplifted tomahawks, and yelling at the top of their voices.

But Wetzel soon had loaded his rifle in his old fashion, and suddenly wheeling around he discharged its contents into the body of his nearest pursuer. The other Indian now rushed forward, thinking to dispatch his enemy immediately, but Wetzel kept dodging from tree to tree, and being more fleet than the Indian managed to keep ahead until his unerring rifle was once more loaded, when turning, he fired, and the last of the party lay dead before him.

He walked about for a little while, then, drawn by an irresistible impulse, he drew towards the open space where he had left the lovers. Far off, radiantly illuminated by the early morning sun, he could see them going lovingly along towards the settlement, the arm of the lover supporting the clinging girl. Long he looked at them, a soft expression on his dark face. Then he turned away.

"It is not for me," he said softly. "This must be my only love and bride," and hugged his trusty rifle to his breast.

CHAPTER XXI.

WETZEL'S BROTHERS.

A FEW words may not be out of place here regarding Lewis Wetzel's brothers. For though the scout was the most prominent member of the family, and the one in whom hatred for their common enemies rankled most strongly, yet the other brothers were not behindhand in bravery, though they earlier settled down to rest and enjoyed the comforts of a fixed home which appears to have ever been denied the scout. They were nearer to the habitation of their mother and sisters, and thought more of the progressive spirit of the West and availed themselves of the many opportunities to become landed proprietors, holding their possessions by lawful fee-simple, and in many ways may be accounted shrewder men than their brother, who in time became almost a stranger to them.

Their sisters looked up to them and almost forgot at times that somewhere in the wilds roved a discontented spirit in whose veins flowed the same blood, and that he protected them afar off as effectually as the stout brothers who were ever within call in time of need.

Leaving Lewis Wetzel for a little while, and confining our story to the other members of his family for the length of one short chapter, it will be found that the hard school which reared the scout might reckon his brothers as adepts in its teachings with small fear of a loss of honor when they were entrusted with the care of its worthy reputation.

It would appear that their mother, having discarded the son who came into these wilds a babe at her breast as thoroughly incorrigible and deaf to the calls of maternal affection, lavished on the remaining children a greater love than had hitherto been theirs—almost as though she expended upon them the share that had once been their brother's, his who wandered through the wilderness an Ishmael whom Hager had grown tired of when he any longer refused to abide with her.

Before her second marriage the mother of the Wetzels never stirred abroad without having one of her sons with her, and her fretful, broken manner was compensated for in the great look of trust and dependence the strapping fellow at her side was ever receiving from her anxious and fear-stricken eyes.

They went on expeditions, and she shuddered for their fate, while she could not withhold them from what she knew was their duty.

The first of these expeditions relating to John Wetzel may be chronicled here, not because of its show of extraordinary bravery on his part, but that there may be a further example of the difference between the brothers. Lewis brooked no interference with his plans and mode of life, while the others viewed any divergence from the law they had laid down to govern them but as a contingency which must be met, and, if it could not be thwarted, then to be turned aside to do as little damage as possible.

Late in the spring of 1786, John Wetzel, who was then about sixteen years of age, coming into his home one day was met by his sister who informed him that a lot of horses had gone astray in the woods, and among them a mare and its foal which had been given to her.

"You can have the colt, if you get the mare for me," she said.

"All right," was the jubilant answer, and the young fellow bounded off.

He sought a companion of his own age, one of the hardy boys of the time, and together they went to the woods on Wheeling Creek. For hours they hunted for the mare and colt, and their search was unavailing, till all at once John Wetzel cried to his companion:

"Hist! I hear a bell."

The other listened intently.

"You are mistaken," he said, "it is the creek washing over the roots of a tree."

"I am not mistaken," asseverated John Wetzel, "for I would know our bells among a thousand."

And so he would. For the settlers who turned their beasts adrift for forage always placed bells on their necks, and so acute had become their sense of hearing that the tinkle of the bells belonging to their own cattle was never mistaken for that of a neighbor's, and, from a herd of animals of the same color and size, the careful housewife or her children could pick out their own cattle by touching the various bells, with very little danger of making the slightest mistake, for each settler trusted this part of the management of his clearing to his wife and children.

And young John Wetzel had not been mistaken in this instance, for he had, indeed, heard the faint tinkle of the bell about the neck of his sister's mare.

"Follow me," he said to his friend, "and we'll see who is mistaken."

They went through the wood, in another direction, for a considerable length of time.

"Queer!" said John Wetzel. "Bess could not have traveled this far since I heard the bell. She knows my voice, too. Ho! Bess, Bess, Bess!"

He stopped to await the result of his calling, but all was quiet once more. Then again came the soft tinkle of the bell, and the lads spurred onward. The bell sounded now quite close.

"Hurrah!" shouted John Wetzel; "the colt is mine," and made for a close covert of dense trees, where he heard the bell plain enough.

He got there only to find it empty of any beast, and the bell tinkled in another direction.

"Strange," he muttered.

"It almost seems as though the bell was leading us deeper into the wood, and for a purpose," said his companion, startled and pausing.

"Come on," cried John Wetzel, for the Wetzels paid little attention to timely warning in those days.

And the two boys followed the bell that, like an *ignis-fatuus*, led them first into one direction, then into another, but leading all the time further and further away from the white settlements.

For the mare and her colt had been come across by a party of marauding Indians and tethered in a thicket, while the bell was detached from the mare's neck and tied to the wrist of a brave, who led the way for the Indians through the under-brush, tinkling the bell at intervals, well knowing that the white settler to whom the beasts belonged would come in early search of them, and would depend upon the sound of the bell to find them. Thus the red-skins soon saw the two boys in search of the missing creatures, and by the sound of the bell they led them into a place of security, where they might easily be captured without any fear of intervention on the part of any rescuing party of the whites.

The horse was ever a favorite object of plunder with the savages, as not only facilitating his own escape from pursuit, but also assisting him in carrying off the spoil.

Into the very heart of the forest these two boys were led by the tinkling of the well-known bell, and they were congratulating themselves upon the rescue of the animals, when there sprang out from the shade four stalwart Indians, who immediately bound the boys with cords.

John, in attempting to escape, was shot through the arm. On their march to the Ohio his companion made so much lamentation and moaning on account of his captivity that the Indians dispatched him with their tomahawks.

The party struck the Ohio River early the following morning, at a point near the mouth of Grave Creek, and just below the clearing of a Mr. Tomlinson. Here they found some hogs, and killing one of them with a rifle, put the carcass into a canoe they had stolen.

Three of the Indians took possession of the canoe with their boy prisoner, while the other Indian was busied in swimming the horses across the river. It so happened that Isaac Williams, Hamilton Carr, and Jacob, a Dutchman, had come down that morning from Wheeling to look after the cattle and hogs left at the deserted settlement at the mouth of the creek.

While at the outlet of Little Grave Creek, about a mile above, they heard the report of a rifle in the direction of the plantation.

"Dod rot 'em!" exclaimed Williams; "a Kentuck boat has landed at the creek, and they are shooting my hogs."

Immediately quickening their pace to a smart trot, they in a few minutes were within a short distance of the creek, when they heard the loud snort of a horse.

Carr being in the prime of life, and younger than Williams, was several rods ahead, and reached the bank in advance of the others.

As he looked down into the creek, he saw three Indians standing in a canoe; one was in the stern, one in the bow, and one in the middle of the boat. At the feet of the latter lay four rifles and a dead hog; while a fourth Indian was swimming a horse across the Ohio, a few rods from the shore. The one in the stern had his paddle in the edge of the water, in the act of turning and shoving the canoe from the mouth of the creek into the river.

Before they were aware of his presence, Carr drew up and shot the Indian in the stern of the boat, and he instantly fell into the water.

The crack of his rifle had scarcely ceased when Williams came on to the bank and shot the Indian in the bow of the canoe, who also fell overboard, as Jacob came up. Carr dropped his own rifle, and seizing that of the Dutchman, shot the remaining Indian who stood in the waist of the boat. He fell over into the water, but still held on to the side of the canoe with one hand. So amazed had been the last Indian at the fall of his companions, that he never offered to lift one of the rifles, which lay at his feet, in self-defense, but acted like one bereft of his senses.

By this time the canoe, impelled by the impetus given to it by the first Indian, had reached the current of the Ohio, and was some rods below the mouth of the creek.

Carr now reloaded his own gun, and, seeing another man lying in the bottom of the canoe, raised it to his face in the act of firing, when he in the bottom of the canoe, seeing the movement, called out:

"Don't shoot, I am a white man."

Carr told him to knock loose the Indian's hand from the side of the canoe and paddle to the shore.

In reply, he said his arm was broken, and that he could not. The current, however, set it near some rocks not far from land, on to which he jumped and waded out.

"Bless my soul!" cried Williams, "if it ain't one o' John Wetzel's boys."

"It's only John, junior," answered the wounded lad, and fell in a faint from the pain in his arm.

Carr now aimed his rifle at the Indian on horseback, who by this time had reached the middle of the Ohio.

The shot struck near him, splashing the water on to his naked skin.

The Indian, seeing the fate of his companions, with the bravery of an ancient Spartan, immediately slipped from the back of the horse, and swam for the abandoned canoe, in which were the rifles of the whole four warriors. This was in fact an act of necessity as well as of noble daring, as he well knew he could not reach his country without the means of killing game by the way.

He gained possession of the canoe unmolested,

crossed with the arms to his own side of the Ohio, mounted the captive horse which had swum to the Indian shore, and, with a yell of defiance, escaped into the woods. The canoe was turned adrift to spite his enemies, and was taken up near Maysville, the dead hog which had been the means of the rescue of the white boy still in it.

The whole of this story is here given, and almost entirely in the exact words of the chronicle, as proving being both interesting and more compressed than most of the stories that have reached us in the verbatim reports of the settlers, who often added to their own personal knowledge of a matter the arguments of any chance settler who came in and proved that he knew as much as the original reporter, only his knowledge was a little fuller and totally at variance with the first man's.

There is a little story of John Wetzel, "junior," meeting a little Indian papoose tied up in its birch-bark box and lying upon the ground in the woods, its mother not being in sight. The boy looked at the grave-eyed child lying in his path, and thought it would be a good plan to steal it. He caught it up and, hugging it closely to him, bore it out of the wood. It kept its great fawn-like eyes on him, and smiled in his face. He bore it on and gained the outer rim of the wood. Here he was confronted by a squaw who held out her arms for the child.

"Mine," she said. "Squaw followed white boy with papoose out of the woods."

Without a word the boy handed her the child, which she eagerly took, raised it above her head and dashed it to the ground, a dead and bleeding thing.

She had no sooner done the fiendish act, when another squaw appeared upon the scene, distraught and wild.

"My papoose," she cried.

She saw it lying upon the ground, and wailed and threw herself beside it in a paroxysm of grief.

All the time the other squaw was looking on unmoved.

Then the grieving one raised herself to her feet again, and turned her blood-shot eyes upon the pair of human beings regarding her.

"Who did that?" she said coldly.

There was no answer.

"White boy did not," she went on; "you did," turning to the squaw.

The one accused did not change her position, standing there gazing calmly at her accuser.

"Did you kill his child because he loved me and did not love you?" asked the mother-squaw, going to her and standing menacingly before her.

The other clearly foresaw a murderous attack, and made no attempt to ward it off, but smiled in the eyes of the woman she had so wronged.

"Kill me!" she said at length; "kill me! I do not want to live. I have not wanted to live since you loved him; kill me, and spare not. Yes, I killed the child; I killed it because I love its father, not because he loves you. I killed it so that I may be killed. Thus do I punish the man who does not love me."

The mother stepped back from her, and moved away.

"Well," cried the other, "what will you do to me? I will make no defense. Kill me."

"Live!" said the mother in a hollow voice; "live! If you kill to punish those you love—then live!"

And, noticing not the body of her child, she turned on her heel and disappeared in the forest.

The other woman appeared as though petrified for an instant, and gazed with eyes, where little speculation lingered, in the direction the woman she had wronged had gone. Then, seeming to realize the position, and casting her eyes upon the ground, with a great burst of passionate grief she threw herself beside the little form and caught it to her, hugging it close, rocking it to and fro, wailing in a grief-stricken tone, and punished more effectually than death ever punishes when it avenges an evil act. The boy, comprehending enough to be rooted to the spot, witnessed a little longer the abandonment of the woman, and then the full horror of the scene came before him and enlightened him with its inmost meaning. Edging a little away from the woman holding the dead child, yet his eyes set upon her, at last, by a supreme effort, he broke the fascination that held him, and with a wild cry of fear turned and fled from the spot, that scene forever stamped upon his brain.

I find that years elapse before any very striking adventure of any of the brothers of the scout are spoken of after the one above mentioned.

But in the year 1791, or possibly 1792, the Indians having made frequent and disastrous incursions into the settlements of the whites along the Ohio River, between the town of Wheeling and the Mingo Bottom, sometimes murdering entire families, at other times capturing them and taking them away to torture and servitude, again making a raid and capturing all the horses belonging to a station or a fort, a little company of fiercely-determined and insulted men, consisting of John Wetzel, Jr., as he called himself, William McCullough, John Hough, Thomas Biggs, Joseph Hedges, Kinzie Dickerson, and a certain Mr. Linn, rendezvoused at a place called the Beach Bottom, which was on the Ohio River, a few miles below where Wellsburg is now situated.

The avowed object of this little band was to proceed to the Indian town and steal horses, in revenge for the beasts taken from the whites.

This horse stealing was considered a legal, honorable profession, as there was then open war against the Indians, and it would only be retaliating on them in their own way.

And possibly the Western frontier could at few other times have furnished seven men whose souls were better fitted, and whose nerves and sinews were better strung, to perform any enterprise of hazard which required resolution and firmness. These men, then, after making the scanty adieus vouchsafed to families and friends on undertaking such adventures, procceded across the Ohio, and went along, with cautious steps and vigilant glances, on their way through the cheerless, black, and almost impenetrable forest in the Indian country, till they came to an Indian town, near where the headwaters of the Sandusky and the Muskingum Rivers interlock.

Here they discovered a paddock, where flowing manes and frisking tails were theirs for the taking. There was no opposition offered, nor did a red-skin put in an appearance.

They took and tethered fifteen horses, and prepared to go off home with their champing freight.

They traveled with all rapidity, for they knew how soon the Indian loss would be discovered, and that a pursuit would take place immediately after the loss was found out, making only the shortest halts, to allow their horses to graze, and to throw themselves down upon the sward to breathe for an instant, to recruit their strength and activity. In the evening of the second day of their rapid retreat they arrived at Wells' Creek, not far from where the busy little town of Cambridge now rears its aspiring and pretty head. Here Linn, one of the seven, was taken ill, and the party were compelled either to stop and administer to his wants or go on and leave him entirely alone to perish in the lonely woods that resounded with the cries of preying animals.

But they were men of too simple a type to desert one of their number in time of necessity, and selfishness was only to come later when civilization made inroads upon the green lengths of wood and field which the first settlers claimed, but were only too often denied by legal measures.

They, therefore, paused in their homeward stretch, and placed sentinels on their back and trail, who remained until late in the night without perceiving any signs of their being pursued. When midnight had passed, and all was quiet, the sentinels on the back trail returned to the camp, where Linn was rolling and tossing in excruciating pain. All the simple remedies in the power of the six pitying men were administered without producing a sensible result or diminishing the pain of the sufferer. Their camp was on the back of a small stream, and therefore naturally guarded in one of its approaches; and, feeling safe from the other three sides, at last worn out, and the sick man sinking into a temporary sleep of exhaustion, they threw themselves upon the ground to snatch a few moments of repose. But one of their party was wakeful, and he constituted himself a guard.

Just before daylight this guard went to the small stream already mentioned, and, taking a small bucket, dipped up some water out of the run. On carrying the bucket back to the camp-fire, he discovered the water to be muddy. The muddy water immediately awakened his suspicion that the red enemy might be approaching them, and might at this instant be walking towards the camp in the midst of the stream, the footsteps coming thus being drowned in the water and rendered noiseless. He aroused the rest of the party, and communicated his suspicions to them.

They arose, examined the stream a short distance, and listened attentively for quite a protracted time.

But neither could they see nor hear anything calculated to alarm them, and they concluded forthwith that it must have been raccoons or some other animals who had swam the stream and stirred it up, and that that accounted for the mud.

After this conclusion they all lay down again, with the exception of the self-constituted guard, who exclaimed:

"You can do as you please, but I watch for the balance of the night," and took up his station just outside the light.

Happily for them, the camp-fire had burned down so low that but a few live coals remained, and offered a dim radiance, merely sufficient to point out where they lay.

For the mud in the stream had not been occasioned by any four-footed denizens of the forest; the enemy had come silently down the little creek, bent on the most ferocious attack on the whites, and were even then far on their way to them, as the sentinel had suspected, and were soon within ten or twelve feet from where they lay, and immediately fired several guns over the bank.

Linn, the sick man, lying with his side towards the stream, received nearly all the balls in his body, and was in the position to afford a slight barricade, protecting the others.

The Indians, after firing once, with tremendous, deafening yells mounted the bank with loaded rifles, tomahawks, and war-clubs, and made for the surprised men, who, giving a glance of sleepy protestation, fled dismayed, and without arms, closely pursued by the enemy.

It is sufficient to say that Linn was already killed, and Biggs and Hedges were murdered a few steps outside the camp.

McCullough ran a short distance further, when he was fired at and fell. But, instead of being prostrated by a bullet, he had, at the moment of firing, precipitated himself into a quagmire. The Indians, supposing they had killed him, rushed past him in pursuit of the other fleeing men, not caring for his scalp until they had finished the whole party and obtained seven trophies.

But their feet had scarcely past him, when McCullough extricated himself from the quagmire and put off in an opposite direction to that taken by the Indians. When day had fully broken, he fell in with Hough, who had also managed to elude the enemy, and the two made their way, haltingly, and with the direst surmises as to the fate of their less fortunate companions, to Wheeling.

John Wetzel and Kinzie Dickerson had also made a partial escape; at least the Indians had gone past them where they lay in the under-brush, and were seeking them further on. They could distinctly hear the expression of anger and disappointment where they lay in the grass, scarcely daring to breathe. They remained where they had fallen all day, all the next night.

At day-break on the second day they heard a tremendous tramping; it was the troop of recaptured horses being driven off by the Indians, and arranged in squads and tramping through the grass in order to crush any of the little undiscovered party who might be in hiding there. Miraculously the two men were unharmed; and waiting till the retreating sounds were hushed entirely, and assuring themselves cautiously that none of the foe remained behind still searching for the escaped men, the two made their way through the grass, foot-sore and nearly famished, on to Wheeling, where they arrived more dead than alive.

As soon as the stragglers had arrived at Wheeling, Captain John McCullough, collecting a party of men, proceeded to Wells' Creek, where they performed the funeral rites of the three unfortunate men who had fallen in or near the camp, and whose dead bodies the Indian miscreants had mutilated in a most horrible manner.

Thus was closed the horse-stealing tragedy.

Then John Wetzel and the hunter named Veach Dickerson associated together to go on an Indian scout. They crossed the Ohio three miles below the present town of Steubenville, with its more than thrifty inhabitants and activity in the march of improvements. The men set off with the avowed intention of bringing in an Indian prisoner. Indeed it seems that while Lewis Wetzel's brothers were as vindictive as he was himself, their vindictiveness had a merry, playful side to it wholly lacking in his case. Their escapades were enjoyed, and created as much amusement as anything else.

For now the two men, Dickerson and John Wetzel, painted their bodies and garbed themselves in complete Indian style, and had no fear of the result, trusting to their fluency in the Indian language to aid materially in the deception and prevent detection.

"We are half Indian anyhow," said they, "and the wonder is we are not wholly so out in this nightmare land."

Whatever induced them thus to undertake the expedition is not known, outside of the novelty and danger of the undertaking and their desire to manifest their contempt for the Indians' gullibility. They were not employed by government nor recognized as scouts. Each man constituted himself a government in himself, bestowing upon himself the authority to act as he thought best and to be fully exonerated in the result. Then, instead of the usual mode in these enterprises,—of killing the foe on sight, and taking no captives,—these two masquerading men determined to bring in a prisoner to make a pet of him as they would a monkey or a cub bear.

Their idea obtained little attention from the serious settlers, but then, as now, there was no gathering of people among whom there were not those whose whole lives appeared to be on the lookout for amusement and delectation. By these Wetzel and Dickerson were much approved, and what was called nonsense by the more sober mind was here regarded as the greatest kind of bravery, seeing that the masquerade was not to be attended by merry dances and junketing.

The two men, keeping their wits about them, in spite of their grotesque appearance, pushed through the hostile Indian country, with silent tread and keen outlook, till they came near the head of the Sandusky River, where they came full-tilt upon a small Indian village.

Their belief in their disguises may have failed them a little here, for it would appear that, instead of pushing on and entering into the village and claiming to be what they assured themselves they represented so well, they concealed themselves near a path which appeared to be considerably traveled, and prepared to wait.

In the course of the first day of their ambush, they saw several small companies of Indians pass by them, almost brushing the grass that hid them. But as it was not their desire to raise an alarm among the enemy, they permitted these small companies to pass by undisturbed. All the next day they waited here undetected. In the early evening of that second day they saw two Indian youths coming sauntering along the road, in the merriest possible moods, wrestling as they came. The two disguised white men immediately stepped from their hiding-place out into the road, and with the most confident air in the world went forward, as if meeting friends, until they were within a few feet of the advancing Indian youths.

"White men, no like Injuns," said one of the Indians at once, thus destroying the hallucinations of the two men.

Without another word, and knowing that they were in immediate danger, Wetzel drew his tomahawk and, with a powerful sweep, knocked one of the Indians down.

Dickerson, at the same instant, threw his arms

about the other Indian, and, by a dexterous movement, tumbled him to the ground. By this time John Wetzel had killed the other Indian, and turned his attention to gagging and 'pinioning the remaining one.

This was speedily accomplished; and, taking the scalp of the dead red-skin, the two white men set rapidly off with their prisoner for home. They traveled all that night on the war-path leading towards Wheeling. In the morning they struck off out of the path, making diverse courses, and keeping on the hardest ground, where their feet would leave the very least of impressions, as this would render their trail more difficult to follow in case of pursuit, which they strongly suspected.

They pushed along until they had crossed the Muskingum, and had left it behind them at some distance, when their prisoner began to show a restive, stubborn disposition. They now removed the gag from his mouth, no longer fearing his shouts.

"Indian no go with white cowards; Indian rather die by Indian hands," he said doggedly. "Indian brave and free. Cords make Indian no prisoner."

His head turned from them, and he looked back, smiling, towards the country he had come from. He finally threw himself upon the ground, and refused to rise.

They coaxed and pushed; he held his head towards them.

"White man may tomahawk Indian," he said, "but Indian go no farther with white man."

They used every argument they could think of to induce him to rise to his feet and proceed with them, but all to no purpose.

He said he would prefer dying in his native woods than to preserve his life a little longer, and at last be tortured by fire and his body mangled for sport when they took him into their towns.

He was assured that his life would not only be spared, but that he would be well-used and treated with all kindness. But nothing could induce him to rise to his feet. The idea that he would be put to death for the amusement of his captors, and in the presence of a vast number of spectators who would enjoy rapturously the struggles in his torture and death, as prisoners were often treated among his own people, had all taken such a strong hold on his mind that nothing would change his idea, and he determined to spoil the possibility of any gratification being had at his expense.

As it was not their desire or intention to kill him, they ceased coaxing, and concluded to try if a hickory switch, well applied by strong hands, would not alter his determination.

"White man coward," he said, with infinite scorn, as he saw the cutting of the switch, and speaking in his broken English—for he had refused to use the Indian language to these men who attired themselves like his people.

They then applied the switch to him, but without producing the slightest effect; he seemed to be as callous and indifferent to the lash as he had been to their arguments and coaxings. Finding all their efforts to get him forward in vain, and determined that he should not have his way and return to his tribe, they then threatened to kill him.

Again he lowered his head and presented it to them—and this time it did not again resume its upright position, for a tomahawk found its way into the brain; and after the scalp had been taken the supine body was left in its native woods which it had never left, a prey to the wild, free beasts of the forest, and the free birds of the free air.

The two masqueraders then returned home, vexed and disappointed, to show only two scalps, and not the dancing prisoner which they had promised to their friends.

The following incident, in which General Simon Kenton appears as the companion of Lewis Wetzel's brother Jacob, is vouched for in Pritt's "Border Life."

Kenton and Jacob Wetzel made arrangements to make a protracted fall hunt together. For that purpose they went, in the month of October, into the wild, furzy, hilly country near the mouth of the Kentucky River, for deer abounded there and few Indians had lately been seen in the immediate vicinity. However, when Kenton and Wetzel arrived there, and had made arrangements for their hunt, they discovered by unmistakable signs that Indians had lately been on the ground, and might be lurking near at hand.

It would have been foreign to the well-known character of a Kenton and a Wetzel to retreat in confusion without first ascertaining the exact position and number of an enemy's party.

They therefore determined, before proceeding on their hunt for venison, to find the Indian camp which they believed to be at no great distance from them. The first night of their encampment on the ground proved that their surmises were correct, for reports of guns had sounded far off, and these reports decided them.

Early the next morning the reports of the guns were repeated, and far off in the air they could see a soft haze which hinted at a camp-fire. With these precursors of the nearness of the red savages, Kenton and Wetzel moved cautiously forward, making as little sign as possible, fearful of the possibility of Indian videttes stationed some distance from the camp, as was usually the case. All day they moved slowly onward, coming inch by inch nearer to the smoke of the camp-fire, and meeting with no opposition nor hint that they had been discovered.

Towards evening they came within full sight of the camp. They kept in closer concealment yet, and determined that as soon as night had fallen, and the vigilance of the Indians had relaxed a little, they would reconnoiter the vantage-ground, find out the number of the enemy, and then govern their future operations as prudence and the circumstances might dictate.

Night had no sooner come than they crept forward and peered into the camp, and by the light of the fire found five men and five blankets—there were then no more than five braves here.

"When shall it be?" whispered Wetzel to his companion impatiently.

"Now, if you say so," was the reply.

Having confidence in themselves, and in their usual good fortune, they determined to attack the Indians boldly, and without any shilly-shallying, for they wanted to begin their hunt for deer. Contrary to all military tactics, they agreed to defer the attack until it was day.

"According to military code, small numbers should attack large in the dark. But we had better have light and an open field," General Kenton had explained.

There was a large fallen tree lying near to the camp of the Indians, and this prostrate monarch of the forest it was determined should serve as a rampart for the defense; and it would also serve to conceal the two attackers from observation until the battle began.

They took up their positions behind the log, and there they lay silent, until light should come, and they should be able to draw a clear bead.

"I am glad I have a double-barreled rifle," whispered Jacob Wetzel once.

"Hush!" said the general.

Daylight struggled through the trees. By the dim light the two ambushed men saw the Indians moving about.

"Now!" whispered the general; "and when my foot moves, fire."

They took aim, the preconcerted signal was given, fired, and two Indians fell dead to the ground. As quick as thought Jacob Wetzel fired his second load, and down fell the third Indian to bite the dust. Their numbers were now equal, and screaming and yelling at the top of their voices to terrify the astonished savages, the two white men bounded from their covert of the log, and were with their remaining enemies before they had recovered from the shock. These two remaining Indians took to their heels, without arms or blankets, and ran in different directions, having completely lost their heads, and becoming panic-struck.

General Kenton pursued one, whom he soon overtook, struck down, and returned to the camp with his scalp. But Wetzel was not in the camp, and the general shouted for him. A faint answer far off assured him of the young man's safety, and in a few minutes Jacob Wetzel came bounding in, the scalp of the fifth Indian in his hand.

"And now let us hurry," said he, "and begin our too-long-deferred deer hunt."

CHAPTER XXII.

THE NEW ORLEANS EPISODE.

SOON after the rescue of the betrothed of his young relative, Simon, Lewis Wetzel, seeming to be possessed by a new phase of unrest, determined to go far away from the scenes that knew him best, and which now seemed to pall on him; so, two days after he had last seen the happy man taking the saved girl on to the settlement, the sun gilding them as they went across the landscape, he engaged passage on a flat-boat just about leaving for New Orleans.

"Let me go on the boat."

"We go to New Orleans," returned the captain.

Wetzel pulled out his purse and paid his passage-money.

"The man looks as excited as though he were running away from his wife and children," said the captain suspiciously. "He did not even answer me civilly when I told him where we were bound for."

"You'd better look out," answered the deck-hand.

"Who knows but we shall have a mother-in-law starting up when we have been out a couple of hours? You had better see into it, captain."

"Look at him now," pursued the captain, "acting as much at home as though he had been born and bred on a flat-boat. See, he don't even look astonished; and it is as likely as not that he never was on such a craft as this in all his life. It is hardly fair to a man's feelings, and that man the captain of a boat like this one, to take so much for granted and not even deign to admire the taut and trim shape of everything about us. What shall I do, Neddy? I don't want to be hauled up before a court of law."

"The best thing you can do, captain," returned Neddy, "is to give the poor chap a chance. So let's pull off immediately."

The boat sailed out from her moorings, and put off for the South. All the way there Wetzel remained on deck, silent and sad. He answered when spoken to, but addressed no one without provocation, and adventured little or no conversation on his own account.

There was a sick man on board, going home to die, his thin, transparent face peculiarly fascinating the strong, robust pioneer. With this man Wetzel consorted most, listening to faint, vague raptures, as the invalid spoke of the sunny South and heaven, till his listener scarcely knew at times which place the sufferer alluded to, so were the two confused—the one his earthly home, the other his spiritual, and both equally beloved.

"You believe in its glories and its great tenderness?" once asked the invalid.

"Yes," answered Wetzel in a low tone of voice, looking out across the water.

"And you know we can lie there day after day, unfearing anything at all, always sure of a mellow light and soft winds, that never disturb. Then the countless songs, the soft, sweet music in the air, and the rest that reminds you of nothing you have ever known; the voices of those you love around you, the odors of a million flowers about you, and above and around all the grateful sense of rest that fears no rude awakening; perfect security and no fear. Then there is no pain there——"

"No pain there," mused the listener.

"And," went on the other, "tears are dried, smiles come easily, and we forget all the dreary longing and the want we have ever had!"

"All the dreary longing and the want we have ever had!"

"And then some one we loved best of all comes with us, hand and hand we go through all the glories scattered so profusely around us, and which are ours for the very enjoying."

"Hand in hand!"

"There is no more disappointment; those we love love us. You believe in all this, do you not?"

"I believe, oh, yes," answered Wetzel; "oh, yes, I believe, though maybe you see it with a sick man's eyes, and suffering here see only in heaven the difference between pain and the total lack of it."

"I did not mean that—I did not speak of heaven. I meant the South, the glorious, warm South," said the other.

Wetzel could only answer that he had seen very little of that South which the sick man lauded.

At New Orleans he would not leave the invalid.

"Have you no friends?" he asked.

"Friends!" echoed the man, smiling, "friends! many—many."

"They are not here to receive you."

"They did not expect me so soon. The captain sailed sooner than he expected to, on your account."

"On my account!"

"He thought you were in a hurry, I believe. Yes, my friends will soon be here. But don't you stay here with me; go to your own dear friends."

"They are not in New Orleans."

"Where are they?"

"I do not know."

The sick man looked up at him, a pang of sorrow crossing his face. He grasped the scout's hand fervently.

"It will all be right some day," he said.

"It is all right now," answered Wetzel.

He came and sat on the wharf with his new friend until loving people hurried there and claimed the invalid. Then the same look came into Wetzel's face that had rested there the time he had looked after the reunited pair going towards the white settlement in the sun. But, as then, he grasped his rifle and trudged on into the heart of the busy place, and was soon lost to the view of the few people who looked after him and his quaint appearance.

Many months elapsed before his friends heard anything of him, and his life while in New Orleans seems never to have been fully known. It was hinted though that he roved the streets of the city gazing on the stately buildings and crowded workshops and busy people. He was said to have thrashed a man for using profanity towards a woman. He found stray children and took them home. He attracted much attention from his garb and his adherence to his rifle in place of a walking-stick, and timid women held aloof from the wild-looking man, who, often observing their repugnance, would hurry away with lowered head.

Then there came news to the West that he was in prison in New Orleans. What the exact nature of the charge was has never been fully ascertained, but it is very certain that he was imprisoned and treated as a common felon for nearly two years.

It was said that he was going along a street one night, and seeing a ruffian insulting a young girl, he had rapped the man over the head with his rifle as a polite reminder that he had better stop his insults. The man stopped the insulting proclivities sufficiently to lie in a gutter and call for assistance, which, when it came, arrested the scout and lodged him in jail.

Again it was said that a stranger, gaudily attired, came up to him in the street one day.

"Halloo, captain," said the stranger, grasping the hand of the confused scout and wringing it cordially.

"I'm not a captain," said Wetzel simply. "I'm only Lewis Wetzel."

"As if I didn't know it," said the still further pleased stranger. "You must allow me to call you Captain Wetzel. And how are bears out your way, captain?"

"There are not so many as there used to be,"

returned Wetzel. "But how do you know me?—and how do you know I came from the Mingo Bottom?"

"Why it's printed in your face, even if everybody did not know who you were beforehand. Why your name is all through New Orleans. I should be ashamed of my own mother's only son if I had not been prolific in spreading the news of Lewis Wetzel's various escapades."

"The people of New Orleans are very kind."

"By the way, captain, would you mind giving me a big gold coin for these little ones? These take up too much room in the shallow pockets our tailors make for us. But your pockets hold a bushel."

"Of course I'll accommodate you," said Wetzel, and did so, and with another hearty shake of the hand, and a promise to see him again, the gaudily-attired stranger hurried off.

"That is a very nice man," said Lewis Wetzel.

He attempted to spend one of the small gold coins which the very nice man had given him for the large piece, and as it was discovered to be counterfeit, and many others being found upon his person, he was apprehended and sentenced to imprisonment for uttering false coin.

Whatever charge it may have been that caused his incarceration, he was finally liberated, and hurried home by way of Philadelphia, to which place he was sent from New Orleans. He shut his eyes sedulously now to all overtures towards friendship, no matter by whom made.

While in Philadelphia he was greeted by a peace society composed of Friends, who, seeing his dreary condition, and hearing his story, offered to befriend him. But he turned away from their gentle, calm faces, and doubted them.

He had liked the quiet, straight streets of Philadelphia, and he had gone and looked at Independence Hall, and felt a thrill permeate every inch of him as he thought of those stirring things enacted there when he was such a young and helpless babe.

He had looked at Christ Church, and thought he could see General Washington going in there of a Sunday to listen to the tender voice of Bishop White, who stood in the pulpit and reckoned the man in the pew, who was now termed "the father of his country," only as a fellow-being who came to him for guidance into the country whose Father spoke to one and all alike, making no distinction in men, if only they appealed to Him and believed in his strength with firmest faith.

Then Wetzel found himself once in the neighborhood of a plain, low building, surrounded by a high wall—a Friends' meeting-house. Here he thought the elm-trees were very fine, particularly that one which had been taken, a slip, from Penn's treaty-tree, up further in Philadelphia. It was gazing on these trees that brought him in contact with some Friends who would have been good to him.

"We do not press ourselves upon thee," said an elder, "though verily we should like thee to come to our business-meeting next fifth-day, in our meeting-house on Twelfth street, and perchance instruct us a trifle about the condition of the frontier, and how best the miserable condition of the Indians may be ameliorated. Thee thyself is a man who has had vast experience, and, peradventure, thee would not refuse to induct us a little into the ways and means of thy part of the United States. We would do well by thee, friend Wetzel, if thee would give us a chance to do so."

But he turned away from them, disregarding their offer.

"You may be all right," he said; "but I thought the nice man in New Orleans all right too. You don't want me to give you a big gold coin for a lot of little ones, do you?"

"Nay," said the drab-coated elder gently, "small coins are much more convenient than large ones."

"Your tailors don't make your pockets so small that you can't find room for your money, do they?"

"Nay, friend, our tailors devise our pockets with sufficient capacity to accommodate all the coin we put into them."

"Well, you may be all right; but I think you'd better leave me alone," said Wetzel firmly.

"It shall be as thee wishes," answered the elder with a sigh. "Fare thee well, friend!"

Wetzel waited impatiently till he got to Wheeling again; he did not feel safe until then.

De Haas in his narrative writes:

"Mr. Rodefer says he saw him immediately after his return, and that his personal appearance had undergone a great change by reason of his long imprisonment."

At Wheeling Creek he visited his mother for two days during the absence of his mother's husband. He was kinder now towards his mother, and listened patiently to her praises of her husband, now a prosperous herder.

"You are more like you were when you were very young, Lewis," said his mother. "Ah, Lewis, I remember the time I sat in the bottom of the wagon and watched our old little home disappearing."

"Well, what are you crying about now, mother? That's all over, years and years ago," he said, not unkindly.

"Cry! why I've always cried about you. I cried

that day in the wagon till you were all damp. Cry! women have always cried about you; when we heard here that you had been arrested in New Orleans——"

"Which arrest I mean to avenge," he said quietly.

"All the women around cried," went on his mother, unheeding the interruption. "Cry! why when you were a baby in your cradle didn't Grizzie Heister come in with a flag and cry over you? You don' remember Grizzie Heister, do you, Lewis?"

"Not very well," he answered smiling.

"Ah, true; you were only two months old. Well, it's not your fault that you don't remember her. Ah, there was a fine figure of a woman; none of your Western breed there!"

"There's nothing against the Western women, mother."

"I didn't say there was. But I hope I am allowed a preference. I am firmly convinced by the way Grizzie cried over you that day that had you chosen to remain you might have married her."

"She was fifteen years old, wasn't she?"

"Yes, a most interesting age."

"I was two months!"

"That's neither here nor there, Lewis; this is New Orleans manners to your mother, likely; and I wish you wouldn't catch me up so quickly. Ah, me! I wonder where Grizzie is now?"

"A grandmother, no doubt."

"It is possible; her family always did marry early. But what is to hinder you from marrying, Lewis? You are getting old and——"

"Ugly," laughed a woman's voice.

It was Mrs. Cookis, a relative coming in.

"Yes, Lewis," she went on, "it's high time you thought of settling down like the rest of us. Now I know the sweetest, dearest, lovingest, smartest, gentlest creature in the world; and she thinks you are the boldest, brazenest, hatefulest, fearfulest man in creation—and that's next to saying that she is over head and ears in love with you. Now, come, let your mother and me fix it up between you two. You surely can't refuse a woman such a trifle! Come! What do you say?"

"There is no woman in this world for me," he said sadly; "but I do hope there may be one in heaven."

He left the room and the house after this, and next day he had disappeared in the old fashion.

He had told a man or two that now he was at home, he felt like an arrant coward, and longed to go back to New Orleans and have revenge of the man who had caused his imprisonment. He was not to be laughed out of it, he was not to be argued out of it; and the very thought that he had been made a dupe of, and that he must be jeered at by the man who had duped him, as not being able to compete with a rascal's duplicity, made him chafe and long to wipe out the disgrace of iron chains and bolts and bars by a free use of his manhood and a speedy satisfaction upon his enemy.

When he disappeared he was called fool-hardy, and he lost friends by this line of action. And those at home waited daily for intelligence of his death in a street brawl in New Orleans, or his arrest as a murderer. But this startling news never came, and month after month passed and there was no report of him whatever. He was given up for lost by some, his mother among the rest, and it was even proposed to send a delegation to New Orleans to ascertain the cause of no news of him.

"Let me go," said Charley Madison, now a well-to-do farmer, and very anxious for a little change in his life.

"Indeed, I won't let you go," said his buxom and comely wife.

"What have you got to say against it, Berta?" he asked.

"Only that you *shan't* go," she replied calmly, and took his arm and led him away.

CHAPTER XXIII.

THE LAST INDIAN.

BUT all this pother and worry was brought to a close after many months of vexatious continuance. For Wetzel one day appeared in the neighborhood, his rifle over his shoulder, as though he had been only on one of his old scouts.

But whether Lewis Wetzel avenged his wrongs, as he had vowed to do, his biographers at this time cannot say. Only it is fair to say that he would not have come across the man who had wronged him by any secret means; and if he took any revenge, it was scarcely less than a manly one.

He never told what he had done, nor if he had come across the man. But he returned this second time with much of his old, well-known strength, and his propensity for the woods seemed redoubled, if possible, to atone for his long absence from them. He was forever hunting, and his deer-hides found ready purchasers; for the more peaceful deer were his victims now. With advancing years and experience, he seemed to regard the taking of human life with more thought, though his hatred for the Indians had never deserted him. The savages were not so plentiful now as formerly, and they had moved further up the country, and were seldom seen around the settlements that claimed Wetzel, for adventurous people had long passed by Wheeling and its environment, and gone out to greater wilds and less settled lands to lay their claims and establish their towns.

Therefore, Wetzel, losing none of his hatred, yet did not follow up his foe with his old cunning and recklessness. He was destined, however, to go to those further wilds, too, after an adventure wherein some of his old taste returned to him. And he it was who was often engaged for months at a time by the settlers furthest removed from the aid of the forts to hunt up and locate their lands.

The incident which seemed to change him from the man loving to brood in the woods while he tracked the deer may be summed up in a little space, and shows that very little of his old cunning had been lost through his long incarceration in New Orleans and the inactivity and gloominess of a hopeless prison discipline to a man like him.

Returning home one day from a hunt north of the Ohio, fatigued, and suspecting no treachery here where he had been for the last week or so, he suddenly espied an Indian, not far off, in the very act of raising his gun to fire on him. Both the Indian and the white man immediately sprang to trees, behind which they stood for more than an hour. There was nothing to be done but to think it out. To remain long in that position was not to the taste nor inclination of Wetzel.

He suddenly hit upon the boldest plan imaginable, the successful carrying out of which displays to the fullest the superiority of the sagacity of the white man over the natural simplicity of the savage.

"I can't help myself," communed Wetzel, for the first time in his life hesitating where the life of an Indian was intended.

He peeped from behind his tree, and saw the Indian doing the same from behind the tree that sheltered him, but with this difference: that the Indian had his rifle lodged in a knot of the tree, aimed directly towards the spot where the white man lay concealed.

"No, I can't help myself," said Wetzel for the second time.

He thereupon removed his bear-skin cap, and very cautiously adjusting it to the ramrod of his gun, with the slightest, most dubious, and hesitating movement, as though fearful of venturing a little glance, he protruded the cap from the side of the tree.

In an instant there was a crack, and the furry cap flew from the ramrod, torn by the bullet from the gun of the ever vigilant savage, whose aim Wetzel even then thought admirable. Quick as lightning Wetzel leaped up, and passed from the side of the tree and advanced upon the confounded Indian.

"White man's ghost," gasped the savage.

At this Wetzel laughed, which laugh seemed to assure the Indian of the flesh and blood quality of his foe; for, raising his tomahawk aloft with the ever-rapid movement, in the twinkling of an eye it leaped from the tawny hand, but not before Wetzel's bullet had sped on its work of death. For as the tomahawk descended, harmless, behind him, Wetzel saw the brave leap convulsively into the air, and, straightening his limbs as he descended, fall prone upon his face, quite dead. Wetzel went up and gazed at him.

"And was my life given to me to do such work as this?" he said. "Are there not nobler ways of dealing with a deadly foe than this? Did not my life in that Southern pest-city show me crime like this where there should have been loving pity and refuge? What did my life in that prison, surrounded by what is called the scum of society,—the scum because it rises rapidly to the surface, while the less hurried body of the water remains below,—

what did that prison-life teach me? Oh, that men of strength like mine would go to crowded towns and use their arms to protect innocence in danger, truth belied, and weakness trodden down! Had I but seen in my early days as I see now, I might have been a better man. If my father had only been content with his poverty when I was born, there might have been shown to me a different line of action than I have made mine. If the girl who wept over my cradle had only influenced my mother to remain, and thus have kept my father! Yet, what might my father have become, over there, in poverty and discontent? Temptation might have made him one of those very fallen ones that men like I should raise. And where might I have been, with a fallen man for a father? In the mire, very likely. But, no; my father was a brave man, not a man like his sons—killers of God's people. My father accepted God's profusion, not God's curse of Cain. Yet am I a murderer? Have not the deaths of certain men been necessary to life since the very beginning? And has not God selected men to avenge his people's rights? Have I not been instrumental in preserving a few innocent lives at the expense of less worthy ones? No, I am not a murderer, but my revenge actuated me too much. But it was not a flippant revenge, and it was for the life of one of God's noblest men—my father! And so I come back to the starting-point, and prove nothing. Who can answer the questions I have asked myself all my life long? I cannot answer them myself, and I dare not ask another's interpretation. Whether I have been wholly wrong or partly right, whether my life will be called wasted or partly useful, I know that such a man as this cooling savage was one short hour ago has possibilities which not I nor any other man alive dare limit or guage by the mistakes and perversions of our own selfish lives."

Then, giving one more look upon the prostrate body, and throwing a few tree branches on it, Wetzel left the woods, and determined on peace, if he could ever obtain it.

CHAPTER XXIV.

VALE.

AS Wetzel's name and prowess had long been the subject of universal regard, and as he was known to be one of the most efficient scouts and practical woodmen of his day, his services, as has been before mentioned, were now most eagerly called for by the new settlers anxious to found their claims in the further West. Their reliance on the man forced him to accede to their wishes, no matter what his own longing after rest may have been. He saw his duty in thus helping the ambitious new men coming in from crowded cities and overburdened countries,—German, Irish, or English,—and he helped them all that he could. Under the protection of the scout they felt safe, for they no sooner landed in the neighborhood that had known him all his life than stories of him were told them, and they were advised "to get Lewis Wetzel, and then they need have no fear of Indian interlopers, for that the Indians held him in mortal dread and always gave him a wide berth wherever he might happen to be."

During his inactivity the savages seem to have formed a more extravagantly exalted opinion of his qualities as a subduer, so that they held aloof and always imagined he was on their trail.

Of those who became largely interested in Western lands about this time, was John Madison, the brother of James, afterwards President Madison. He employed Lewis Wetzel to accompany him through the Kanawha region. During their expedition they one day came across a deserted hunter's camp, into which they penetrated and found a lot of goods concealed.

"I think I'll help myself to a blanket," said young Madison, and did so.

That day in crossing Little Kanawha they were fired upon, and Madison was killed. Strange as it may appear, Wetzel failed to pursue the Indians who committed the deed. He took the body to Madison's friends and went home to Wheeling, where he spent days and weeks alone in the woods. The birds became used to him, and would hop upon him as he rested there. There was a lame, delicate little doe that used to come and rest its face beside his, looking at the fierce man out of tender, melting eyes, and unafraid.

General Clarke, in the celebrated tour across the Rocky Mountains, had heard much of Lewis Wetzel in Kentucky, and determined to secure his services in the perilous enterprise. A messenger was sent for him, but he was reluctant to go. However, he finally consented, and accompanied the party during the first three months' travel, but then declined to go any further, and returned home.

Shortly after this, his old restlessness returning with redoubled force, he made up his mind to leave his part of the country. He went to his mother and sisters, and made his simple good-bye's.

"When shall you return?" was asked of him.

"Return!" he answered, "I do not know. Wherever I may be of most use, there I remain."

"We need you here."

"I do not think so. A new civilization has sprung up, and a new mode of settlement has come about. The Indians are more peaceful, and killing them while they are so is nothing short of murder. They may be wilder and fiercer further West, but I shall not go there, I am too old."

"Old! you at forty years of age?"

"I have lived more than my age in many things."

"If nothing else kept you near the new settlers, it should be that your vow has never been laid aside."

"I have never broken my vow, as the Lord

knows, and I love my father as much now as I ever did when he was with me. But I should not be keeping that vow to leave this, my own part of the country, and seek after Indians. I have kept the oath I made—to kill any Indian that came across my path!"

He took passage on a flat-boat going down the river, and his friends came to see him off. They said that he smiled that day such as he had never smiled before—the smile of an old man having nothing before him but hope of rest. There were women who wept at parting with him.

"You know, Lewis Wetzel, that I was always proud of you for a brave man," sobbed Charley Madison's wife.

"You were always a kind friend, Mrs. Madison" he replied.

"Mrs. Madison!" she said, reproachfully.

"Berta, then," he smiled.

"Come, Berta, the boat is about leaving," urged her husband.

"What do I care!" cried she. "It's all your fault, Charley Madison."

Wetzel's young relative, Simon's young wife, now came up.

"I owe so much to you. I pray for you always," she said simply, and left his side.

"Well, Lewis," said his mother, "the world is wide, but it always sends us back to where we started from. Good-bye, my son, and come again in the spring."

So they all left him, and grouped together on the shore, watching him sailing away from them.

"Here, let us give him three cheers," cried Charley Madison.

"Don't you dare to," shrieked his wife. "Why do you want to cheer him? He is not going out in happiness! Can't you see his face, and the sorrow there?"

"But, Berta, it's our good-will for him that makes me want to cheer him," exclaimed her husband, "as a sort of send-off."

"Send off! Ugh, you disagreeable thing, you! It's all your fault."

"What is my fault?"

"Everything—that's what."

But there was no cheering, as they watched him there. Slowly, slowly down the stream he sailed, calmly and gently, the ripples the boat made in moving floating up against the shore in little, whispering wavelets. Slowly, slowly down the stream he sailed, under the heavy shadows of the clustering trees on the shore. Far out the silent watchers on the shore saw a golden spot on the waters where the trees ceased to shadow the path of the boat, and the sun played in all its glorious light, that mocked at shadows. Into this golden spot the boat sailed softly, and the sun lit up the figure standing at the prow like a halo; lit up the dark face till they said it shone with a strange, weird expression; lit up the gun-barrel till it was like a flash of lightning, as the boat rocked and made the light strike it every instant from a new direction; lit up the long, black hair and the fierce eyes that were softer, dimmer now. He took his hat from his head, out there in the golden spot on the waters, and held it up to those far away on the shore, and held it so till the boat went further and further, rounded a curve, and he was gone; and the ripples still coming into the feet of the group on the shore alone told that he had been here and was gone away from the land that knew him so well, never, never to return.

For he never did come back. Shortly after he had gone he was heard from at intervals—merely that some one had heard of him in some out-of-the-way place. He is known to have visited a relative living about twenty miles in the interior from Natchez, and here he lived until the summer of 1808, when he died, at the age of forty-four years, in the prime of a life that had never been happy and seldom satisfied.

That the description of him attempted in these pages may be less full than the reader may like, the author is well advised. But it has been very carefully done, and has closely followed a mass of notes and papers detailing the exploits narrated here.

More seems to have been thought of the extraordinary length of his hair and his fury, as though it were an acknowledged fact that length of hair and fury were always connected, than to the more generous points in the man. The matter in the hands of the author has helped to show the fallacy of much of this belief, and it is hoped that murder and revenge will not be conceded as the whole tenor of Lewis Wetzel's life.

For the very work of destruction to which Lewis Wetzel's life was devoted was, at the same time, a service to the frontier settlers. There is no doubt that his prowess, and the influence of his name, struck a wholesome fear into the minds of the Indians, and saved the pioneers from many a hostile incursion. Let those who shudder as they think of the Indian scout,—a true hero and benefactor in his day and way,—reflect upon the times and circumstances as narrated in these pages; and let them grapple with that profounder and more mysterious problem of the conquest of civilization over barbarism, and they may be enabled to see in this child of the forest the elements that in another age and under happier circumstances are revered in philanthropists and benefactors of mankind.

That others than the readers of this volume found good in the man may be vouched for by a note of De Haas with which the author closes:

"When Lewis Wetzel professed friendship, he was as true as the needle to the pole.

"He loved his friends and hated their enemies.

"He was a rude, blunt man, with but few words before company; but with his friends, not only sociable, but an agreeable companion.

"Such was Lewis Wetzel; his name and fame will long survive, when the achievements of men vastly superior in rank and intellect will slumber with the forgotten past."

THE END.

CPSIA information can be obtained
at www.ICGtesting.com
Printed in the USA
LVHW011000100121
675968LV00009B/132

9 780353 538405